Communities and Counterterrorism

This book highlights a wide range of community-related counterterrorism initiatives undertaken in England, Northern Ireland, and Australia.

The book continues established scholarship in terrorism studies about the importance of considering communities when understanding, responding to, and preventing politically, religiously, and other ideologically motivated violence. Terrorists are in competition with communities and sociopolitical—religious movements for proactive and passive support for their causes, membership, and resources. The book is particularly relevant in the aftermath of a series of jihadist terror attacks, alongside terror acts committed by far-right extremists. There has been an increased emphasis upon the role of communities in combatting terrorism, with 'Communities can defeat terrorism' becoming a well-known mantra.

This book was originally published as a special issue of *Studies in Conflict & Terrorism*.

Basia Spalek is a Professor of Conflict Transformation at the University of Derby, UK. She has undertaken extensive and in-depth research into community-based approaches to counterterrorism, including community policing initiatives, mentoring, and deradicalisation interventions. She is a British Association for Counselling and Psychotherapy (BACP) accredited psychotherapist at the University of Leicester Counselling Service, UK, and also has her own private practice.

Douglas Weeks is a Lecturer at California State University, Long Beach, USA, and a Visiting Research Fellow at London Metropolitan University, UK. He specialises in radicalisation, deradicalisation, counterterrorism policing, and counterterrorism policy. Within those fields, his research has broadly centred on the convergence of counterterrorism policy delivered by public safety agencies, and how mainstream and radicalised individuals respond.

Communities and Counterterrorism

Edited by
Basia Spalek and Douglas Weeks

LONDON AND NEW YORK

First published 2019
by Routledge
2 Park Square, Milton Park, Abingdon, Oxon, OX14 4RN

and by Routledge
52 Vanderbilt Avenue, New York, NY 10017

Routledge is an imprint of the Taylor & Francis Group, an informa business

© 2019 Taylor & Francis
Chapter 6 © 2017 Carmel Joyce and Orla Lynch. Originally published as Open Access.

With the exception of Chapter 6, no part of this book may be reprinted or reproduced or utilised in any form or by any electronic, mechanical, or other means, now known or hereafter invented, including photocopying and recording, or in any information storage or retrieval system, without permission in writing from the publishers. For details on the rights for Chapter 6, please see the chapter's Open Access footnote.

Trademark notice: Product or corporate names may be trademarks or registered trademarks, and are used only for identification and explanation without intent to infringe.

British Library Cataloguing-in-Publication Data
A catalogue record for this book is available from the British Library

ISBN13: 978-0-367-18470-4

Typeset in Minion Pro
by codeMantra

Publisher's Note
The publisher accepts responsibility for any inconsistencies that may have arisen during the conversion of this book from journal articles to book chapters, namely the possible inclusion of journal terminology.

Disclaimer
Every effort has been made to contact copyright holders for their permission to reprint material in this book. The publishers would be grateful to hear from any copyright holder who is not here acknowledged and will undertake to rectify any errors or omissions in future editions of this book.

Contents

Citation Information		vi
Notes on Contributors		viii
	Introduction: Community-Based Counterterrorism *Basia Spalek and Douglas Weeks*	1
1	The Role of Communities in Counterterrorism: Analyzing Policy and Exploring Psychotherapeutic Approaches within Community Settings *Basia Spalek and Douglas Weeks*	5
2	Campaigning on Campus: Student Islamic Societies and Counterterrorism *Tufyal Choudhury*	18
3	Police and Community Cooperation in Counterterrorism: Evidence and Insights from Australia *Adrian Cherney and Kristina Murphy*	37
4	Community-Led Counterterrorism *Aziz Z. Huq*	52
5	Community-Based Counterterrorism Policing: Recommendations for Practitioners *Robert Lambert and Tim Parsons*	68
6	"Doing Peace": The Role of Ex-Political Prisoners in Violence Prevention Initiatives in Northern Ireland *Carmel Joyce and Orla Lynch*	86
7	U.K. Foreign Fighters to Syria and Iraq: The Need for a *Real* Community Engagment Approach *Tanya Silverman*	105
	Index	123

Citation Information

The chapters in this book were originally published in the *Studies in Conflict & Terrorism*, volume 40, issue 12 (September 2018). When citing this material, please use the original page numbering for each article, as follows:

Introduction
Community-Based Counterterrorism
Basia Spalek and Douglas Weeks
Studies in Conflict & Terrorism, volume 40, issue 12 (September 2018) pp. 987–990

Chapter 1
The Role of Communities in Counterterrorism: Analyzing Policy and Exploring Psychotherapeutic Approaches within Community Settings
Basia Spalek and Douglas Weeks
Studies in Conflict & Terrorism, volume 40, issue 12 (September 2018) pp. 991–1003

Chapter 2
Campaigning on Campus: Student Islamic Societies and Counterterrorism
Tufyal Choudhury
Studies in Conflict & Terrorism, volume 40, issue 12 (September 2018) pp. 1004–1022

Chapter 3
Police and Community Cooperation in Counterterrorism: Evidence and Insights from Australia
Adrian Cherney and Kristina Murphy
Studies in Conflict & Terrorism, volume 40, issue 12 (September 2018) pp. 1023–1037

Chapter 4
Community-Led Counterterrorism
Aziz Z. Huq
Studies in Conflict & Terrorism, volume 40, issue 12 (September 2018) pp. 1038–1053

Chapter 5
Community-Based Counterterrorism Policing: Recommendations for Practitioners
Robert Lambert and Tim Parsons
Studies in Conflict & Terrorism, volume 40, issue 12 (September 2018) pp. 1054–1071

CITATION INFORMATION

Chapter 6
"Doing Peace": The Role of Ex-Political Prisoners in Violence Prevention Initiatives in Northern Ireland
Carmel Joyce and Orla Lynch
Studies in Conflict & Terrorism, volume 40, issue 12 (September 2018) pp. 1072–1090

Chapter 7
U.K. Foreign Fighters to Syria and Iraq: The Need for a Real Community Engagment Approach
Tanya Silverman
Studies in Conflict & Terrorism, volume 40, issue 12 (September 2018) pp. 1091–1107

For any permission-related enquiries please visit:
http://www.tandfonline.com/page/help/permissions

Notes on Contributors

Adrian Cherney is an Associate Professor in the School of Social Science at the University of Queensland, Brisbane, Australia. He has completed evaluations of programs aimed at countering violent extremism and is undertaking research on the supervision of terrorist offenders who have been released into the community on parole.

Tufyal Choudhury is an Assistant Professor at Durham Law School at Durham University, UK. He is also a Senior Research Affiliate of the Canadian Terrorism, Security and Society Research Network, and a member of the UK Foreign and Commonwealth Office External Review Panel. His teaching and research focuses on issues of counterterrorism, radicalisation, racial and religious discrimination, and integration.

Aziz Z. Huq is a Professor of Law at The Law School at the University of Chicago, USA. His teaching and research interests include constitutional law, criminal procedure, federal courts, and legislation. His scholarship concerns the interaction of constitutional design with individual rights and liberties.

Carmel Joyce is a Psychologist and an IRC award recipient, currently researching peripheral involvement in terrorism at University College Cork, Ireland. She was previously a Postdoctoral Researcher in the Centre for the Study of Terrorism and Political Violence (CSTPV), Department of International Relations at the University of St Andrews, UK.

Robert Lambert was previously a Research Fellow at the University of Exeter, UK, and held teaching posts in the Handa CSTPV at the University of St Andrews, UK, and in John Grieve Policing Centre at London Metropolitan University, UK. He was the Co-founder and Head of the Metropolitan Police Muslim Contact Unit until retirement at the end of 2007.

Orla Lynch is the Head of Criminology at University College Cork, Ireland. Until 2015, she was the Director of Teaching and a Lecturer in Terrorism Studies in CSTPV at the University of St Andrews, UK. Her research interests lie in individual and group desistance from political violence, including issues related to *deradicalisation*, the role of grand narratives in justifying involvement in violence, and psychosocial understandings of the transitions from violence to peace.

Kristina Murphy is a Professor of Criminology at Griffith Criminology Institute at Griffith University, Brisbane, Australia. Her current research interest focuses on the policing of ethnic minority communities.

NOTES ON CONTRIBUTORS

Tim Parsons is an independent adviser on police reform and an Honorary Visiting Lecturer in Police Studies at Liverpool John Moore's University, UK.

Tanya Silverman is a Coordinator at the Institute for Strategic Dialogue (ISD) where she manages the Against Violent Extremism (AVE) network and supports the Institute's counter-narratives projects, in partnership with grass roots and social media companies. Previously, she researched new approaches to counter-radicalisation and played a key role in ISD's policy programmes.

Basia Spalek is a Professor of Conflict Transformation at the University of Derby, UK. She has undertaken extensive and in-depth research into community-based approaches to counterterrorism, including community policing initiatives, mentoring, and deradicalisation interventions. She is a British Association for Counselling and Psychotherapy (BACP) accredited psychotherapist at the University of Leicester Counselling Service, UK, and also has her own private practice.

Douglas Weeks is a Lecturer at California State University, Long Beach, USA, and a Visiting Research Fellow at London Metropolitan University, UK. He specialises in radicalisation, deradicalisation, counterterrorism policing, and counterterrorism policy. Within those fields, his research has broadly centred on the convergence of counterterrorism policy delivered by public safety agencies, and how mainstream and radicalised individuals respond.

INTRODUCTION

Community-Based Counterterrorism

Basia Spalek and Douglas Weeks

Fifteen years of intensive studies following 11 September 2001 (9/11) has advanced many aspects of the academic knowledge and practitioner practices within the counterterrorism domain. On a collective basis, both strands continue to advance in understanding, application, and capability. However, despite those advances, the threat of violent extremism remains high with little sign of abatement. Moreover, since 9/11 governments around the globe are increasingly focusing on the threat from within. Seemingly not a day passes where there is not some mention in the media of the internal threat posed by radicalization, returning foreign fighters, someone arrested on suspicion of planning a terror attack, or an actual attack. In response to those realities, governments continue to search for better ways to manage the risk. Constrained by legal frameworks, governments are increasingly looking to partner with communities in their counterterrorism efforts. This special edition highlights some of those efforts and gives insight to some of the ways that is occurring.

At a community level, terrorism-related discussions are ubiquitous. This is probably most true in Muslim communities where hard power policing mechanisms have resulted in the watchful eye of the community being ever-present. Information and opinion are passed by word of mouth and through a vibrant network of social media. Government actions, police and intelligence service activity and accountability, the wars in Syria and Iraq, radicalization and extremism in the West, and current terror-related events reported by citizen journalists are dominating a large part of discussions within the Muslim public sphere. Not only are people monitoring the things that affect them locally, they are monitoring events taking place around the world. Moreover, there is an active and vibrant debate taking place by individuals within virtual and traditional communities on those same topics. The point to be made here is that the topics of radicalization, terrorism, and counterterrorism are no longer the sole purview of government. Communities are not only embroiled in the debate; they passively monitor the individuals around them and the events that affect their community.

Given the attentive nature of communities, coupled with the fact that policing and legislative actions alone have been unable to stem the tide of individuals adopting radicalized belief, some of whom go on to engage in violent extremism, the natural evolution of government is to partner with communities in their counterterrorism efforts. Although the benefits that come from such partnerships is clear, partnering with the community is not a simple task nor is it a foregone conclusion. Years of hard power policing methods, invasive legislation, securitization policies, slanted media representation, and political rhetoric directed at Muslims have left many Muslim communities with a sense that they have become the suspect "other." Collectively that has eroded trust in the community/government relationship, leaving partnership a difficult task to negotiate. Undeterred by that reality, governments around the globe are attempting to place strained relationships in the past and broker new effective partnerships with Muslim communities in their fight against terrorism.

In the seven articles that follow, a cross-section of experiences and approaches used in community-based counterterrorism are explored. These articles are not provided to suggest that these are the only mechanisms worthy of consideration but rather provide examples of a broad array of approaches that have been used. Despite the prominence of terrorism, the concerns over radicalization, and the clear move by governments to exploit what may be its last untapped resource, little is actually written about community-based counterterrorism. This special edition serves to highlight some of the initiatives, partnerships, and challenges contained in this environment, and add to the academic body of knowledge regarding the role of communities in counterterrorism.

The first article, "The Role of Communities in Counterterrorism: Analyzing Policy and Exploring Psychotherapeutic Approaches within Community Settings," provides an overview of the legislative environment in the United Kingdom and the steps government is taking to stem the tide of extremism while simultaneously advocating the need to develop a stronger government/community relationship. The article highlights the similarity of goals between government and community and the different mechanisms used to realize those goals. The imposition of responsibility placed on communities by government is discussed as well as how community-based resources are being used to engage and mentor those at risk of extremism and those who have ventured into criminal activity. Examples of police led community engagement initiatives including those that backfired are also included. The article similarly explores how psychotherapeutic approaches can be used in the counterterrorism environment to change police culture, understand the pathways into and out of extremism more effectively, and build stronger community/policing bonds. The discussion includes how psychotherapeutic approaches might be used to engage and intervene at various stages as individuals are drawn to violent extremism. It concludes with a discussion about how psychoeducation techniques can be used to develop critical thinking skills which in turn may help build resilience to violent narratives.

The second article, "Campaigning on Campus: Student Islamic Societies and Counterterrorism," discusses the evolution and role that the Federation of Student Islamic Societies (FOSIS) plays on college and university campuses across the United States. The discussion is set against the backdrop in which the British government has articulated that universities are locations where extremist recruiters exploit vulnerable people. The discussion also takes in the requirements imposed by the Counter-Terrorism and Security Act of 2015, which places statutory responsibilities on universities to identify and prevent people vulnerable to being drawn into extremism. The article first provides some background on FOSIS before delving into the sometimes ambiguous nature of U.K. counterterrorism law, how that plays out on university campuses, the activism of FOSIS to ensure fairness and equal treatment of Muslim students, and how those things combine to shape the student/government relationship. Key areas of discussion include radicalization on university campuses, the application of Prevent, and FOSIS activism off campus to campaign against Schedule 7 stops.

The third article, "Police and Community Cooperation in Counterterrorism: Evidence and Insights from Australia," explores the police/community relationship in Australia. This article draws from a recent large quantitative study conducted by the University of Queensland and Griffith University, Australia. The article begins by profiling an in-depth quantitative assessment of Muslim sentiment in Australia and how that has affected the police/community relationship. Core areas of exploration include the sense of unfair treatment felt by Muslims and how that has affected the willingness of Muslims to participate in counterterrorism efforts. Using that as its starting point, the remainder of the article discusses how police proactively addressed the problem. The article concludes with a discussion on the outcomes of the police initiatives and boundaries of successful engagement.

The fourth article, titled "Community-Led Counterterrorism," explores the idea that nonstate actors have a distinctive and largely untapped role in responding to terrorist recruitment in North America and Europe. The article begins with a discussion on how community-led counterterrorism should be conceived. The author argues that "community-led counterterrorism" works through at least two causal channels, ideological competition and ethical anchoring, and that current policing models typically fail to embrace either. The arguments for and against community-led counterterrorism are discussed, as are the differences between community-led counterterrorism and community policing for counterterrorism. The article concludes with a discussion about the ethical issues facing both government and Muslim communities.

The fifth article, "Community-Based Counterterrorism Policing: Recommendations for Practitioners," is written by two former police officers. They provide a very practical and practitioner view of engagement based on their own experiences. As career police officers, they reflect on the evolution of policing and the lessons learned after thirty years of conflict with Northern Irish Republicanism. They apply that knowledge and experience to the current threats associated with radical Islam. The authors discuss the implications and limitations of policing by consent and the need to understand and respect the legitimate religious beliefs of all communities. They conclude with a discussion on the need to provide meaningful community feedback to the police and policymakers so that risk is minimized, trusted relationships are maintained, and more informed policies can be developed.

The sixth article is titled "Doing Peace: The Role of Ex-Political Prisoners in Violence Prevention Initiatives in Northern Ireland." The article discusses the role of ex-political prisoners in Northern Ireland who are now doing violence prevention and counterterrorism work. This article is written by two psychologists with extensive research history in Northern Ireland. They explore the transition in identity that former combatants have gone through and the roles they now take on to ensure that transgenerational violence is avoided. The article is based on fifty-two interviews they did with Loyalist and Republican ex-prisoners who are now involved in support organizations committed to restorative justice. Intermixed within the discussion is how ex-prisoners establish legitimacy with the communities they interact with. The article concludes with a discussion on how the identity of the those doing the work and the identity of the community are simultaneously changed through the complex process of deradicalization.

The last article is "U.K. Foreign Fighters to Syria and Iraq: The Need for a Real Community Engagement Approach." This article discusses the initiatives and limitations of government to dissuade young adults from traveling to Syria and Iraq. The author exposes the raw emotion that many young people are feeling, how that emotion is shared within communities, and argues that because of that shared sense of emotion they are best positioned to provide the necessary positive engagement to deter people from traveling abroad to fight. Included is a discussion on the need by both community and government to partner with one another and why choosing the right institutions to partner with is essential. The article closes with a discussion on how the government community partnership is maximized through open dialogue, transparency, and the need to work locally.

Collectively, the seven articles provide a good cross-section of community-based initiatives that lend themselves well to positive examples in the counterterrorism environment. As mentioned, they are not the only mechanisms available but do offer some insight to what is possible. They also highlight some of the challenges that are equally abundant in this environment. Through these examples it is hoped that practitioners, academics, and policy-makers will find this collection relevant and thought provoking.

The Role of Communities in Counterterrorism: Analyzing Policy and Exploring Psychotherapeutic Approaches within Community Settings

Basia Spalek and Douglas Weeks

ABSTRACT
The role of communities in preventing or responding to terrorism and political violence is increasingly finding prominence within government strategies, nationally and internationally. At the same time, implementation of effective community-based partnerships has been nominal. Adding additional complexity to this problem are policies such as Prevent in Britain, which was arguably developed with good intentions but has received significant and sustained criticism by the very communities it sought to engage with. The result has been ongoing discussions within community practice and research arenas associated with radicalization, extremism, and terrorism, as to the role, if any, that communities might play in the counterterrorism environment. This article explores that environment and highlights some of the community-based perceptions and initiatives that prevail in the United Kingdom. In particular, innovations around the development of psychotherapeutic frameworks of understanding in relation to counterterrorism are discussed, alongside the role of connectors.

In recent years there has been an increasing shift in various government strategies to include narratives about engaging communities in their counterterrorism efforts. Although terrorism is nothing new for many countries, the decline of Al Qaeda as the preeminent threat did little to minimize concern. The rise of the Islamic State (IS) in Syria and Iraq immediately reinforced the perception that an existential threat and increasingly internal threat of terrorism exists. Furthermore, the barbaric nature of IS displayed in the media combined with the migration of thousands of "foreign fighters" from the West going to Syria and Iraq has resulted in high levels of anxiety for those in government. Those in Europe are particularly concerned because of the large numbers of "foreign fighters" leaving from and returning to European countries where the Schengen Agreement permits free and unobstructed travel across borders.

In response to the ongoing and the newest threat posed by the current foreign fighter phenomenon, governments are proposing more penetrating legislation while simultaneously attempting to impose additional "responsibilities" on communities in order to maximize their counterterrorism efforts. This is particularly true in the United Kingdom, where the government recently published its newest counterterrorism strategy. The newest rendition of the United Kingdom's CONTEST strategy is simply titled Counter-Extremism Strategy.[1] Intended to be broader than previous iterations the newest strategy purports to address "the full spectrum of extremism: violent and non-violent, Islamist and neo-Nazi—hate and fear in all their forms."[2] And, although the newest strategy is decidedly broader than previous iterations, the government makes clear from the start that their focus will remain fixed on Muslim communities when it states, "The greatest current challenge comes from the global rise of Islamist extremism."[3]

The United Kingdom's most recent counterterrorism strategy is built around four key pillars: countering extremist ideology; supporting mainstream voices; disrupting extremists; and building more cohesive societies.[4] The strategy also references introducing new laws designed to challenge the most troublesome groups and individuals, explores the possibility of revoking citizenship, and strengthens the Office of Communications to regulate and take punitive action against television and radio stations that broadcast unacceptable material.[5] Although it is not always possible to disaggregate the interconnected parts, of particular relevance here is that the strategy seeks to build more cohesive societies through a proposed Cohesive Communities Programme that will promote opportunity and integration through government/community engagement.[6]

The possible reasons behind the shift to strengthening community-based counterterrorism solutions are numerous and could be argued from a variety of different perspectives. Undoubtedly, the government would argue that policing and ultimately crime reduction has long established roots within the United Kingdom and is exemplified in its Peelian policing model. Whether the police are still seen as peers within the community is debatable but the U.K. government continues to promote the legacy of Robert Peel who advocated that the police are merely citizens in uniform.[7] An alternative and perhaps more cynical view is that government is realizing that despite fifteen years of adopting increasingly invasive and controversial counterterrorism laws it has been unable to legislate or police its way out of the problem of Islamist extremism. Individuals continue to radicalize despite efforts to the contrary. As mentioned above there are surely other arguable positions but regardless of which explanation seems closest to explaining the environment it is clear that the U.K. government is exercising all of its hard and soft power resources to manage its perception of the threat.

From a conceptual standpoint, it can be said that government and communities have very similar goals when it comes to counterterrorism in so much as violence is never a tolerable alternative in any robust democratic society. Additionally, because human nature is universal in that no one wants to feel vulnerable, the notion of security can be similarly argued as universal at the governmental, community, and individual levels. However, problems do arise when one person's security is reinforced through the erosion of another person's security.[8] Moreover, this can happen at the individual, group, community, and societal levels. Thus, while security is arguably a universal part of human nature, its application is not.[9]

At the community level the methods to achieve the sense of security can be both remarkably similar to government and at the same time significantly different. As an example, community resources do not possess the same traditional hard power resources that government has, such as the power of arrest. At the same time they do possess similar and arguably more effective soft power approaches, which include defining mainstream boundaries and passive observation of the environment.[10] Moreover, despite the current political rhetoric that one's acceptability in society is measured predominantly by one's adherence to "British values" it is the broader social sphere that defines the acceptable margins of society.

Especially in a country as diverse as the United Kingdom, there is also an argument that the margins of society are not universal; what is acceptable in one community is potentially not acceptable in another. That acceptability can occur for any number of religious, cultural, gender, sexual, or ethic reasons.[11] Examples might include halal or kosher foods, the acceptance of women working outside the home, male and female segregated professions, the approval of same-sex unions, or what clothes are acceptable. Thus, not only do communities establish the boundaries of what is acceptable and what is not, they passively monitor that environment to ensure compliance.[12] When individuals fall outside of defined communal boundaries they are seen as outliers and eyed with scrutiny. This is not entirely dissimilar to government, which must attempt to manage those whom it considers "insufficiently socialized" and take steps to control them through force or conversion.[13] Whether viewed from a governmental or community perspective, those outside of the margins arguably become the socially excluded "other."[14] Thus governments and communities are similarly involved in defining, monitoring, and validating the social order. More directly, those within the mainstream are accepted while those outside are not.[15] Another similarity is that each strive to make sure that there are limited unchallenged spaces where individuals can be recruited, plan, or execute violent acts. In most cases the police do that through securitization whereas communities, faith groups, and community activists do that from a social justice perspective.[16]

Despite the idea that government and communities each have mechanisms in place to monitor and ultimately manage the risk of terrorism, their commitment to working with one another to achieve the common goal of safety and security for all has not been a homogenous process. Although the notion of countering violent extremism (CVE) through the soft power mechanisms of community engagement has gained momentum quickly in the policy environment, the practical side of that momentum has proven to be far more challenging to implement. As if each are negotiating with the other, communities, the police, and policymakers are each attempting to define what that partnership should look like. Moreover, although all parties want to broker the best deal for their side, all simultaneously realize that it will be the communities who ultimately decide whether government is a viable partner. Last, even though there is a desire by communities to engage, government's past prioritization of security over engagement has left communities suspicious over any newly articulated desire to work together.[17]

Backdrop to Engaging Communities

Historically, there has been a reliance on the ability of the police and security services to disrupt criminal activity, or as is more often the case, investigate crimes once they have been committed with the goal of arresting those responsible.[18] Once arrested, individuals are prosecuted and imprisoned for their crimes. This approach is classically considered the retributive justice model; arrest, conviction, and imprisonment.[19] The basis of the retributive justice model is that individuals convicted of a crime must be punished and thus experience the consequences of their actions. This leads to the reality that most policing resources are not organized on the prevention of criminal activity but rather the investigation of crimes already committed.

However, this traditionally based reactive rather than proactive policing model is politically and professionally unacceptable in the counterterrorism environment.

Counterterrorism work necessitates that individuals be interdicted before their plot is carried out, which puts tremendous pressure on the police and intelligence services to seek every and all means to disrupt plots before they mature while simultaneously attempting to gather sufficient evidence for arrest and conviction.[20] Thus, from both the political perspective and policing perspective there is a constant search for ways to mitigate threats so that risk is managed at an acceptable level. The result is that the police and security service are perpetually uncomfortable about what it is that they do not know. This reality is not dissimilar to the infamous 2002 quote by former U.S. Secretary of Defense Donald Rumsfeld, who made reference to the unknown unknowns as a way to explain his uneasiness regarding possible weapons of mass destruction in Iraq.[21] The concerns over the unknown unknowns not only epitomize the counterterrorism working environment for law enforcement and security services personnel but also explains at least some of the motivation for leveraging every possible resource, including those in the community. This concept is fully understood by communities as well.

To be sure, in recent years there has been growing emphasis placed on building social resilience to extremist ideologies and organizations. Several policy documents in Britain, the United States, Australia, and other liberal democratic societies relate the view of the centrality of communities in the prevention or support of terrorism. In Britain, for example, rooted within the Northern Ireland experience, "communities defeat terrorism" has become a well-entrenched counterterrorism maxim as evidenced by the Prevent Strategy.[22] There has been, and continues to be, a significant onus placed on the community's ability to thwart terrorism through campaigns such as "See something, say something" in the United States and the "Anti-Terrorist Hotline" in the United Kingdom. Moreover, to impose a sense of duty, governments are openly advocating that citizenship carries with it certain sets of responsibilities, one of which is counterterrorism.[23] In the United States the Empowering Local Partners strategy invokes a sense of duty when it makes the statement "it becomes the collective responsibility of the U.S. Government and the American people to take a stand."[24] In the United Kingdom, the sense of duty is captured in the statement "our society does not just confer rights; it demands responsibilities of us too. You have the freedom to live how you choose to live—but you must also respect the freedom of others to live how they choose to live."[25] Linking those responsibilities with the government's interpretation of "British Values" the strategy asserts its demand that all citizens subscribe to those values by further stipulating that "we will also consider … how we can more easily revoke citizenship from those who reject our values."[26]

One of the key linkages to community-based counterterrorism efforts can be found in the 2011 review of the Prevent Strategy. In that review, the government articulated that vulnerability to violent extremism was more likely in some places and communities but simultaneously concluded that resilient people, groups, and communities have the capability to "rebut and reject proponents of terrorism and the ideology they promote."[27] Similarly, in another 2011 report, the U.K. government stated that "challenging and tackling extremism is a shared effort. We welcome the spontaneous and unequivocal condemnation from Muslim community organisations and other faith groups in response to the Woolwich attack."[28,29] The most recent and direct demonstration of the U.K. government's desire to partner with the community in the counterterrorism arena is found in its 2015 Counter-

Extremism Strategy whereby partnering with the community is one of the four key strategic pillars. The strategy states that it would "support the individuals and groups who have credibility and experience fighting extremism within their communities, by amplifying their voices and helping them where required."[30] Thus there is ample evidence that the U.K. government has promoted community partnerships within the counterterrorism arena for at least the last four years and arguably as far back as 2007 when the Prevent workstream was first introduced into the CONTEST strategy.

The United Kingdom has not been alone in its actions. The United States adopted a very similar approach and borrowed significantly from the United Kingdom when it published its Empowering Local Partners strategy in 2011. Although far less detailed than the United Kingdom's Prevent Strategy the Empowering Local Partners strategy again emphasizes the role of communities by saying "we will continue to assist, engage, and connect communities to increase their collective resilience abroad and at home."[31]

Whether in the United States, United Kingdom, or beyond, engagement efforts have included a wide range of initiatives. Those initiatives are too numerous to list here but actively seek to involve communities, schools, universities, youth justice agencies, police agencies, and others to counter all forms of terrorism, but particularly Al Qaeda–inspired and now IS-inspired terrorism. Widening the net even further, engagement efforts have often included the families of violent offenders, those considered nonviolent extremists, and those at risk of radicalization. Examples include Indonesia, Singapore, Saudi Arabia, and Malaysia, which all have government-sponsored de-radicalization programs that seek to provide counterterrorism intervention for mid-ranking and grassroots members of radical organizations. Supporting families is typically included as an integral part of those programs as well. Although the family and the offender have different needs, stability and support for both is believed to be required if successful de-radicalization is to be achieved.[32]

Returning once again to the United Kingdom, the 2015 Counter-Terrorism and Security Bill made the Prevent program a statutory responsibility for a variety of community-based and governmental resources that include: local authorities, schools, universities, healthcare providers, social services, and police agencies.[33] Within the Prevent workstream the Channel Programme was created as a pilot program in 2007 and is now one of the cornerstones of the government's counterterrorism efforts.[34] Channel is designed to support teens and young adults who are at risk of radicalization but only in the pre-criminal space.[35] Channel interventions work on a bespoke framework that allows Channel review panels to deliver individualized support based on the needs of the individual. The review panels are made up of a wide range of statutory partners but are always led by the police and chaired by a local authority representative.[36] That support might include a variety of mechanisms that range from mentoring, life skills counseling, anger management training, education opportunities, sports, job placement/employment assistance, family support, drug and/or alcohol rehabilitation programs, or housing support.[37]

The original Channel concept has also potentially changed with the latest iteration of the United Kingdom's Counter-Terrorism Strategy. In previous versions, Channel's aim was always stated as "supporting people at risk of radicalisation."[38] In the most recent publication on Channel Guidance it appears the government has changed the stated aim of Channel to "Protecting vulnerable people from being drawn into terrorism."[39] Whether this is simple mission creep, an undisclosed plan to expand the Channel Programme, or the conflation that radicalization is a precursor to terrorism is unclear. However, if the intent is to expand

Channel, helping move individuals away from radicalization to protecting those at risk of terrorism represents a large conceptual leap for the Channel Programme. Although those that mentor youth in the pre-criminal space and those that mentor those coming out of prison after serving sentences related to terrorism both come from community-based resources, they require completely different skill sets.[40]

As inferred above, a similar program exists within the United Kingdom's National Offender Management Service (NOMS) whereby individuals convicted on terrorism-related charges, charges considered terrorism related, or those that have been identified as being radical or extreme are being paired with community-based intervention providers as a condition of their license agreements.[41] Although the mentoring of youth and those that have progressed sufficiently to the point of engaging in criminal activity requires significantly different skill sets, one similarity is that those that employ a more holistic approach including social mentoring, employment and housing assistance, and educational activities appear to have greater success rates.[42] Whether there is a plan to merge Channel and the post-criminal mentoring services is unclear but changes do appear to be forthcoming. In the United Kingdom's latest Counter-Extremism Strategy (2015), the document states,

> Individuals further down the path to radicalisation need a particularly intensive type of support. When necessary this support will be mandatory. The Home Office will therefore develop a new de-radicalisation programme to provide this support by spring 2016. This scheme will be available to be used in conjunction with criminal sanctions.[43]

Interesting too is that despite the U.K. government's commitment to providing support and mentoring services, there is no measurement of efficacy for either program.[44]

Aside from mentoring, the U.K. government has engaged in several outreach programs through its Prevent workstream. Since its inception in 2007 the aim of Prevent has remained consistent; to "stop radicalization, reducing support for terrorism and discouraging people from becoming terrorists."[45] At its peak, there were 8–10 different nationalized community engagement programs operating in the United Kingdom and most were run by the police. Programs varied in content and covered a spectrum of issues, such as: having community members play the role of a counterterrorism investigation team so that they better understood the process; having the police guide local authority representatives as they developed and took action on a fictional counterterrorism case so that local government officials understood the process more thoroughly; workshops on radicalization case studies so that members of the public better understood the process; internal programs for police so that they could minimize community impacts when counterterrorism arrests are made; profiles of missed opportunities where statutory partners might have alerted authorities to those planning attacks; engagement with women's groups to create a network of informed and active community members; and bringing together individuals from a range of statutory bodies to explain their role in Prevent.[46]

The references above demonstrate that, increasingly, the U.K. government has been investing heavily in its community support and engagement activities. Whether that is out of need or out of a desire to maximize its counterterrorism efforts is unknown but there is clear engagement and support activity occurring. That is not to suggest that the role of traditional policing within the counterterrorism environment is being changed but rather is to suggest that the police have expanded their role to include community-based resources. There are several reasons for that but certainly one key element is that communities have the credibility and capability to effectively monitor and engage with at risk and high risk individuals that the police just do not have.

Although it can be argued that government is clearly asserting its soft power mechanisms to co-opt community-based individuals and resources in its counterterrorism activities, it can also be argued that it has been somewhat slow in developing that resource. As far back as 1981, academics such as Crenshaw[47] and more recently Galam[48] highlighted the reality that extremists and those involved in terrorism are in fact competing with government for community support. Whether that support is active or passive is simply a matter of scale. Moreover, the importance of that support should not be underestimated. A recent report by the New America Foundation in response to data obtained from the Snowden leaks concluded that the single largest identifiable source for initiating a terrorism investigation came from the category of community/family, not the intelligence or police services.[49] In fact, the community/family category outranked law enforcement by more than a 3:1 margin. Not only does this bring into question the issue of efficacy and value for money, it highlights the need for the police to develop more trusting relationships within the competitive community environment.

Nothwithstanding the discussion thus far, efforts for effective engagement with community groups have not gone as planned. In the United Kingdom, the Prevent agenda has backfired in many ways. According to Kundnani, the Prevent agenda has destabilized police/community relations by casting Muslims as the "suspect other," undermined community cohesion, eroded the notion of shared values and personal security, and generated widespread mistrust and community pushback resulting in additional space for antigovernment sentiment; the exact opposite of its intended purpose.[50] These kinds of reactions, coupled with antigovernment sentiment, should be reason to take pause. According to Crelinsten "an important element … in understanding the emergence of terrorism in any society is an appreciation of the forms that counter-terrorism has taken in that society."[51] These examples not only demonstrate the importance of community-based solutions to counterterrorism but speak to the unintended consequences that can occur when things go wrong.

In many ways the United Kingdom has become the proverbial canary in the coal mine when it comes to its counterterrorism efforts. Reacting to its perception of the "Islamist threat," in 2000 it began adopting some of the most comprehensive terrorism laws of any country in the West. In a succession of legislative actions between 2000 and 2015 it has adopted six pieces of terrorism law and in doing so it began exercising its hard power prerogative with determination. Despite those efforts, there is no sign that the threat is abating. In fact, as argued by individuals like Kundnani and those in government, the threat has actually increased both domestically and abroad. In response, since 2007 the U.K. government has put forth significant resources into expanding its community partnerships and utilized a variety of community-based resources to leverage its soft power, especially where it has neither the trust, capability, or capacity to operate. Thus, partnering with community is not only the best option, in many cases it is the only option.

While there are clear successes in some of its mentoring schemes and outreach programs, there have also been clear failures. As noted by Kundnani those failures have challenged the government/community relationship and brought widespread and significant criticism to the Prevent agenda as a whole.[52] Acknowledging some of its shortcomings, the U.K. government continues to seek engagement with communities across Britain asking once again for them to place their trust in government. However, despite acknowledging that communities are critical partners in the counterterrorism environment and that government has limited ability to monitor or influence unchallenged spaces, what seems to be missing is government's ability to put its trust in the community. Arguably, that is a key factor that will have to be negotiated before any meaningful progress and ultimately partnership can be achieved. However, the ability of government to relinquish power and/or extend trust is decidedly challenging in the current politicized environment. Similarly, because the Muslim communities are decidedly heterogeneous, deciding who the community leaders are and which ones to engage with creates a whole new set of challenges for communities and government alike. As a result, the most likely scenario moving forward seems to be an ad hoc approach whereby communities and government exploit opportunities when it is mutually beneficial. Although the scope and function of that relationship will be limited, it has the promise of building the necessary trust that will be required for a longer, more sustainable, and effective relationship.

The relationship between government and communities as discussed is certainly not without its specific challenges. However, interdiction and/or disruption is only the first half of the problem. Managing those at risk of radicalization and/or those extreme cases that may opt to use violence as a means to communicate their grievances is the second half of the problem. Although government sources suggest that programs like Channel are effective, they are clearly limited in both scope and capacity. Similarly, even when momentarily setting aside the negative aspects of Prevent, it is arguably limited in its effectiveness at "stop[ing] radicalisation, reducing support for terrorism and discouraging people from becoming terrorists."[53] As a result, a new approach is needed that can augment existing capabilities. One promising option may be to incorporate a more holistic psychotherapeutic approach.

Therapeutic Approaches for Communities in Relation to Counterterrorism

The importance of the role of communities within counterterrorism efforts offers the potential for innovative approaches to be developed. So far, one under-explored area in research, policy, and practice has been the application of psychotherapeutic frameworks of understanding and interventions within counterterrorism. Psychotherapeutic approaches offer insights into the connections between thoughts, emotions, and behavior, alongside understandings of how individuals experience and undergo change, and as such counterterrorism efforts could be enhanced by the incorporation of psychotherapy. The contention of these authors is that an integrative psychotherapeutic framework is most appropriate for applying to nonclinical settings such as counterterrorism. Integration involves going beyond the confines of any one psychotherapeutic school of thought, to combine a mixture of different approaches into a larger framework.[54] An integrative program of activity enables the most appropriate psychotherapeutic tools to be applied depending on the individual, organization, group, and wider social context. Currently, there are a few examples of single school psychotherapeutic approaches being applied to nonclinical settings. For example, a compassion-focused therapeutic approach is being developed in the United States in relation to police training, in order to promote and develop a police culture that is motivated by compassionate competency, especially in light of many instances of abuses of power committed by police officers. Increasing competency in emotional intelligence and emotional regulation is a core aspect of a compassion-focused approach, with the argument being that as a result of increased competence here police officers will be able to manage more effectively conflict, and they will be able to manage their own stress, frustration, and anger better, among other things.[55] Integration enables a richer combination of therapeutic tools in order to potentially have a greater impact.[56]

Regarding counterterrorism, an integrative psychotherapeutic approach would draw on a wide range of different psychotherapeutic traditions in order to develop greater understanding about the processes involved in radicalization, and in order also to then create new programs of intervention within community settings. One integrative framework that can be applied to counterterrorism is that of the Transtheoretical Model (TTM) as developed by Prochaska and Norcross.[57] The TTM is a biopsychosocial model explaining intentional change, and as such can be applied to understanding individuals' journeys into and out from radicalization. According to the TTM, psycho-behavioral change can be conceptualized through stages, levels, and processes of change. There are six stages of change—pre-contemplation, contemplation, preparation, action, maintenance, and termination. There are five levels of change that a person can experience—at the level of their situational problems, their cognitions, their interpersonal relationships, their family relationships, and their own, intra-personal, conflicts. The processes of change within the TTM explain how people undergo psychological and behavioral change: through consciousness raising; dramatic relief; self re-evaluation; environmental re-evaluation; self-liberation; social liberation; counterconditioning; a helping relationship; among others. Applying the TTM to radicalization research and practice can therefore helpfully provide understandings about the different stages, levels, and processes of change that individuals experience and moreover, can then inform the kinds of interventions given to individuals who have been radicalized or who are being drawn into extremism. For instance, a person may be at pre-contemplation stage (meaning that they are unconsciously aware) regarding family dynamics and any connections to them being radicalized, while being at the preparation stage in terms of becoming prepared to commit acts of violence. Different processes of change can be applied to the different stages of change in this example, as different processes of change are more effective when applied at particular stages of change.[58] So consciousness raising is most appropriate for a person at pre-contemplation stage whereas counterconditioning might be most appropriate for a person at a preparation stage of change. Thus, the suggestion here is that pre-crime and post-crime interventions can be more effective if informed by the TTM. Clearly, there needs to be research exploring the TTM in relation to counterterrorism efforts in order to build up an evidence base. While the TTM cannot provide any causal explanations of radicalization and de-radicalization, it can provide insights into the ways in which individuals have experienced change. Interestingly, researchers applying the TTM to deal with drug addiction have suggested people can go through the different stages of change in a matter of minutes.[59] Certainly, this would potentially also apply to people experiencing radicalization.

Another example of how an integrative psychotherapeutic approach can be applied to counterterrorism efforts is the integration of compassion-focused therapy with cognitive-behavioral approaches. Compassion-focused therapy has been developed by Gilbert.[60] This involves understanding how the brain works and then developing a compassion-focused approach to the challenges of being human. There are three types of affect regulatory systems within the human body: drive/excite/vitality (wanting, pursuing, achieving), content/safe/connected (soothing), and threat focused (protection, safety seeking). Compassion-focused therapy raises awareness within individuals about the nature of their brains and bodies and how individuals' threat systems can be over-stimulated. Techniques to encourage social safeness are promoted in order to encourage parasympathetic activity, especially in the myelinated vagal nerve.[61] Such techniques (including breathing, safe space, and compassionate imagery) seem extremely relevant for community-based counterterrorism initiatives in that they could increase individuals' resilience to violent narratives that are perhaps evoking a threat-based response within recipients. At the same time, a compassion-focused approach can help to ease inter- and intra-community tensions.

Turning to the integration of cognitive-behavioral psychotherapeutic knowledge, a core theme from cognitive-behavioral approaches is that individuals' reactions to events are as, if not more, important than the actual events themselves. This theme has a long history in that in 75 A.D. Roman philosopher Epictetus argued that "people are not disturbed by events, but by the view they hold about them."[62] In order to raise understanding within individuals as to how their thoughts are linked to their behavioral and emotional responses, an ABC model of cognitive-behavioral therapy has been developed, arising from the work of Albert Ellis.[63] A stands for an activating event, B refers to a belief that responds to that event, C being the consequences, an individual's feelings, behaviors and symptoms. Importantly, this model posits that it is possible to distinguish between a rational and irrational, and a healthy and unhealthy belief. Irrational, unhealthy beliefs are inflexible, illogical, dogmatic, and often self-critical, whereas rational, healthy beliefs are flexible, logical, and consistent with reality. This model allows a focus on an activating event and then exploring how that event has made a person feel through an exploration of their thought processes. Individuals can then be empowered to swap irrational, unhealthy beliefs with rational and healthy ones, thereby impacting positively on their subsequent feelings, behaviors, and symptoms.[64]

Clearly, there are potential connections between cognitive-behavioral therapeutic approaches and that of complexity theory in relation to radicalization. Complexity theory posits that funadamentalism and extremism are processes of complexity shutdown.[65] Individuals start to develop inflexible and dogmatic views, they make generalizations that are not supported by any concrete evidence, and then ignore alternatives. From some intervention programs, it has been found that participants can be encouraged to maximize a wider range of their own values in order to increase the complexity of their thinking.[66] New programs are currently being suggested that will draw on cognitive-behavioral therapeutic models in relation to developing critical thinking skills among young people in particular, so that they can be more resilient to radicalization. Such programs include psychoeducation about rational and irrational thoughts and common thinking errors, an exploration of the relaitonship between thoughts and emotions, and an exploration of healthy and unhealthy emotions and how these link to thinking patterns.[67] It is important to roll out such programs across school and also community settings because often there is a limited number of national intervention providers.

Additionally, connectors can be trained in psychotherapeutic frameworks and techniques. The importance of the role of connectors within counterterrorism initiatives within community settings has been previously discussed.[68] Connectors "may act within contexts characterised by low political and social trust. … As such, connectors carry the risk of being considered to be informants for the police." Connectors also are not necessarily community leaders because they can challenge social injustice; however, connectors can have the trust of disenfranchised and marginalized individuals who may be at risk of radicalization. A more recent study of connectors[69] has found that connectors seem to share similar social, geographical, and cultural backgrounds to the young people that they support, and this gives them the credibility to reach out to young people who are distrustful of more formal mechanisms of engagement. The connectors themselves have experienced radicalization, domestic violence, alcoholism, economic deprivation, and violence, and it seems to be these experiences that not only inspire them to support young people but also these experiences serve as the social glue, connecting them to young people. It is important to stress that the response of connectors is often informal in that they rarely seek help from the authorities and are keen to keep young people away from the attention of statutory agencies. The work that connectors undertake in relation to keeping young people safe from violence and from radicalization can therefore be enhanced by training them in integrative therapeutic approaches, including training them about the TTM, compassion-focused and cognitive-behavioral approaches. This might be one way of enhancing individual and community safety within a counterterrorism context where there is distrust of the authorities.

Conclusion

Despite government acknowledgments that community engagement and community-based counterterrorism efforts are critical in stemming the tide of radicalization and potential violence, the ability to engage effectively, promote trust, and support the role of organically driven community-based counterterrorism initiatives remains a work in progress. Whereas government efforts in places like the United States remain in their infancy, places like the United Kingdom have a substantial history of developing a variety of programs and approaches but with varied success. Moreover, some programs have been found to be not only unsuccessful, but in some cases detrimental. Thus, the mix and balance of hard and soft power mechanisms is a complex one that is not easily achieved.

Although security remains the ultimate goal of both government and communities, the manner in which that goal is achieved differs; governments largely seek security through legislation and policing whereas communities seek security through social justice mechanisms. These varied approaches epitomize the often dichotomous notions of human security versus state security. Similarly, in the counterterrorism environment there is the growing argument that state security will only be achieved when sufficient levels of human security are in place. Moreover, because human security is ultimately perceived though one's thoughts and emotions, and those ultimately drive behavior, there may be a place for a variety of nongovernment interventions such as therapeutic methods in the counterterrorism environment.

Therapeutic frameworks of understanding clearly have a potential significant contribution to make to community-based approaches to counterterrorism. It is important for policymakers, practitioners, and community members to be informed about the insights and interventions that therapeutic approaches can provide. This will involve gaining a political and social acceptability of using therapeutic approaches outside of a clinical setting.

Regardless of what approach is used or how hard and soft power is utilized, collaboration and cooperation is only likely to occur when there is mutual trust. Moreover, governments will have to put their faith and trust in communities before communities will restore their faith and trust in government. If and when that happens, more widespread and effective community-based counterterrorism will begin.

Notes

1. Home Office, *Counter Terrorism Strategy* (London: Her Majesty's Stationery Office, 2015).
2. Ibid, p. 11.
3. Ibid, p. 9.
4. Ibid.

5. Ibid.
6. Ibid.
7. Paul Wilkinson, *Homeland Security in the UK* (Oxon: Routledge, 2007).
8. Didier Bigo and Anastassia Tsoukala, *Terror, Insecurity, and Liberty: Illiberal Practices of Liberal Regimes after 9/11* (Oxon: Routledge, 2008).
9. Ibid.
10. Douglas Weeks, *Radicals and Reactionaries: The Polarisation of Community and Government in the Name of Public Safety and Security* (St Andrews: University of St Andrews, 2013).
11. Jennifer Jackson Preece, "Cultural Diversity and Security after 9/11," in William Bain, ed., *The Empire of Security and the Safety of the People* (London: Routledge, 2006).
12. Ibid.
13. Veena Das and Deborah Poole, eds., *Anthropology in the Margins of the State* (Santa Fe, NM: School of American Research, 2004).
14. William Bain, *The Empire of Security and the Safety of the People* (London: Routledge, 2006).
15. Talal Asad, "Where are the Margins of the State," in Veena Das and Deborah Poole, eds., *Anthropology in the Margins of the State* (Santa Fe, NM: School of American Research, 2004).
16. Douglas Weeks, "The Victimisation Experience and the Radicalisation Process. Findings from England," in Orla Lynch and Javier Argomaniz, eds. (The Hague: European Commission, forthcoming 2015).
17. Weeks, *Radicals and Reactionaries*.
18. David Garland, *The Culture of Control: Crime and Social Order in Contemporary Society* (Chicago: University of Chicago Press, 2002).
19. University of Portsmouth, "Types of Justice: 'Retributive Justice' v. 'Restorative Justice,'" Available at http://compass.port.ac.uk/UoP/file/c7ffec37-0632-475f-84ba-ae018a2f0f38/1/Types_of_law_I MSLRN.zip/page_11.htm (accessed 5 November 2015).
20. Lord Alex Carlile, "Recent Changes in Terrorism Law: An Insiders Perspective," Lecture, Kings College London, 3 September 2011.
21. Donald Rumsfeld, *Known and Unknown: A Memoir* (New York: Penguin Press, 2011).
22. Rachel Briggs, Catherine Fieschi, and Hannah Lownsborough, *Bringing it Home: Community Based Approaches to Counter-Terrorism* (London: Demos, 2006).
23. Home Office, *Counter-Terrorism Strategy*.
24. The White House, *Empowering Local Partners to Prevent Violent Extremism in the United States* (Washington, DC: The White House, 2011), p. 1.
25. Home Office, *Counter Terrorism Strategy*, p. 10.
26. Ibid., p. 47.
27. Home Office, *Prevent Strategy* (London: London: Her Majesty's Stationery Office, 2011), p. 108.
28. Cabinet Office, *Tackling Extremism in the UK: Report from the Prime Minister's Task Force on Tackling Radicalisation and Extremism* (London: Cabinet Office, 2011), p. 2.
29. Michael Adebolajo and Michael Adebowale were found guilty of murdering a British soldier, Lee Rigby, on the street near Woolwich barracks in South London in the first Al Qaeda–linked attack to claim a life on British soil since th July 2005. See Vikram Dodd and John Halliday, "Lee Rugby Murder," *The Guardian* 19 December 2013. Available at http://www.theguardian.com/uk-news/2013/dec/19/lee-rigby-murder-michael-adebolajo-adebowale-guilty (accessed 10 January 2014).
30. Home Office, *Counter Extremism Strategy*, p. 31.
31. The White House, *Empowering Local Partners*, p. 10.
32. Jolene Jerard, "Future Challenges in Fighting Radicalism: Roles of Non-Muslims in Community Engagement Efforts in Singapore, in A. Kader, ed., *Countering Radicalism: The Next Generation and Challenges Ahead* (Singapore: Singapore Malay Youth Library Association, 2009), pp. 95–106.
33. U.K. Parliament, *Counter-Terrorism and Security Bill* (London: Her Majesty's Stationery Office, 2015).
34. Home Office, *Counter Terrorism Strategy*.
35. Home Office, *Prevent Strategy*.
36. Home Office, *Channel Duty Guidance: Protecting Vulnerable People from being Drawn into Terrorism* (London: Her Majesty's Stationery Office, 2015).

37. Ibid.
38. Home Office, *Prevent Strategy*, p. 2.
39. Home Office, *Counter Terrorism Strategy*, p. 3.
40. Weeks, "The Victimisation Experience and the Radicalisation Process."
41. National Offender Management Service (NOMS), *MAPPA Guidance* (London: Ministry of Justice, 2012). Available at http://www.justice.gov.uk/downloads/offenders/mappa/mappa-guidance-2012-part1.pdf (accessed 14 February 2015).
42. Weeks, "The Victimisation Experience and the Radicalisation Process."
43. Home Office, *Counter Extremism Strategy*, p. 29.
44. Weeks, "The Victimisation Experience and the Radicalisation Process."
45. Home Office, *Pursue Prevent Protect Prepare: The United Kingdom's Strategy for Countering International Terrorism* (CONTEST 2009) (London: Her Majesty's Stationery Office, 2009).
46. Weeks, *Radicals and Reactionaries*.
47. Martha Crenshaw, "The Causes of Terrorism," *Comparative Politics* 13(4) (1981), pp. 379–399.
48. Salim Galam, "The September 11 Attack: A Percolation of Individual Passive Support," *The European Physical Journal B—Condensed Matter & Complex Systems* 26(3) (2002), pp. 269–272.
49. Peter Bergen, David Sterman, Emily Schneider, and Baily Cahall, *Do NSAs Bulk Surveillance Programs Stop Terrorists?* (New York: New America Foundation, 2014).
50. Arun Kundnani, *Spooked: How Not to Prevent Violent Extremism* (London: The Institute forRace Relations, 2009).
51. Ronald D. Crelinsten, "Analysing Terrorism and Counter-Terrorism: A CommunicationModel," *Terrorism and Political Violence* 14(2) (2002), pp. 77–122.
52. Kundnani, *Spooked: How Not to Prevent Violent Extremism*.
53. Home Office, *Prevent Strategy*, p. 2.
54. James Prochaska and John Norcross, *Systems of Psychotherapy: A Transtheoretical Analysis*, 7th ed. (Belmont: Brooks Cole/Cengage Learning, 2010).
55. Ariel Cowan, "The Impact of Police Compassion Competency," *White Paper* (The International Centre for Compassionate Organizations, 2015). Available at https://www.compassionate.center/ (accessed 17 November 2015).
56. Prochaska and Norcross *Systems of Psychotherapy*.
57. Ibid.
58. Ibid.
59. L. Mckie, E. Laurier, S. Lennox, and R. Taylor, "Conceptualising Smoking and Health: Eliciting the Smokers Agenda." Paper presented at the BSA Medical Sociology Group Annual Conference, University of York, 24–26 September 1999.
60. Paul Gilbert, *Compassion Focused Therapy: The CBT Distinctive Features* (London: Routledge, 2010).
61. Ibid.
62. Epictetus, quoted in Windy Dryden, "Rational Emotive Behavior Therapy," in *Encyclopedia of Cognitive Behavior Therapy*, eds. S. Felgoise, A. Nezu, C. Nezu, & M. Reinecke (New York: Springer, 2005), 322.
63. Albert Ellis Institute. http://albertellis.org/ (accessed 4 January 2017).
64. Avy Joseph, *Cognitive-Behavioural Therapy* (Chichester: Capstone Publishing, 2009).
65. Lynn Davies, *Education and Conflict: Complexity and Chaos* (London: Routledge, 2004).
66. Jose Liht and Sara Savage, "Preventing Violent Extremism through Value Complexity: Being Muslim Being British," *Journal of Strategic Security* 6(4) (2013), pp. 44–66.
67. Basia Spalek, Fiona Hammins, and Robina Khan, *Think to Challenge* (forthcoming).
68. Basia Spalek, "Community Engagement for Preventing Violence: The Role of Connectors," *Conflict and Terrorism Studies* 37(10) (2014), pp. 825–841.
69. Basia Spalek, *Crime Victims and Trauma* (London: Palgrave Macmillan, 2016).

Campaigning on Campus: Student Islamic Societies and Counterterrorism

Tufyal Choudhury

ABSTRACT
Cooperation in counterterrorism policing increases when communities can be confident that legislation and policy is not implemented in an arbitrary or discriminatory fashion: the ability to challenge executive overstretch, abuse, or misapplication of powers is vital for maintaining procedural justice. Through examining the experiences of the Federation of Student Islamic Societies, one of the oldest British Muslim civil society organizations, we see how key structural features of the counterterrorism legal and policy framework—the wide definition of terrorism, the broad discretion in the use of stop and search powers at ports, and the expansion of Prevent into the opaque terrain of nonviolent extremism—undermine cooperation.

Since 2001, government policymakers and security practitioners have recognized the need to work with individuals and organizations in Muslim communities to protect the United Kingdom against the threat of international terrorism.[1] The potential benefits of effective partnership and cooperation include the improved flow of information and intelligence to the police, a reduction in the backlash against state actions, and increased community capacity for countering violent extremism.[2] This article focuses on the legal and policy framework of counterterrorism, which shapes the terrain within which partnerships are negotiated and trust is built. Careful calibration is needed to ensure that broad legal powers and policies support rather than undermine cooperation and partnership with community organizations.

Research on cooperation between the public and the police finds strong and consistent links between public willingness to cooperate and evaluations of the legitimacy of the police. Such legitimacy is shaped by experiences and expectations of procedural fairness.[3] Furthermore, evaluations of procedural justice link to social group identity; thus, it is not only how an individual is treated that impacts their evaluation of procedural fairness, but how others belonging to their social group and community organizations representing that group are treated.[4] Key features of fairness include the application of policies and rules in a way that is seen to be consistent and transparent. Such transparency and consistency is important in avoiding the perception that rules are applied on the basis of personal prejudice or bias but are instead seen to be the result of the application of objective information and criteria.[5] The realistic possibility of identifying and challenging the abuse of executive powers is therefore important for procedural justice. The relationship between procedural fairness and cooperation appears to be particularly strong in the context of counterterrorism policing in the United Kingdom, as "procedural justice concerns ... prove better predictors of cooperation of British Muslims in counter-terrorism policing than either instrumental or ideological" reasons for cooperation.[6]

The British government has identified universities as a key site for recruitment by extremist organizations. This has made cooperation and partnership with both universities and student Islamic societies a primary focus in its counterradicalization strategy. The Counter-Terrorism and Security Act 2015 steps beyond voluntary cooperation and partnership and places a legal duty on universities to prevent people from being drawn into terrorism. Resistance to this, from teaching and student unions, highlights the potential for new legal and policy tools to undermine rather than support cooperation.

Through a focus on the experience of the Federation of Student Islamic Societies (FOSIS)—an umbrella body representing student Islamic societies active in colleges and universities across the United Kingdom—and their encounter with counterterrorism law and policy, this article suggests that perceptions of fairness and equal treatment, vital to cooperation, are undermined by the fundamental structural features of the United Kingdom's counterterrorism legal and policy framework. It argues that the legal framework generates perceptions of arbitrary and discriminatory application. This arises from having ill-defined and broad offenses, operating alongside wide discretionary powers that are sustained and deployed through constructing categories of suspicion in which Muslim identity plays a central role. Furthermore, it argues that a key shift in counterterrorism policy, the refocusing of the Prevent policy from an emphasis on violent radicalization toward challenging nonviolent extremism, has widened the scope of those falling within the reach of counterterrorism policy and created conditions in which the social welfare activities and activism of Islamic societies can become interpreted as indicators suggesting the potential for radicalization. The final part of the article examines FOSIS's campaign to draw attention to the extensive use, or from their perspective misuse, of counterterrorism stop and search powers at airports. The FOSIS campaign, responding to the experience of its members, aimed at greater accountability of the use of executive powers through greater transparency. However, it could not overcome the structural features embedded in the architecture of the legal powers that allow for no-suspicion stops. Their campaign, while successful in forcing a government review on the use of stop and search powers, nevertheless highlights how key features of the counterterrorism legal and policy framework make it difficult for Muslims, as individuals or through collective civil society organizations, to challenge executive overreach or abuse.

The Federation of Student Islamic Societies

FOSIS is one of Britain's oldest grassroots Muslim civil society organizations. Founded in 1962, the early period of postwar largely postcolonial labor migration to Britain, FOSIS was created to serve the pastoral needs of the growing number of Muslim students from overseas studying in Britain. In its early period, the group's political activism focused on political developments in the Middle East, drawing it to the attention of the Muslim Brotherhood and Jama'at-i Islami, thus creating an "Islamist legacy" that continues to color its public reputation.[7] For example, after 2005, those arguing for government to disengage from partnership with Islamist organizations cautioned against working with FOSIS. They argued that it was part of "a sophisticated strategy of implanting Islamist ideology among young Muslims in Western Europe."[8] The British government's review of the influence of the Muslim Brotherhood in the United Kingdom was tellingly brief and careful in its evaluation of the influence of the Muslim Brotherhood, noting that associates and affiliates to the Brotherhood had "at times" influenced FOSIS.[9] It provided no further details on whether this was a reference to its early or more recent history, nor the nature and type of influence. However, the contrast with the review's more detailed account of the influence of the Muslim Brotherhood on other U.K. organizations suggests that the links with FOSIS are limited and historic. It is perhaps also a reflection of the change and diversity to be found in any student organization, including student Islamic societies, where membership changes rapidly over short periods of time.

Today, FOSIS operates as an umbrella body that seeks to represent and serve Muslim students; its membership consists of affiliated student Islamic societies operating in British colleges and universities. These have a visible and active presence on many campuses. Three quarters of Muslim students in London reported the presence of an Islamic society in their college and half said that they took part in its activities.[10] Students join Islamic societies for a variety of reasons. Many enjoy the chance to network and meet other Muslim students; Islamic societies also provide an opportunity for charitable and other humanitarian work.[11] They lobby and advocate on issues arising from the religious needs of Muslim students, most notably in relation to provision of prayer space. Relationships with university authorities can become strained when they mobilize students to protest against university policies that impact religious practice.

In the 1990s, the growing participation of British Muslims in higher education should have created a greater role for student Islamic societies and FOSIS in the relationship between universities and Muslim students. Instead, growing concerns about the threat of religious fundamentalism and the visible presence of *Hizb-ut-Tahrir* on campuses culminated in a report from university authorities on extremism and intolerance and a National Union of Student's handbook on racism. Both documents were developed without consultation with FOSIS, even while other bodies seen as representatives of students that were the victims of the threat from Muslim religious fundamentalism were consulted.[12] The conspicuous absence of FOSIS in the consultations implied the culpability of Muslim students generally in the extremist problem.[13]

After the July 2005 London bombings, concerns about extremism and radicalization on campuses increased and universities became an arena of action for the Prevent policy. With the revision of Prevent in 2011, signaling a further shift in focus in the strategy from violent extremism to nonviolent extremist ideas, universities have become a focal point for addressing concerns of radicalisation by identifying and challenging nonviolent extremism. The government's relationship with FOSIS has therefore been a mixed one. On the one hand, there is recognition that FOSIS does represent a significant section of Muslim students and so there is a need for government to engage with such grassroots organizations. One indicator of the importance of FOSIS within the broader eco-system of British Muslim civil society organizations has been the willingness of senior British Muslim politicians from across the political parties to speak at FOSIS conferences despite negative media coverage.[14] Senior civil servants and police officers attended and addressed the 2011 "Radical Thinking" conference on extremism on campuses organized by FOSIS and the University College London Union

Islamic Society.[15] On the other hand, the role of FOSIS and student Islamic Societies has come under intense scrutiny, particularly for the platform or space that some Islamic society events have given to speakers or organizations viewed as extremist. The government review of Prevent concluded that FOSIS "could and should do more to ensure that extremists will be no part of any platform with which it is associated" and go to greater lengths to demonstrate their rejection of extremism.[16]

For Muslim civil society organizations, cooperation and engagement on counterterrorism entail a number of risks. Some community-based organizations are wary of working on counterterrorism as they believe this reinforces the perception of Muslims as a suspect community. There are also fears that counterterrorism initiatives are used for gathering intelligence and information about Muslim communities.[17] Furthermore, there is a belief that those organizations dependant on state funding will self-censor and curtail criticism of government counterterrorism policies. For grassroots community groups, their effectiveness and therefore credibility as partners for cooperation can require that they retain space to remain vocally critical of aspects of government policy they disagree with while cooperating on common issues. For FOSIS this means engaging on issues of counterterrorism, through conferences and workshops, while reflecting the concerns and criticism of their members on aspects of counterterrorism policy.

Government demands for action and cooperation from Muslim civil society in addressing the threat to "national" security ignores the gap that can exist between state and community perceptions of threats to safety and security.[18] Such cooperation is also made more difficult when the concepts at the core of counterterrorism policy—terrorism, extremism, and the relationship between the two—remain fluid, elastic, and imprecise.

Staying Within the Law: The Broad Definition and Wide Scope of Terrorism Offenses

The ability of a grassroots advocacy group like FOSIS to challenge any executive or institutional overreach, important for procedural justice, requires legal powers and duties to be defined with sufficient precision to identify and challenge their misuse. A legal duty on those involved in higher education to prevent terrorism, or prevent people from being drawn into terrorism, rests on the ability to clearly identify actions that constitute terrorism.

This section examines the lack of clarity in the definition of terrorism. It argues that the wide range of actions that fall within the definition of terrorism and that could be prosecuted for "terrorism offenses," as well as the broadening of Prevent to cover nonviolent ideas that lead to terrorism, expands the net of "suspect" groups to organizations like FOSIS. The low threshold of a capacious definition also contributes to permitting the extensive use of stop and search powers at airports. The impact of this on Muslim students, particularly international students, triggered FOSIS's campaign challenging the use of these powers.

Fundamental to the architecture of British antiterrorism legislation is the definition of terrorism contained in the Terrorism Act 2000 (TA 2000). This definition provides the basis for constituting serious criminal offenses out of actions that do not otherwise attract criminal liability; it also provides the trigger for the mobilization of the full panoply of coercive executive actions from Terrorism Prevention and Investigation Measures (TPIMs) and the proscription of organizations through to powers to stop and search individuals without the need for reasonable suspicion. The definition of terrorism is also relevant to the Prevent strategy, and the Prevent duty on universities, as this is aimed at preventing people from supporting terrorism or being drawn into terrorism.

The TA 2000 defines terrorism as any action (or the threat of action) that is "made for the purpose of advancing a political, religious, racial or ideological cause."[19] Furthermore, the action must be "designed to influence the government or an international governmental organisation or to intimidate the public or a section of the public." The definition encompasses "action" that involves serious violence either against a person or against property, as well as "action" that creates "a serious risk to the health or safety of the public or a section of the public," or is designed seriously to interfere or disrupt an electronic system.[20] Thus, it includes violence against property and actions affecting health and safety that fall short of endangering life. Furthermore, the "action" may be physical action but can also be, for example, the publication of ideas.[21]

The types of action that can constitute terrorism are broadened further by the lack of any geographical limitations; the definition covers actions *anywhere in the world* that seek to intimidate the public or section of the public *anywhere in the world* or to influence *any government in the world.*[22] The legislation makes no normative distinction between democratic states and dictatorships; thus, a defendant possessing material likely to be useful for terrorism directed at the overthrow of the Libyan regime of Colonel Gaddafi was guilty of an offense even though the U.K. government enabled and welcomed the subsequent regime change.[23] The definition of terrorism contained in the TA 2000 outlined above has been described as "remarkably" and, in some instances, "absurdly" broad.[24] In the U.K. Supreme Court, Lords Neuberger and Judge agreed that "[T]he definition of terrorism in section 1 in the 2000 Act is, at least if read in its natural sense, very far reaching indeed ... the definition of "terrorism" was indeed intended to be very wide ... [and] is indeed as wide as it appears to be."[25]

Such a wide definition poses obvious problems for organizations, like FOSIS, that are concerned with procedural fairness in the application of the law. The definition is far from self-executing; it provides no clear indication about which of the actions that fall within the definition of terrorism will actually be treated as terrorism by the state. The academic, parliamentary, and legal debate over the definition is populated with examples that highlight the potential reach of the law beyond anything that would be regarded as the proper focus of antiterrorism law. For example, violence in the course of the 1983–84 miners' strike, or direct action against refugee detention centres or nuclear weapons facilities that involved damage to the perimeter fences of such locations fall within the scope of the definition of terrorism. To illustrate the far-reaching breadth of the definition, David Anderson QC, the Independent Reviewer of Terrorism Legislation, gives the example of a blog that argues (on religious or political grounds) against the vaccination of children for certain diseases, noting that "if it were judged to create a serious risk to public health, and if it was designed to influence government policy, its publication would be classed by the law as a terrorist action."[26] As the earlier examples indicate, many of the actions that fall within the broad definition of terrorism are rarely treated as terrorism; some may be dealt with through the ordinary criminal law and public order offenses, and others are unlikely to attract any official sanction or attention. The fact that actions that fall within the definition of terrorism are not pursued as such is not due to legislative precision but the exercise of executive discretion and restraint.[27]

The danger is that the wide discretion afforded to the state in the application of counterterrorism laws has the potential to lead to discriminatory practices, with the term terrorism determined by the identity or assumed identity of the individual rather than the nature of their actions. There is a risk that the term terrorist is reserved for "categories of perpetrators with which it is stereotypically associated."[28] For example, while the definition does not provide for any hierarchy between the different types of political, religious, racial, or ideological causes, in practice not all causes are treated the same. Anderson notes that in Northern Ireland it was widely believed that Republican violence was viewed through the lens of terrorism while Loyalist actions were more often dealt with as issues of public order or ordinary criminality. He goes on to suggest that "in Great Britain, there may also have been a tendency to categorise Islamist-inspired violence as terrorism more readily than what is still often referred to as 'domestic extremism.'"[29] Furthermore, the definition encompasses actions motivated by political or ideological beliefs such as animal rights, yet as Lord Carlile, Anderson's predecessor as Independent Reviewer of Terrorism Legislation, notes, "it has become the practice to deal with animal rights terrorism not using terrorist provisions ... but under criminal law."[30] While it is possible to argue that the law should not treat all forms of possible terrorism with moral and legal equivalence, the current legal framework avoids such normative judgements.

Ordinary criminal law already covers violence against property and person as well as any attempt, incitement, or conspiracy of such offenses. However, the scale of the harm that a terrorist action can entail has provided justification for extending the reach of the criminal law beyond directly harmful actions to the conduct leading up to that harm. The wide definition of terrorism is central to a growing number of offenses that include the dissemination of terrorist publications,[31] acts preparatory to terrorism,[32] training for terrorism,[33] attending a place used for terrorist training[34] or failing to disclose information that might be of material assistance "in preventing the commission by another person of an act of terrorism."[35] The law, in these cases, is criminalizing activities and conduct on the basis that they are likely to lead to terrorist action that is so harmful in its scale that it justifies this early intervention.

These developments can also be seen as part of a wider shift from a post-crime society, in which "crime is conceived principally as harm or wrongdoing" to a pre-crime society, which "shifts the temporal perspective to anticipate and forestall that which has not yet occurred and may never do so."[36] Such offenses may be better characterized as aimed at "pre-emption" rather than "prevention" as it points toward an outcome that cannot be proven.[37] MacDonald refers to these as "precursor crimes," noting that the ordinary criminal law of attempts "criminalises acts that are more than merely preparatory" while "precursor crimes focus on various forms of preparatory conduct."[38] The problem with such offenses is that they "hold a person responsible now for her possible future actions."[39] The further away temporally from the harmful action, the less reliable the prediction of future harmful acts that the offense is seeking to preempt. In such circumstances, "measures based on what is described as 'circumstantial evidence' come perilously close to criminalising risky types (rather than acts) and thoughts (rather than deeds)."[40]

The need to exercise discretion combined with a lack of clear guidelines on how it is exercised can add fuel to perceptions among some within Muslim communities that counterterrorism legislation is applied in a discriminatory fashion against Muslims.[41] Such concerns are reinforced with examples of cases where actions of non-Muslims that fall within the definition of terrorism do not appear to be treated as such. Notable cases include Robert Cottage, former member of the far right, British National Party, who was found with a stockpile of chemicals in his home and charged with possession of the chemicals under the Explosive Substances Act 1883,[42] and the lack of action against former Special Air Service (SAS) officer Simon Mann and Mark Thatcher (son of the former prime minster, Margaret Thatcher), both of whom were involved in 2004 in plans to overthrow the government of President Obiang of Equatorial Guinea.[43]

For those who face prosecution for terrorism offenses, the "discrepancy between the wrong that the offence targets and what it actually encompasses" also means that the basis of their selection for prosecution does not lie in their actions alone.[44] Thus, great weight is placed on the discretion of the state on who to prosecute and this will be decided on the basis of whether or not the individual is seen to pose a threat to "national security." However, while the national security consideration is relevant for the prosecuting authorities in selecting a particular individual for prosecution, once that person is charged they will be judged by the law as set out in the statute. They cannot argue that the offense was not aimed at people like them, or that they have been unfairly selected for prosecution. This denies "individuals the opportunity to address the reasons they have been selected for prosecution" and undermines "the courts' ability to deliver procedural justice."[45]

For student Islamic societies a key concern is around the offense of encouragement of terrorism that was introduced in the Terrorism Act 2006 (TA 2006). The TA 2006 makes it an offense to "publish" or cause to be published a "statement that is likely to be understood by some or all members of the public to whom it is published as a direct or indirect encouragement or other inducement to them to the commission, preparation, or instigation of acts of terrorism."[46] The statute itself remains largely silent on the crucial issue of what constitutes direct or indirect encouragement or other inducement. In respect of indirect encouragement there is some limited elucidation; it includes "every statement which glorifies the commission or preparation (whether in the past, in the future or generally) of acts of terrorism."[47] What is particularly concerning is the fact that the offenses can be committed recklessly,[48] and irrespective of whether or not anyone is in fact encouraged.

In determining whether a statement is "likely to be understood" by some of the members of the public to whom it is made as an encouragement or inducement, the context and audience become critical factors. During the passage of the legislation the government explained that "no offence will be committed if a member of an audience at an academic lecture thinks, 'Well, I am not encouraged to commit terrorist acts, but I can quite imagine that, *if this sentiment was expressed at a gathering of young Muslim men*, it could have an encouraging effect on them' (emphasis added)."[49] The minister's comment, while trying to alleviate concerns about the chilling effect of the offense on free speech, inadvertently points toward the way in which statements made in the course of a student Islamic society talk or debate could be unlawful by virtue of the largely Muslim audience at such events, while the same statements would be unproblematic if made at other student society events.

A further concern is that the offense, while it does not have direct extra-territorial application, does apply to statements made in the United Kingdom in relation to actions overseas. This brings within the scope of the legislation statements by individuals that provide direct or indirect encouragement of acts of terrorism to those involved in violent political resistance to any government, irrespective of the nature of the regime or the opportunities for nonviolent resistance. Through the membership of its affiliates, FOSIS became aware of the impact of the geographical breadth of the offense on Muslim students from countries with nondemocratic, authoritarian, or military rulers. The ability for such students to express support for radical political change is curtailed by the risk that the government of such states can request that the U.K. authorities take action where there is any indirect incitement against them.

For FOSIS and student Islamic societies, a further concern is the potential for any organization that encourages or promotes terrorism to be proscribed under the TA 2000.[50] The promotion or encouragement of terrorism "includes any case in which activities of the organisation include the unlawful glorification of the commission of preparation of acts of terrorism" or where the organization's activities "are carried out in such a manner that ensures that the organisation is associated with statements containing any such glorification."[51] The wide scope of these offenses leaves student Islamic societies uncertain about the boundaries of the criminal law and may have a chilling effect on the discussion and debates they host and the speakers they invite. As proscription is an executive action, it lacks the same safeguards that would apply to a criminal prosecution.

Concerns noted in this section regarding the broad legal definition of terrorism are amplified further by the expansion of counterterrorism policy to include "extremism." The lack of clear definition creates a broad discretionary space in which individuals or organizations can be labeled as extremist with limited scope of effective external challenge to the exercise of such power. It is within this context that the warning to FOSIS, in the 2011 Prevent Strategy, that it had "not always fully challenged terrorist and extremist ideology within the higher and further education sectors," and the demand that FOSIS members take "a clear and unequivocal position against extremism and terrorism" could be seen as particularly worrying.[52]

Extremism and Radicalization on Campus

Prevent has been a strand of Contest, the UK counterterrorism strategy, since its inception in 2003; however, it was only after the 2005 London bombings, and the involvement of young British men, that Preventing Violent Extremism (PVE) took on a more central role in the overall strategy.[53] Prevent aims to stop radicalization, reduce support for terrorism, and discourage people from becoming terrorists.[54] Under the Labour government, Prevent focused on countering "violent radicalization" and at times involved working with groups and organizations that clearly opposed violence but shared aspects of ideological views of those involved in violence. The Coalition government that came into power in 2010 published a revised Prevent Strategy in 2011. This strategy signaled a shift and widening in the focus of Prevent to include the broader set of ideas that it argued underpinned radicalization. Thus, "preventing terrorism" involved challenging nonviolent extremist ideas "that are also part of a terrorist ideology."[55]

The need to work with communities on counterterrorism was recognized in the period after the July 2005 London bombings, as a wide range of individuals active across Muslim civil society participated in the Preventing Extremism Together working groups that met over the summer of 2005. Starting in 2007, the Prevent Strategy involved an investment of £150 million in Prevent projects, much of which went toward developing partnership or providing grants developing the leadership and capacity of Muslim civil society organizations. It is estimated that 44,000 individuals, mainly young Muslims, had participated in PVE programs during its pilot year alone.[56] Concerns about the policy's focus on funding toward Muslim civil society led to criticism that it was "stigmatising, potentially alienating" and failed "to address the fact that that no section of a population exists in isolation from others."[57] Such criticisms contributed to the decision to separate Prevent and Cohesion policy, with responsibility for Prevent being placed with the Office of Security and Counterterrorism (OSCT) within the Home Office.

The relocation of Prevent to the OSCT reinforced concerns that Prevent projects were being used to develop an apparatus of state surveillance, gathering information about Muslim communities.[58] At the same time, the attempt to develop partnership with communities appears to have given way to a far greater emphasis on the role of public sector agencies in identifying young people "at risk" of radicalization.

This is solidified through the Counter Terrorism and Security Act (CTSA) 2015. The CTSA places a legal duty on public bodies, including universities, requiring them, in carrying out their functions, to have "due regard to the need to prevent people from being drawn into terrorism."[59] The statutory guidance accompanying this duty makes clear the expansive scope of this duty as it elaborates that "being drawn into terrorism includes not just violent extremism but also non-violent extremism, which can create an atmosphere conducive to terrorism and can popularise views which terrorists exploit."[60] Thus, the concern is not with all forms or expressions of nonviolent extremism that can lead to violence; rather, it is only concerned with nonviolent extremism related to the risk of terrorism. The need for a link with the potential for terrorist violence ensures that expressions of homophobia, anti-Semitism, and sexism by Muslims can become a concern for security and counterterrorism policy while similar views from other students would be challenged through equality, diversity, and antiracism policies. The duty requires "frontline staff who engage with the public" to "understand what radicalisation means and why people may be vulnerable to being drawn into terrorism as a consequence of it" as well as the "relationship between extremism and terrorism." Universities are required to "provide appropriate training for staff involved in the implementation" of the duty.[61] The specific guidance for universities calls on the need to manage the risk of radicalization off campus from radicalized students, noting that "change of behaviour and outlook may be visible to university staff."[62] The Russel Group of Universities, in their response to the consultation on the draft guidance, noted that "students often undergo a developmental period in their lives whilst at university and their time there can prove to be a transformational experience. It is not at all unusual for students to display changing behaviours which are a natural part of their development."[63]

One of the problems in creating a statutory duty that applies across the education sector is the policy's reliance on assumptions about radicalization that remain deeply contested.[64] Radicalization is identified by Prevent as "the process by which people come to support terrorism and, forms of extremism leading to terrorism."[65] Research on radicalization highlight different factors that are understood to contribute to the process, and posit various models of the relationship between ideological, social, and psychological factors as well as group and individual dynamics.[66] Unable to identify which individuals holding radical ideas will cross the line from radical ideas to terrorist violence, counterradicalization policies fall back on identifying "indicators." As there is no typical profile of an extremist and no single indicator of when a person could move from holding extremist views to violent action, the reach of counterterrorism policies is wide and is used to justify greater levels of surveillance, deeper into Muslim communities and support preemptive intervention against those deemed to be "at risk."[67] The narrative of radicalization can lead to signs of what would otherwise be normal processes of childhood and adolescences or expressions of anger at social injustice becoming pathologized into indicators of risk and possible future terrorist violence.[68] Such models of radicalization lead to universities (where young people are often away from home for the first time and are experimenting with new ideas and identities) being seen as sites of vulnerability to radicalization.[69]

Soon after the July 2005 London bombings there were reports expressing concerns about the threat of violent radicalization on British campuses.[70] Prevent and Contest both identify university campuses as sites of radicalization. The fear of violent radicalization on campus soon led to accusations that student Islamic societies were incubators of violence and terrorism. However, the evidence to support this claim remains mixed. The Centre for Social Cohesion's 2010 report drew attention to the extremist preachers that have spoken at Islamic society events and the number of individuals convicted of terrorism that have been involved in student Islamic societies, assuming the link between a propensity to violence and holding extremist ideas. Their claim is undermined by their own data, which finds that 15 percent of convicted "Islamist terrorists" had attended universities in the United Kingdom.[71] As more than 40 percent of Muslims leaving school at the age of 18 pursue higher education the data have been interpreted as showing that universities increase resilience, rather than vulnerability, to radicalization.[72]

The case of Umar Farouk Abdulmutallab, whose attempt in 2009 to detonate a bomb on an airplane in Detroit illustrates the problems in drawing a clear link between universities and radicalization. Contrary to the Centre for Social Cohesion's claim—that Abdulmutallab's radicalization while studying at University College London (UCL) was an established fact— the universities minister revealed that the Security Services had not been able to "pinpoint whether the university experience was the specific trigger."[73] This was echoed by the Caldicott inquiry, which found no evidence to support the claim that Abdulmutallab was radicalized while studying at UCL or that "conditions at UCL during that time or subsequently are conducive to the radicalisation of students."[74] Similarly, the 2012 Home Affairs Select Committee Report found there "may be a much less direct link than was thought in the past" between university education and terrorist activity.[75] This led them to conclude that "the emphasis on the role of universities by government departments is now disproportionate."[76]

With no clear and direct link between Abdulmutallab's university activities and subsequent terrorist violence, the focus shifts on to the broader notion of extremism and extremist activities. Thus, he is described as falling into the category of students that were "attracted to and influenced by extremist ideology while at university" but who engaged in violence after leaving university.[77]

It is within this wider focus on unacceptable *extremism* (rather than violence), that the 2011 Prevent Strategy singles out FOSIS for failing to "fully challenge … extremist ideology," and demands that FOSIS members take "a clear and unequivocal position against *extremism*" (emphasis added).[78] The 2011 Prevent Strategy only goes some way toward identifying some of these unacceptable extremist ideas: this includes the claim that the West is perpetually at war with Islam, ideas that oppose the legitimacy of interactions between Muslims and non-Muslims and claims that Muslims "cannot legitimately and or effectively participate in our democratic society." More opaquely it includes "problems" that "Islamist extremists can purport to identify … to which terrorist organisations then claim to have a solution."[79] The Prevent Strategy also notes that extremist narratives exploit perceived or real grievances at the local level, including claims of discrimination. Similarly, Lord Carlile argued that "support for extremism is often associated with a perception of discrimination ... a sense of victimhood sometimes created, and always preyed upon by extremists."[80] This creates a danger of deterring or silencing organizations that attempt to identify and challenge discrimination and Islamophobia by implicating them in inadvertently furthering, if not deliberately propagating, extremist narrative of Muslim victimhood and grievance.

Of particular concern to FOSIS and student Islamic societies is the potential that their core welfare activities, including advocacy and lobbying for the accommodation of religious needs, is reframed as providing support for extremist narratives of grievance and Islamophobia. For example, the former Higher Education Minster Bill Rammell argued that the "unreasonable" demands for the accommodation of religious needs of Muslim students created grievances that can be exploited and push students toward extremism.[81] This locates disputes over the right of Muslim female students to wear the *niqab* and disputes over the provision of adequate prayer space into the landscape of extremism.[82] In doing so, it exemplifies "the way strategies of ... 'preventing' 'terror' have become so broad in scope as to include mundane requests for Muslim provisions."[83] The legitimacy of such campaigns is brought into question when they are viewed through the prism of extremism as contributing to or perpetuating a terrorist narrative of Muslim victimhood. In fact, such a characterization fails to see the extent that campaigns challenging discrimination and Islamophobia reflect claims of equal rights and engagement by Muslims as active citizens that are in fact a direct and effective challenge to any extremist narrative of disengagement or disempowerment.[84]

Challenging Stop and Search at Airports

The ability of civil society advocacy organizations to challenge the discriminatory or arbitrary use of discretionary powers is important to ensuring procedural fairness, a key determinant of cooperation with the state. This section explores the role of FOSIS in leading a grassroots Muslim civil society campaign to challenge the use of powers to stop and search individuals at ports and airports.

As a community-based organization that is rooted in, and connected to, the lived experience of Muslim students through members of affiliated student Islamic societies, FOSIS became aware of the impact of airport stops under Schedule 7 of the TA 2000 at a time when this was not on the radar of mainstream human rights organizations. The impact and use of Schedule 7 remained largely unnoticed in mainstream public examination of counterterrorism law and policy until 2011: Schedule 7 was not included in the 2010 government Review of Counter-Terrorism and Security Powers; it barely featured as an issue of concern in Lord Carlile's 2009 report as Independent Reviewer of Terrorism Legislation;[85] nor was it included in the Equality and Human Rights Commission report on the operation of Stop and Search powers in England and Wales.[86] FOSIS's campaign played a key role in raising the profile of Schedule 7 stops.

Schedule 7 enables examinations to be carried out at ports and the border areas "for the purpose of determining whether [the person being examined] appears to be a terrorist"; in other words, is or has the person stopped "been concerned in the commission, preparation or instigation of acts of terrorism." The definition of terrorism noted earlier ensures that the scope of people this power can be used to identify for questioning is broad. Crucially, while the purpose of these stops is to determine whether the person is a terrorist, there is no requirement to have reasonable suspicion of the person that is being stopped. This therefore grants significant and broad discretion to an examining officer in deciding which individuals to stop. In effect it requires the identification of individuals whose appearance, actions, or behavior make them look like a terrorist. The Schedule 7 power is therefore not comparable to the body search of passengers and the screening of cabin baggage at airports as these are applied to all airport passengers and so do not involve the exercise of any significant discretion or selection.

The emergence of stops at airports as an issue for FOSIS reflected the demographic profile of its members: most are young British students largely in their late teens and early twenties; like other British students many travel abroad, in groups, often for long periods with no clear itinerary or purpose (i.e., backpacking); the membership also includes international students from counties with undemocratic and authoritarian rulers.

By 2009 FOSIS were sufficiently concerned about airport stops to create a Civil Liberties Division within their organization to lead their campaign on Schedule 7. There were a number of elements to the campaign. First, through workshops and information packs FOSIS sought to raise awareness among Muslim student of their legal rights if they found themselves stopped at an airport. This was particularly important as there is no right to a lawyer for a person stopped and examined under Schedule 7. Furthermore, refusing to answer questions is an offense under the TA 2000. Second, they developed their contacts with other campaign organizations and student groups. FOSIS's civil liberties officer became a key participant in the nongovernmental organization (NGO) Stopwatch, an umbrella group for organizations that campaign for accountability in the use of police stop and search powers. Third, they utilized existing public and institutional accountability mechanisms. They raised their concerns directly with David Anderson, the Independent Reviewer Counter Terrorism Legislation. According to Anderson, the "main pressure for reform" of Schedule 7 came from FOSIS.[87] The impact of Schedule 7 featured prominently in the Independent Reviewer's 2012 and 2013 reports, as well as in research by the Equality and Human Rights Commission.[88] FOSIS's work led Anderson to commend them for their "strong and constructive campaigning record" in drawing attention to concerns about the use of stop and search powers at airports, he also urged that in any government consultation reviewing the powers, FOSIS's voice is "clearly heard"[89] FOSIS also gave evidence to the Metropolitan Police Authority's (MPA) examination of police use of DNA data. The evidence from FOSIS appears to be the primary source for the MPA report's discussion around community concerns arising from the collection of DNA data from those stopped at airports under Schedule 7.[90]

A key part of their strategy was to increase the information in the public domain regarding the use of Schedule 7. Crucial to this was the use of Freedom of Information Act requests to obtain the release of data on the number of stops. The data released revealed the extensive use of the power. Between 2009–2014 over 338,000 people were "examined."[91] Furthermore, half a million people each year are estimated to have been asked screening questions but not formally "examined."[92]

Taking a cue from the challenge to the use of counterterrorism stop and search power in the street under section 44 TA 2000, FOSIS sought to establish that the power was used disproportionality against minority ethnic groups. However, no data on the ethnicity of those stopped was collected until 2009. An application for the release of post-2009 data was initially denied on grounds of national security. Its eventual release gained significant media attention.[93] It featured as a front page story in the Guardian and led to calls by David Lammy MP and Hamza Yusuf MSP for a review of Schedule 7. Anderson also gave greater attention to the impact of Schedule 7 stops and called for a review of the use of the power. The pressure paid off; a formal government review of Schedule 7 was undertaken in 2012. This led to some important changes in the legal framework for the use of the power as well as a significant reduction in its use.[94]

The FOSIS campaign, while successfully contributing to the pressure for a review of Schedule 7, brings into sharp focus the difficulties of challenging the misuse of a power that rests on a structure of broad discretion. The inability to prove improper exercises of the power inherent within the structure of the discretion it created undermines any possibility of securing procedural fairness.

Judicial comments on the exercise of discretion to stop people using powers under s44 TA 2000 are relevant to Schedule 7, as both allow for stops without the need for reasonable suspicion.[95] In a case before the House of Lords and then the European Court of Human Rights, challenging the use of s44, it was argued that the wide discretion granted to police officers in selecting individuals for stops meant that the power could be exercised in an arbitrary manner, leaving the "public … vulnerable to interference by public officials acting on any personal whim, caprice, malice, predilection or purpose other than that for which the power was conferred."[96] The House of Lords, when considering the case had commented that s44 stops should be used to selectively target "those regarded by the police as most likely to be carrying terrorist connected articles"[97] and "cannot, realistically, be interpreted as a warrant to stop and search people who are obviously not terrorist suspects."[98] It endorses the use of profiles that provide predictive assessments of who is likely to be a risk. While risk-based profiles are a legitimate tool, where the profile is developed to include data about the characteristics of those who have been convicted of terrorism-related offenses, caution is needed as it is likely to include individuals convicted of preemptive offenses, which themselves criminalize activities and actions based on assumptions about the profile of risky individuals. The Strasbourg Court, in its judgement of the case concluded that the "breadth of discretion conferred on individual police officers" created a "clear risk of arbitrariness." They also noted that "in the absence of any obligation on the part of the officer to show a reasonable suspicion, it is likely to be difficult if not impossible to prove that the power was improperly exercised."[99]

Furthermore, the fact that there may be good reasons for the profile that gives rise to the suspicion does not prevent it from being stigmatizing. A stop that is targeted, because it is based on a carefully developed profile or other evidence, is simultaneously more stigmatizing when it is a false positive and contributes to feelings of humiliation and alienation.[100] For Muslims such stops "raise painful questions about how they are seen and positioned by others": they experience shock, hurt, and confusion from the failure of the state to see them as "respectable, moderate, law-abiding and contributing members of society."[101] The lack of complaints and challenges may reflect strategies for managing "risky" Muslim identities through performances of "safe" identities.[102]

Until the FOSIS campaign highlighting the scale of Schedule 7 stops, its impact remained largely unnoticed and below the radar of civil society activists and watchdog bodies. The limited number of formal complaints were noted as an indicator of the "remarkable docility with which passengers for the most part submit to police questioning."[103] The lack of complaints conceals the profound anger and resentment that many British Muslims felt from their experiences of Schedule 7.[104] Furthermore, in a context where disproportionality is to be expected and accepted as evidence of effective policy implementation rather than discrimination, the lack of complaints reflects the difficulty Muslims in particular are likely to encounter in establishing that their stop is based on the unlawful discriminatory or arbitrary exercise of the discretion. It is perhaps not surprising that the high profile test cases that mainstream civil liberties campaign groups have used to challenge the use of s44 (Gillian and Quinton) and Schedule 7 (Miranda), and that have gained public attention, concern non-Muslims; in other words, people that so obviously do not fit the profile of those who are likely to be terrorist suspects.

Acknowledging the limits and difficulties that Muslim students face in mounting a credible legal challenge to the use of Schedule 7 powers, FOSIS, as a grassroots organization, has focused its advocacy and campaigning in working with student Islamic societies to raise awareness among young Muslims of their rights when they are stopped. By raising the profile of the use of the power in the media, campaigning with other NGOs and through dialogue with the Independent Reviewer of Terrorism Laws they contributed directly to the government's decision to review Schedule 7. Their campaigning places them in the broader British tradition of seeking social change and defending civil and political rights by applying "pressure through law"[105] The success of their advocacy on Schedule 7 highlights the vital role of grassroots community organizations in drawing attention to issues that directly affect Muslim communities.

Conclusion

Cooperation in counterterrorism policing increases when communities can be confident that legislation and policy is not implemented in an arbitrary or discriminatory fashion: the ability to challenge executive overstretch, abuse, or misapplication of powers is vital for maintaining procedural justice. This article has argued that the wide definition of terrorism, the broad discretion in the use of stop and search powers at ports, and the expansion of Prevent into the opaque terrain of nonviolent extremism, are all key structural features of the counterterrorism legal and policy framework that operate to deter cooperation.

For over 50 years FOSIS has been involved in providing services and support for Muslim students in British colleges and universities. Its experience of the counterterrorism legal and policy framework provides insight into how these structural weaknesses impact on students and how a community organization resists and responds. The overreliance on executive discretion in the "targeting" of prosecution on "real" cases of terrorism reinforces perceptions that decisions to prosecute are based on unacknowledged or unarticulated factors and generates uncertainty. Key activities undertaken by FOSIS—advocacy, student mobilization, protest around the accommodation of religious needs, campaigning against discrimination and Islamophobia, partnership with the National Union of Student in leading the "Students not Suspects" campaign against the implementation of the statutory duty on Prevent in universities—when viewed through the prism of the need to challenge nonviolent extremism, risk becoming seen as contributing to an extremist narrative of grievance. These actions can, however, be better understood as examples of direct civic engagement. As such, they provide an effective challenge to those who reject democratic and civic engagement in favor of violence. Such an interpretation challenges the perception that FOSIS is not doing enough to address extremism; it acknowledges that the different modes, methods, and approaches adopted by community organizations can be effective in supporting greater participation and integration. They contribute to deliberative politics by bringing the concerns and experiences of marginalized groups into the public domain, showing how community organizations, "attuned to how societal problems resonate in the private life spheres," are able to "distill and transmit such reactions in amplified form to the public sphere."[106]

Acknowledgments

Sincere thanks for comments on earlier drafts to Thom Brooks, Zin Derfoufi, Helen Fenwick, Ian Leigh, Basia Spalek and Doug Weeks.

Notes

1. See: Rachel Briggs, Catherine Fieschi, and Hannah Lownsbrough, *Bringing it Home: Community-Based Approaches to Counter-Terrorism* (London: Demos, 2006); Martin Innes, "Policing Uncertainty: Countering Terror through Community Intelligence and Democratic Policing," *The ANNALS of the American Academy of Political and Social Sciences* 205 (2006), pp. 222–241; Department of Communities and Local Government, *Preventing Violent Extremism—Winning Hearts and Minds* (London: DCLG, 2007); Robert Lambert, *Countering Al-Qaeda in London: Police and Muslims in Partnerships* (London: Hurst and Co., 2011); Floris Vermeulen, "Suspect Communities—Targeting Violent Extremism at the Local Level: Policies of Engagement in Amsterdam, Berlin, and London," *Terrorism and Political Violence* 26(2) (2014), pp. 286–306.
2. Adrian Cherney and Jason Hartley, "Community Engagement to Tackle Terrorism and Violent Extremism: Challenges, Tensions and Pitfalls," *Policing and Society* (2015), pp. 1–14.
3. Jason Sunshine and Tom R. Tyler, "The Role of Procedural Justice and Legitimacy in Shaping Public Support for Policing," *Law & Society Review* 37(3) (2003), pp. 513–548; Tom Tyler and Jeffrey Fagan, "Legitimacy and Cooperation: Why Do People Help the Police Fight Crime in their Communities?," *Ohio State Journal of Criminal Law* 6(1) (2008), pp. 231–275.
4. Adrian Cherney and Kristina Murphy, "Policing Terrorism with Procedural Justice: The Role of Police Legitimacy and Law Legitimacy," *Australian & New Zealand Journal of Criminology* 46(3) (2013), pp. 403–421.
5. Tom Tyler and Avital Mentovich, *Mechanisms of Legal Effect: Theories of Procedural Justice*, A Methods Monograph (Public Health Law Research Programme: Temple University Beasley School of Law, 2011).
6. Aziz Z. Huq, Tom R. Tyler, and Stephen J. Schulhofer, "Mechanisms for Eliciting Cooperation in Counterterrorism Policing: Evidence from the United Kingdom," *Journal of Empirical Legal Studies* 8(4) (2011), pp. 728–761, at p. 749.
7. Shaida Nabi, "Federation of Student Islamic Societies, (FOSIS) UK," in Frank Peter and Rafeal Ortega, eds., *Islamic Movements in Europe* (London: IB Tauris, 2014).
8. Martin Bright, *When Progressives Treat with Reactionaries: The British State's Flirtation with Radical Islam* (London: Policy Exchange, 2006), pp. 29–30.
9. HM Government, *Muslim Brotherhood Review: Main Findings* (London: The Stationary Office, 2015).
10. Serena Hussein, Ewan King, Sanah Sheikh, and Chloe Cook, *The Experience of Muslim Students in Further and Higher Education in London* (London: Greater London Authority, 2009).
11. Miri Song, "Part of the British Mainstream? British Muslim Students and Islamic Student Associations," *Journal of Youth Studies* 15(2) (2012), pp. 143–160.
12. Shaida-Raffat Nabi. *How is Islamophobia Institutionalised? Racialised Governmentality and the Case of Muslim Students in British Universities*, University of Manchester, Ph.D. thesis, 2011.

13. Nabi. *How is Islamophobia Institutionalised?*, p. 109.
14. Andrew Gillighan, "Baroness Warsi and the Demons of Hate," *The Daily Telegraph*, 27 April 2013. Available at http://www.telegraph.co.uk/news/politics/conservative/10022536/Baroness-Warsi-and-the-demons-of-hate.html (accessed 1 May 2016).
15. Federation of Student Islamic Societies. Available at: http://fosis.org.uk/press-releases/1317-fosis-and-uclu-islamic-society-to-hold-radical-thinking-conference (accessed 1 May 2016).
16. Lord Carlile of Berriew QC, *Report to the Home Secretary of Independent Oversight of Prevent Review and Strategy* (London: The Stationary Office, 2011), p. 11.
17. Arun Kundnani, *Spooked: How Not to Prevent Violent Extremism* (London: Institute for Race Relations, 2009).
18. Tufyal Choudhury and Helen Fenwick, *The Impact of Counterterrorism Measures on Muslim Communities in Britain* (London: Equality and Human Rights Commission, 2011).
19. Terrorism Act 2000, s1(1)(c).
20. Ibid., s1(2).
21. *David Miranda v Secretary of State for the Home Department and the Commissioner of the Police of the Metropolis* [2014] EWHC 255.
22. Terrorism Act 2000, s1(4).
23. *R v F* [2007] EWCA Crim 243.
24. David Anderson, *The Terrorism Acts in 2012: Report of the Independent Reviewer on the operation of Terrorism Act 2000 and Part 1 of the Terrorism Act 2006* (London: Independent Reviewer of Terrorism Legislation, 2013), p. 53.
25. *R v Gul* [2013] UKSC 64.
26. David Anderson, *The Terrorism Acts in 2013: Report of the Independent Reviewer on the Operation of Terrorism Act 2000 and Part 1 of the Terrorism Act 2006* (London: Independent Reviewer of Terrorism Legislation, 2014), p. 30.
27. Ibid.
28. Ibid., p. 80.
29. Ibid.
30. Lord Carlile, Hansard HL vol 705, col 606 11 November 2008.
31. Terrorism Act 2006, s2.
32. Ibid., s5.
33. Ibid., s6.
34. Ibid., s8.
35. Ibid., s38B(1)(a).
36. Lucia Zedner, "Pre-Crime and Post-Criminology?," *Theoretical Criminology* 11(2) (2007), pp. 261–281, at p. 262.
37. Jude McCulloch and Sharon Pickering, "Pre-Crime and Counter-Terrorism Imagining Future Crime in the 'War on Terror,'" *British Journal of Criminology* 49(5) (2009), pp. 628–645.
38. Stuart Macdonald. "Prosecuting Suspected Terrorists: Precursor Crimes, Intercept Evidence and the Priority of Security," in Lee Jarvis and Michael Lister, eds., *Critical Perspectives on Counter-Terrorism* (Abingdon: Routledge, 2015) pp. 130–149, at p. 132.
39. Ibid., p. 134.
40. Jude McCullouch and Sharon Pickering, "Counter-Terrorism: The Law and Policing of Pre-Emption," in Nicola McGarrity, Andrew Lynch, and George Williams, eds., *Counter-Terrorism and Beyond: The Culture of Law and Justice after 9/11* (Abingdon: Routledge, 2010), p. 21.
41. Asim Qureshi, "PREVENT: Creating 'radicals' to Strengthen Anti-Muslim Narratives," *Critical Studies on Terrorism* 8(1) (2015), pp. 181–191.
42. http://news.bbc.co.uk/2/hi/uk_news/england/lancashire/6923933.stm (accessed 15 August 2016).
43. Clive Walker, *Terrorism and the Law* (Oxford: Oxford University Press, 2011), p. 45; see also http://www.independent.co.uk/news/people/profiles/simon-mann-my-biggest-mistake-was-approaching-mark-thatcher-6255035.html (accessed 15 August 2016).
44. Macdonald, "Prosecuting Suspected Terrorists," p. 137.
45. Ibid., p. 138.
46. Terrorism Act 2006 s1.

47. Ibid., s1(3) and s2(4).
48. Ibid., s.1(2)(b) and s.2(1).
49. House of Commons Hansard 09 November 2005, col 391, Hazel Blears
50. Terrorism Act 2000, s3.
51. Ibid., s21.
52. HM Government, *Prevent Strategy* Cm 8092 (London: The Stationary Office, 2011), pp.74-75.
53. Department for Communities and Local Government, *Preventing Violent Extremism: Winning Hearts and Minds* (London: DCLG, 2007).
54. HM Government, *Pursue, Prevent, Protect, Prepare: The United Kingdom's Strategy for Countering International Terrorism* (London: The Stationary Office, 2009).
55. HM Government, *Prevent Strategy*, p. 6.
56. Paul Thomas, "Failed and Friendless: The UK's 'Preventing Violent Extremism' Programme," *The British Journal of Politics & International Relations* 12(3) (2010), pp. 442–458.
57. House of Commons Communities and Local Government Committee, *Preventing Violent Extremism*, Sixth Report of Session 2009–10, HC 65 (London: The Stationary Office, 2010), p. 3.
58. Kundnani, *Spooked: How Not to Prevent Violent Extremism*.
59. Counterterrorism and Security Act 2015, s. 26(1).
60. HM Government, *Revised Prevent Duty Guidance: for England and Wales* (London: The Stationary Office, 2015) p. 3.
61. Ibid., p. 4.
62. HM Government, *Prevent Duty Guidance: For Higher Education Institutions in England and Wales* (London: The Stationary Office, 2015), p. 4.
63. The Russell International Excellence Group, *Russell Group Response to the Consultation on the Counter-Terrorism Bill Draft Statutory Guidance*, 2015, p. 3. Available at https://www.russellgroup.ac.uk/media/5252/57-russell-group-response-to-consultation-on-the-prevent-duty-guidance-as-described-by-the-counter-terrorism-and-securrity-bill-2015.pdf (accessed 15 August 2015).
64. HM Government, *Pursue, Prevent, Protect, Prepare*, p. 9.
65. HM Government, *Prevent Strategy*, p. 3.
66. Marc Sageman, *Leaderless Jihad: Terror Networks in the Twenty-First Century* (Philadelphia: Philadelphia University Press, 2008); Quinton Wiktotowicz, *Radical Islam Rising: Muslim Extremism in the West* (Oxford: Rowman and Littlefield, 2005).
67. Arun Kundnani, *A Decade Lost: Rethinking Radicalisation and Extremism* (London: Claystone, 2015); Jonathan Githens-Mazer and Robert Lambert, "Why Conventional Wisdom on Radicalization Fails: The Persistence of a Failed Discourse," *International Affairs* 86(4) (2010), pp. 889–901; Charlotte Heath-Kelly, "Counter-Terrorism and the Counterfactual: Producing the 'Radicalisation' Discourse and the UK PREVENT Strategy," *The British Journal of Politics & International Relations* 15(3) (2013), pp. 394–415.
68. Viki Coppock, and Mark McGovern, "'Dangerous Minds'? Deconstructing Counter-Terrorism Discourse, Radicalisation and the 'Psychological Vulnerability' of Muslim Children and Young People in Britain," *Children & Society* 28(3) (2014), pp. 242–256; Orla Lynch, "British Muslim Youth: Radicalisation, Terrorism and the Construction of the 'Other'" *Critical Studies on Terrorism* 6(2) (2013), pp. 241–261.
69. House of Commons, *Roots of Violent Radicalisation*, Home Affairs Select Committee Nineteenth Report of Session 2010–12 HC 1446 (London: The Stationary Office, 2012), p. 15.
70. Polly Curtis, "Minister Urges Action on Campus Extremism," *The Guardian* 20 July 2005. Available at http://www.guardian.co.uk/education/2005/jul/20/highereducation.uk (accessed 15 August 2016).
71. The report, *Radical Islam on Campus: A Comprehensive List of Extremist Speakers at UK Universities*, claimed that almost one third of those involved in Islamist terrorism were university educated. However, this conflates those educated in the United Kingdom and those educated elsewhere: "More than 30% of individuals (30.71%) involved in Islamist terrorism in the UK were educated to degree level or higher. *Of these, 19 individuals studied at a UK university* [emphasis added]" (London: Centre for Social Cohesion, 2010), p. 1.
72. House of Commons, *Roots of Violent Radicalisation*, p. 13.

73. Robin Brand, "How Wide is Campus Extremism?" *BBC News* 7 February 2011. Available at http://www.bbc.com/news/uk-politics-12337531 (accessed 15 August 2015).
74. Dame Fiona Caldicott, *Umar Farouk Abdulmutallab: Report to UCL Council of the Independent Inquiry Panel* (London: University College London, 2010), p. 3.
75. House of Commons, *Roots of Violent Radicalisation*, p. 13.
76. Ibid., p. 18.
77. HM Government, *The Prevent Strategy*, p. 73.
78. Ibid., pp. 74–75.
79. Ibid., p. 20.
80. Lord Carlile, *Report to the Home Secretary of Independent Oversight of Prevent Review*, p. 4.
81. Bill Rammel, "Beyond Unreasonable Expectations," *The Guardian*, 11 September 2006. Available at http://www.theguardian.com/education/2006/sep/11/students.uk (accessed 15 August 2016).
82. "Rammel Backs University's Muslim Veil Ban," *The Guardian* 11 October 2006. Available at http://www.theguardian.com/education/2006/oct/11/highereducation.uk2 (accessed 15 August 2015).
83. Nabi, *How is Islamophobia Institutionalised?*, p. 120.
84. June Edmunds, "'Elite' Young Muslims in Britain: From Transnational to Global Politics," *Contemporary Islam* 4(2) (2010), pp. 215–238.
85. Lord Carlile of Berriew, *Report on the operation in 2008 of the Terrorism Act 2000 and Part 1 of the Terrorism Act 2006* (London: The Stationary Office, 2009).
86. Equalities and Human Rights Commission, *Stop and Think—A Critical Review of the Use of Stop and Search Powers in England and Wales* (London: Equality and Human Rights Commission, 2010).
87. Anderson, *The Terrorism Acts in 2013*, p. 418.
88. Choudhury and Fenwick, *The Impact of Counter-Terrorism Measures on Muslims in Britain*.
89. David Anderson QC, *The Terrorism Acts in 2011: Report of the Independent Reviewer on the Operation of the Terrorism Act 2000 and Part 1 of the Terrorism Act 2006* (London: The Stationary Office, 2012), p. 100.
90. Metropolitan Police Authority, *Protecting the Innocent: The London Experience of DNA and the National DNA Database* (London: Metropolitan Police Authority, 2011).
91. Anderson, *The Terrorism Acts in 2013*, p. 41.
92. Anderson, *The Terrorism Acts in 2011*, p. 103.
93. Vikram Dodd, "Asian People 42 Times more Likely to be Held under Terror Law," *The Guardian* 23 May 2011. Available at http://www.theguardian.com/uk/2011/may/23/counter-terror-stop-search-minorities
94. David Anderson, *The Terrorism Acts in 2014: Report of the Independent Reviewer on the operation of Terrorism Act 2000 and Part 1 of the Terrorism Act 2006* (London: Independent Reviewer of Terrorism Legislation, 2015), pp. 24–35.
95. The Supreme Court commented (obiter) that the power to stop under Schedule 7, "is not subject to any controls," and that before examining a passenger "the officer is not even required to have grounds for suspecting that the person concerned falls within section 40(1) of the 2000 Act," *R v Gul* [2013] UKSC 64, para 64.
96. *R (on the application of Gillan and another v. Commissioner of Police for the Metropolis and another* [2006] UKHL 12, para 34.
97. *Gillan*, para 97.
98. *Gillan*, para 35.
99. *Gillan and Quinton v The United Kingdom* (2010) 50 EHRR 45, para 86. Following this ruling, the Protection of Freedoms Act 2013 repealed section 44 powers and replaced them with new powers under s47A-C and Schedule 6B.
100. Katerina Hadjimatheou, "The Relative Moral Risks of Untargeted and Targeted Surveillance," *Ethical Theory and Moral Practice* 17(2) (2014), pp. 187–207, p. 190.
101. Leda Blackwood, Nick Hopkins, and Steve Reicher, "I Know Who I Am, but Who Do they Think I Am? Muslim Perspectives on Encounters with Airport Authorities," *Ethnic and Racial Studies* 36(6) (2013), pp. 1090–1108.

102. Gabe Mythen, Sandra Walklate, and Fatima Khan, "'Why Should We Have to Prove We're Alright?': Counter-Terrorism, Risk and Partial Securities," *Sociology* 47(2) (2013), pp. 383–398; Gabe Mythen, Sandra Walklate, and Fatima Khan, "'I'm a Muslim, but I'm not a Terrorist': Victimization, Risky Identities and the Performance of Safety," *British Journal of Criminology* 49(6) (2009), pp. 736–754.
103. Anderson, *The Terrorism Acts in 2011*, p. 115.
104. Choudhury and Fenwick, *The Impact of Counter-Terrorism Measures*.
105. Carol Harlow and Richard Rawlings, *Pressure Through Law* (London: Routledge, 1992).
106. Jurgen Habermas, *Between Facts and Norms* (Cambridge: Polity Press, 1996), p. 367.

Police and Community Cooperation in Counterterrorism: Evidence and Insights from Australia

Adrian Cherney and Kristina Murphy

ABSTRACT
Effectively engaging the Muslim community is a challenge for police given many Muslims feel unfairly targeted by counterterrorism policies and laws because of their faith. This article explores how such perceptions influence the willingness of Muslims to voluntarily cooperate in counterterrorism efforts, drawing on data collected from Muslims living in Australia. We test whether *procedural justice policing* can help buffer this perception of being targeted as a security threat and whether it can enhance Muslims' willingness to cooperate with police. Efforts by the Australian Federal Police to engage Muslim communities in Australia are also examined. The implications of the results for community-based approaches to counterterrorism are discussed.

It is recognized that community cooperation is essential to mitigating the risks of terrorism and threats arising from violent extremism.[1] For example Sir Ian Blair, former Commissioner of the UK Metropolitan Police Service once stated: "The most single important component in the domestic defeat of terror in the next decade is the ability of the police to work with communities to do just that."[2] An assistant commissioner of the Australian Queensland Police Service also commented to the first author: "we know we can't arrest our way out of this problem"[3]—the problem being terrorism and violent extremism. In another interview an Australian Federal Police officer also made the following comment: "Because the Muslim community … have felt very targeted for probably the last 12 years … I think you have to start with grass roots engagement of let's just talk."[4]

Community outreach and engagement with Muslim communities has therefore become a central component of police counterterrorism efforts both in Australia and abroad.[5] Objectives of community engagement include breaking down police and Muslim community hostilities and misunderstandings, enhancing the collection of community intelligence on terrorist risks, improving Muslims' perceptions of police, garnering community support for counterterrorism efforts and mobilizing Muslim organizations and leaders to take a lead in countering violent extremism.[6] Given these aims an important question to consider is how the police can most effectively win the cooperation and support of the Muslim community?

Answering this question has practical significance because research indicates that community-based approaches to counterterrorism are fraught with tension.[7] Muslims often report suspicion and resentment toward counterterrorism policing and laws and efforts by police to engage Muslim leaders.[8] These sentiments have been exacerbated by the social and political response to the "War on Terror" that has led to the stigmatization of Muslims and Islam being associated with extremism and terrorism.[9] Hence, generating cooperation in such an environment can be challenging.

This article explores factors that have an influence on the ability of police to effectively engage the Muslim community. While community-based approaches to counterterrorism have taken different forms,[10] understanding the antecedents of Muslims' willingness to cooperate with police, and how such cooperation is promoted or eroded, can help to understand why community-based counterterrorism efforts succeed or fail. In this article we draw on quantitative and qualitative data collected in the context of Australia's counterterrorism policing of Muslim communities.

Given the field of terrorism studies has mainly focused on examining terrorist risks and profiles,[11] it has tended to overlook how studies on policing can inform understanding of how terrorism is sustained, detected, and disrupted. While many experts accept that Muslim communities are essential to defeating terrorism the question of how authorities can effectively mobilize key community groups, and the challenges in doing so, is less well understood. It is these gaps that the current article aims to fill.

The article is structured as follows. First, the data sources underpinning the analysis of Australian Muslims' attitudes toward counterterrorism are described. The sense of being "targeted" that characterizes how Muslim communities feel in Australia is then investigated; we will show how Australia's counterterrorism laws and policies have exacerbated this situation. In this article we use the term "targeted" to refer to a shared perception among Muslims that they are being increasingly singled out through counterterrorism policy and discourse as posing a terrorist risk due to their Islamic faith. In another context we have referred to this as a sense of being "under siege."[12] The ways in which Australian Muslims express this feeling of being targeted is explored, including its source. It is hypothesized that the feeling of being "targeted" can affect a community's willingness to voluntarily cooperate in counterterrorism efforts, with this claim empirically tested. If feeling targeted impacts on subsequent cooperation, how then do police effectively engage and win the support of the Muslim community in a context where Muslims feel stigmatized? Survey data comprising Muslim respondents is used to examine this issue and we test whether *procedural justice policing* can: (1) help diminish the perception among Muslims that they are perceived as objects of suspicion and (2) enhance Muslims' willingness to voluntarily cooperate with police in counterterrorism. Further insights and lessons are drawn from a discussion on how the Australian Federal Police (AFP) engage Muslim communities. While the data and insights reported in this article are derived from the Australian context, they provide useful insights for authorities wanting to engage other Muslim populations living in the West.

Data Sources and Methodology

The primary data analyzed here were drawn from two sources. The data were collected as part of a project examining the impact of counterterrorism policing and laws on Muslim communities in Australia. This involved the collection of qualitative and quantitative data via the use of focus groups and a survey with Muslims living in Brisbane, Melbourne, and Sydney. The cities of Brisbane, Sydney, and Melbourne were chosen as the sites for data collection because the majority of Australia's Muslims live in the states where these cities are located (i.e., Queensland, Victoria, and New South Wales). Fourteen focus groups were conducted in 2013/14, with a total of 104 participants (37 females; 67 males) spanning youth (18–26 years of age), "new arrivals" to Australia (18+ years of age), and middle-aged participants (35–50 years of age). Participants were drawn from a variety of ethnic backgrounds and were recruited through Mosques and Muslim community centers. Muslim moderators, who were trained in the aims of the research and the use of the focus group interview schedule, completed nine of the fourteen focus groups. The first author also undertook five additional focus groups, which were facilitated through *imams* and community contacts.[13] All participants were given a $50 department store gift voucher in recognition of their time. The focus group data were coded thematically in Nvivo.[14]

A face-to-face survey was also conducted in 2014. A total of 800 surveys were completed by members of Australia's Muslim community. Two hundred respondents were from Brisbane, 300 from Sydney, and 300 from Melbourne. A survey administration company specializing in the sampling of culturally and linguistically diverse populations administered the survey on behalf of the authors. Participants were selected using the Australian Electronic White Pages using an ethnic/Muslim naming system. This method identified for the Muslim religion given surnames in the Islamic religion often denote religious affiliation with Islam. A total of 525 Muslim surnames were used to generate the sample. A total of 8,765 sample records (name and telephone number) were generated and attempts were made to contact participants from this list by telephone. Of these records, however, only 8,090 were found to be valid phone numbers. After adjusting for the invalid cases and other out-of-scope participants ($N = 3,566$; i.e., those who were not contactable or ineligible to participate because they were not Muslim) an overall response rate of 18 percent was achieved. Overall, therefore, 800 respondents completed a survey.[15] Trained interviewers (all of whom were Muslim) conducted the survey in each participant's preferred language at an agreed time and location. All participants were 18 years or older and paid for their time.[16]

In summary, 50.5 percent of survey respondents were male and 49.5 percent were female. The average age of respondents was 34.9 years old. Most respondents reported that they were born in Australia (58 percent), and 99 percent reported being an Australian citizen. Thirty-one percent reported belonging to the Shi'a Muslim faith, while 69 percent reported being Sunni Muslim. This sample composition matches the broader Muslim population in Australia.[17] More than 50 percent of the sample (53.2 percent) reported attending a Mosque on a weekly basis.

A "Targeted" Community and Its Impact on Cooperation

Scholars have noted that since 9/11 the general feeling among Muslims living in the West is one of a heightened sense of anxiety and belief that their communities are "under siege."[18] In Australia this has been exacerbated by the enactment of a large number of counterterrorism laws. By the end of 2014 successive Australian governments have passed 64 pieces of separate counterterrorism legislation since 9/11 (more than any other Western nation). This has been characterized as a form of hyper-legislation.[19] Many of these laws have raised concerns among legal experts and Muslim organizations. These concerns relate to their impact on individual freedoms, expanding the powers of police and intelligence services, and their potential to be used disproportionately against Muslims.[20] Since the advent of Islamic State of Iraq and Syria (ISIS) and arrests of Muslim youth in Australia for terrorism offenses[21] the need to expand counterterrorism legislation is a priority of both major political parties in Australia (i.e., labor and liberal). Efforts by serving governments to consult the Muslim community about the need for counterterrorism legislation has not always been characterized as amicable. Muslim leaders in some instances have boycotted government consultations in protest.[22] The political rhetoric used by Australian politicians has been branded as divisive with comments by politicians that Muslims are not "doing enough to speak out against terrorism or take the risk of radicalisation seriously" exacerbating tensions.[23] In early September 2014, one of the largest counterterrorism operations occurred in Sydney. This operation reportedly involved 800 police and was seen by some Muslims as adding to the fear and anxiety that Australian Muslims were experiencing.[24]

The hyper-legislation and political rhetoric surrounding the "War on Terror" has implications for Muslims' sense of belonging and the degree to which they believe society regards them as valued citizens.[25] This can fuel beliefs among Muslims that majority groups hold implicit biases toward them, and regard them and their religion as a threat to social harmony and security.[26] In the focus groups, Muslim participants expressed a general feeling that Islam was "under attack." Participants noted that Muslims in Australia (and elsewhere across the world) were labeled as security threats through the media, and they expressed feeling stigmatized by the way national security debates were dominantly framed as a response to Islamic extremism. Participants spoke about feeling they were tarnished as terrorists socially and politically and that their religion was seen as inherently archaic and violent by the Australian public. The form of collective attribution being imposed on Muslim communities was regarded as impossible to resist or counter no matter how often Muslims defended their faith as a *"religion of peace"* or denounced terrorism attacks as not in the *"name of Islam."* For many participants this only exacerbated a general feeling that governments were deliberating targeting Muslims. For example, one participant emotively stated:

> When I hear all of the attacks you just mentioned [in reference to events like 9/11, 7/7, Mumbai] it really makes me angry a lot. Why is the world against us, why are we seen to be the bad people? ... God does not accept people blowing themselves up in the name of God. This is the evil that people use Islam to say, that it was done for the sake of Allah. Perhaps had we had the chance to reflect and say for example, why are Muslims being treated like this ... Muslims around the world ... being subjected to bad treatment from their own leaders. The whole notion is to destroy Islam and its followers. The whole world is against us. (female)

Another participant expressed their feelings about how difficult it was to escape being stigmatized by stating:

> It's upsetting because they tangle us in something that we have nothing to do with, you know being born and brought up here and that's something that happens overseas [in reference to terrorist attacks such as 9/11, 7/7] that we have nothing to do with, just because we have the same faith although they did this. So it really has nothing to do ... it's upsetting that you have to be judged and being judged based on something that really you don't even practise or believe in. (gender not recorded)

In order to explore the feeling of being "targeted" further, survey respondents were presented with a series of seven statements assessing the level of scrutiny they believe they experience from police, authorities and the public (e.g., "I feel at risk of being accused of terrorist activities because of my faith").[27] On average, Muslim respondents felt under pressure, with many reporting they felt subjected to enhanced scrutiny by police and the public due to their faith (7-item "feeling targeted" scale; a higher score on this scale indicates greater feelings of being targeted; Mean = 3.52; SD = 0.91; see Appendix for all items in this scale). Overwhelmingly, 75 percent of the sample reported a high sense of their community being targeted.

Such perceptions should be of concern to authorities because if a group feels they are being arbitrarily and deliberately targeted due to some personal attribution (in this case because of their faith) it can generate a range of negative reactions. This can include perpetuating a sense of victimhood, it can result in reduced identification with Australia, it can provide fertile ground for conspiracy theories to flourish, it can create defensiveness and suspicion toward authorities, and can even perpetuate conflict between groups.[28] In the context of counterterrorism such outcomes are not helpful in a heightened security environment when police are looking to work with Muslim groups. Dismissing such perceptions as unfounded or lacking an objective foundation ignores the fact that the feelings of being targeted can also result from vicarious experience. What Muslims observe around them in the context of the social and political atmosphere and institutional responses surrounding terrorism can influence perceptions.

A number of additional scales were constructed to test whether a sense of being "targeted" is related to Muslims' trust in police, feelings of being treated fairly by police (i.e., procedural justice), and their willingness to cooperate with police in counterterrorism efforts. These additional scales were: "trust in police to combat terrorism," "procedural justice," and two measures of cooperation: (1) willingness to "work" with police in community-based efforts to combat terrorism (i.e., labeled as "work" in Table 1) and (2) willingness to report suspicious terrorism-related activities to police (i.e., labeled as "report" in Table 1). Both cooperation measures are self-report measures, rather than actual cooperation with authorities. The individual survey items used to construct all of these measures are reported in the Appendix. Table 1 presents the mean and standard deviation scores for each measure, and the Cronbach alpha reliability scores report how reliable the scale is (a score closer to 1 indicates a strong and reliable scale; those above 0.8 are considered to be strong and reliable scales). Note that the maximum mean score possible for each scale is 5, with higher scores on the trust and cooperation measures indicating greater levels of trust and a greater self-reported willingness to cooperate with police in their counterterrorism efforts. Table 1 also indicates the bi-variate relationships between reported measures of feeling targeted, trust in police to combat terrorism, and the two cooperation measures.

Table 1 shows that feeling "targeted" has a negative impact on people's trust in police and their willingness to cooperate with police. That is, respondents who felt more targeted were less trusting of police when it came to combating terrorism. Muslims who felt more targeted were also less likely to think police treated them fairly. They were also less likely to want to work with police to combat terrorism and they were less likely to want to report suspicious terror-related activity to police. While it is recognized these relationships do not demonstrate causation due to the cross-sectional nature of the survey data, the data do demonstrate that feeling targeted is related to Muslims' skepticism toward the police. Such a finding begs the question: How, under such circumstances, can police win the support of the Muslim community and encourage their collaboration in counterterrorism? This issue is explored in the next section.

Table 1. Descriptive statistics and bi-variate correlations between scales.

	Mean (SD)	Cronbach α	1	2	3	4	5
1. Feeling targeted	3.52 (0.91)	0.92	1				
2. Trust in police	3.83 (0.78)	0.90	−.35*	1			
3. Procedural justice	3.93 (0.74)	0.95	−.34*	.82*	1		
4. Work with police	4.15 (0.80)	0.92	−.27*	.67*	.66*	1	
5. Report	3.96 (0.84)	0.96	−.35*	.74*	.73*	.66*	1
6. Age	34.89 (15.51)						
7. Income	9.99 (3.57)						
8. Police Contact	0.40 (0.92)						
9. Mosque attendance	5.31 (2.04)						
10. Education	5.32 (2.03)						
11. Muslim faith	69.4%						
12. Country of birth	57.9%						
13. Marital Status	46.3%						
14. Gender	50.5%						

Note. *$p \leq .001$; higher scores on scales indicate more favorable assessments; Gender (0 = female; 1 = male); Country of Birth (0 = overseas; 1 = Australia); Muslim Faith (0 = Shi'a; 1 = Sunni); Marital Status (0 = not married; 1 = married); Income (1 = $11,000 to 20 = $110,000+); Mosque attendance (0 = never to 8 = daily). Percentages shown for dichotomous variables, with percentage referring to the "1" category.

Winning Trust and Cooperation

One aim of this research is to understand the type of police practices that can be used to: (1) build trust with the Muslim community and (2) overcome the barriers to collaboration to encourage greater levels of cooperation in community-based counterterrorism. Of interest is the effectiveness of *procedural justice policing* in a counterterrorism context.

Procedural justice refers to the perceived fairness of decision making and the perceived treatment one receives from a decision maker. The fairness of police treatment depends on how police interact with the public. There is a wealth of research showing that when police use procedural justice in their dealings with members of the public it leads to greater levels of cooperation with police and a greater willingness to defer to police decision making and rules.[29]

There are four key dimensions to procedural justice. One is *neutrality*, which relates to police acting in a neutral fashion during encounters with members of the public. If police decisions are bias-free and Muslims see they are being treated in the same manner as others then police will be seen to be acting in a neutral manner. For example, racial profiling against Muslims signals to them they are being treated differently and that police are not acting in a neutral fashion. Another dimension is *fairness*, which relates to the view that authorities are benevolent in their actions toward individuals by demonstrating they have their best interests at heart when making decisions. For instance, police officers who display concern for Muslims (e.g., about the needs of Muslim youth) and explain that they want to do to the right thing by them and their community, will demonstrate fairness. People are also extremely sensitive to signs that police treat them with *respect*. Respectful and dignified treatment communicates to people that the authority values them. In the case of Muslims this might include police removing their shoes when entering a mosque or a Muslim's home and carefully handling the Koran. This displays respect for Muslims and their religious practices. *Voice* is the fourth principle of procedural justice. People value the opportunity to have a say in situations that affect them. Being able to voice one's concerns and seeing that police are taking those concerns into account is viewed positively by citizens. Hence, when police provide the opportunity for Muslims to have a say about issues that concern them and act on those concerns they are displaying the opportunity for voice.

Research shows that these four elements of procedural justice are important to Muslims when it comes to their interactions with authorities.[30] Existing research with U.S., U.K., and Australian Muslim populations shows that procedural justice is a significant predictor of Muslims' willingness to cooperate with the police in counterterrorism initiatives.[31] One of the key reasons given for why this occurs is that procedural justice can help build trust between police and Muslim communities because it communicates to Muslims that they are valued members of society.

Our study takes this procedural justice research one step further by examining whether procedural justice can buffer the effect of perceived targeting on the negative attributes that Muslims display toward police and counterterrorism. Specifically, we test whether: (1) procedural justice mediates the relationship between feeling targeted and trust in police and whether (2) procedural justice mediates the relationship between feeling targeted and Muslims' willingness to cooperate with police. If procedural justice does buffer the effect of feeling targeted on trust and cooperation then this will be an important finding. It will show that police can use procedural justice to reduce the negative effects that feeling targeted has on attributions toward police counterterrorism efforts.

To test these relationships a series of regression analyses were completed. As noted earlier, the survey items used to measure perceived "targeting," "trust in police to combat terrorism," and the two cooperation measures ("work" and "report") are presented in the Appendix. To measure procedural justice, survey respondents were presented with 10 survey items on a 1 = strongly disagree to 5 = strongly agree scale (e.g., "When dealing with you or people in your community concerning issues of terrorism, the police give people a chance to express their views before a decision is made"). The Appendix lists the items used to construct the procedural justice measure; a higher score on this scale indicates a greater perception that police use procedural justice when interacting with members of the Muslim community. Table 1 presents the mean and standard deviation score for this measure and how it relates to the other scales constructed in this article.

A number of control variables were also included in the regression analyses. These were used to control for demographic and background differences between survey respondents. These variables were: age; gender (0 = female; 1 = male); Mosque attendance (measured as how often the participant attended Mosque each year; 0 = never to 8 = daily); number of contacts respondents had with police in the previous 12-month period (Mean = 0.40; SD = 0.92); Muslim faith identified (0 = Shi'a; 1 = Sunni); country of birth (0 = overseas; 1 = Australia); marital status (0 = not married; 1 = married); income level (1 = $11,000 to 20 = $110,000+); and educational status (0 = no schooling to 10 = postgraduate degree).

Results

The first regression analysis entered all of the control variables and the "feeling targeted" variable at Step 1, followed by the "procedural justice" measure at Step 2 to predict Muslims' "trust in police to combat terrorism." The results of this analysis are presented in Table 2. The second and third regression analyses used these same variables as predictors of Muslims' "willingness to work with police in counter-terrorism" (see the "Work" columns in Table 3), and "willingness to report suspicious terrorism related activities to police" (see the "Report" columns in Table 3).

Turning to Table 2 first, it is shown in Step 1 of the regression model that a few of the demographic and control variables predicted Muslims' trust in police. Specifically, the

Table 2. OLS regression of independent variables on "trust" in police to combat terrorism.

	Step 1 B (SE)	Step 1 β	Step 2 B (SE)	Step 2 B
Intercept	4.50 (.18)		.88 (.15)	
Age	.00 (.00)	.08	.00 (.00)	.01
Gender (0 = female)	−.14 (.06)	−.09*	−.04 (.04)	−.02
Muslim faith (0 = Shi'a)	.01 (.05)	.00	−.01 (.03)	−.01
Country of birth (0 = overseas)	.11 (.07)	.07	.06 (.04)	.04
Marital status (0 = not married)	.20 (.07)	.12**	.09 (.04)	.06*
Income	−.01 (.01)	−.02	−.01 (.01)	−.05
Education	.00 (.02)	.01	.01 (.01)	.02
Mosque attendance	.03 (.01)	.07*	.01 (.01)	.02
Police contact	−.19 (.03)	−.22***	−.07 (.02)	−.08***
Feeling targeted	−.28 (.03)	−.32***	−.07 (.02)	−.08***
Procedural justice	—	—	.81 (.02)	.76***
Adjusted R²		.21		.69
R² change		.21		.48
F change		21.29***		1209.6***
df		10, 789		1, 788

*p ≤ .05 **p ≤ .01; ***p ≤ .001

gender, marital status, mosque attendance, and police contact variables predicted feelings of trust. Those who are female ($\beta = -0.09$), married ($\beta = 0.12$), and who attend a mosque more regularly ($\beta = 0.07$) are more trusting of police. The negative coefficient for the police contact variable is also quite large ($\beta = -0.22$), indicating that those who have more personal contact with police are less trusting of police. Importantly, the "feeling targeted" variable is also a strong negative predictor of trust ($\beta = -0.32$). Those who feel more targeted are less trusting of police.

Table 3. OLS regression of independent variables on intentions to "work" with police and "report" suspicious activity to police.

	Work Step 1 B (SE)	Work Step 1 β	Work Step 2 B (SE)	Work Step 2 B	Report Step 1 B (SE)	Report Step 1 B	Report Step 2 B (SE)	Report Step 2 β
Intercept	4.92 (.19)		1.92 (.21)		4.89 (.19)		1.50 (.19)	
Age	−.00 (.00)	−.03	−.00 (.00)	−.08	.00 (.00)	.04	−.00 (.00)	−.02
Gender	−.14 (.06)	−.09*	−.06 (.05)	−.04	−.20 (.06)	−.12***	−.11 (.05)	−.07*
Muslim faith (0 = Shi'a)	.02 (.06)	.01	.01 (.05)	.00	.04 (.06)	.02	.03 (.04)	.02
Country of birth (0 = overseas)	.07 (.07)	.04	.03 (.06)	.02	−.02 (.07)	−.01	−.07 (.06)	−.04
Marital status (0 = not married)	.21 (.07)	.12**	.12 (.06)	.07*	.16 (.08)	.09*	.06 (.06)	.03
Income	.01 (.01)	.03	.00 (.01)	.01	−.00 (.01)	−.02	−.01 (.01)	−.04
Education	−.03 (.02)	−.07	−.02 (.01)	−.06	−.00 (.02)	−.00	.00 (.01)	.01
Mosque attendance	.01 (.02)	.03	−.00 (.01)	−.01	.02 (.02)	.05	.01 (.01)	.01
Police contact	−.21 (.03)	−.24***	−.11 (.02)	−.13***	−.19 (.03)	.21***	−.08 (.02)	−.09***
Feeling targeted	−.20 (.03)	−.23***	−.04 (.03)	−.04	−.29 (.03)	−.31***	−.10 (.02)	−.11***
Procedural justice	—	—	.67 (.03)	.61***	—	—	.75 (.03)	.66***
Adjusted R²	.14		.45		.19		.56	
R² change	.15		.31		.20		.36	
F change	13.81***		452.32***		19.82***		654.96***	
df	10, 789		1, 788		10, 789		1, 788	

*p ≤ .05; **p ≤ .01; ***p ≤ .00

When the procedural justice scale is entered into the regression model at Step 2, it can be seen that it has a very large positive effect on trust ($\beta = 0.76$). Those survey respondents who feel the police are more likely to use procedural justice when interacting with the Muslim community feel more trusting of police. Interestingly, the size of the coefficient for the "feeling targeted" variable dropped substantially on entry of procedural justice into the model (from $\beta = -0.32$ at Step 1 to $\beta = -0.08$ at Step 2). Such a large reduction in the size of the coefficient from Step 1 to Step 2 suggests that procedural justice may be a partial mediator of the relationship between feeling targeted and trust. In other words, if people feel the police use procedural justice then their feelings of being targeted come close to being negated. Such a finding suggests procedural justice plays an important buffering effect for countering a sense among Muslims that they are increasingly being singled out by counter-terrorism policy and discourse due to their faith.

Turning now to Table 3 with willingness to cooperate ("work" and "report," respectively) as the dependent variables, the models show that the "police contact" and the "feeling targeted" variables both predict the "willingness to work with police" and "report suspicious terror-related activities to police" scales. Those who have had more contact with the police in the previous 12-month period, and those who have greater feelings of being targeted are less likely to want to cooperate with police. For both models, gender and marital status also predicted self-reported cooperative behavior. Women and those who are married indicated a stronger willingness to work with police.

The procedural justice variable was entered at Step 2 for each cooperation model (see Table 3). For the willingness to "work" with police model—procedural justice is a strong positive predictor of cooperation. If Muslims feel the police use procedural justice in their dealings with Muslims then they will be more willing to work closely with police in their fight against terrorism. Likewise, Table 3 shows that procedural justice is also positively related to "reporting" behavior. Those who feel police use procedural justice are also more willing to report suspicious terror-related activities to police. Importantly, at Step 2 of both cooperation models the size of the regression coefficients for the "feeling targeted" variable dropped significantly. For the "work with police" cooperation model, the previously significant effect of "feeling targeted" on cooperation became insignificant on entry of the procedural justice variable at Step 2. This indicates that procedural justice fully mediates the relationship between feeling targeted and willingness to work with police. In other words, if police use procedural justice when dealing with Muslims then this can negate the negative effect of feeling targeted on Muslims' willingness to work with police. Table 3 also shows that procedural justice partially mediates the relationship between perceived targeting and reporting behavior. Again, this suggests if police use procedural justice when dealing with Muslims then this can come close to negating the negative effect that feelings of being targeted can have on Muslims' willingness to report suspicious terrorist related activity to police.

Discussion: The Practice of Engagement and Trust Building

The regression results reported in the previous section indicate that procedural justice has the potential to mediate the effect of feeling targeted on Muslims' trust in police and their willingness to cooperate with police in a counterterrorism context. Such findings across three different dependent variables (i.e., trust in police; working with police; reporting to police) demonstrate the importance of police adopting practices that display procedural justice when engaging Muslims. The results illustrate there are practices police can adopt to build trust with Muslim communities and also that they can potentially engage in ways that help to mitigate the reactions among Muslims that are the outcome of being socially and politically constructed as a suspect community.

Police services in Australia are attempting to incorporate procedural justice into key aspects of their work.[32] One should not underestimate the challenges of adopting practices based on procedural justice into aspects of counterterrorism. However, if police want to partner with Muslims so they can work more cooperatively together through grass-roots initiatives, it is here that the principles of procedural justice readily apply. Displays of procedural justice are particularly important given Muslims feel they have been unfairly singled out by counterterrorism policing and laws.

What might these practices look like when it comes to police engagement of the Muslim community? To answer this question attention is now turned to examining efforts made by the AFP to build partnerships with Muslim communities in Australia. The aim is to examine how principles of procedural justice might be reflected in actual practice. The AFP is Australia's national law enforcement body. The AFP takes a national lead role in counterterrorism investigations and operations. One aspect of the AFP's counterterrorism efforts includes community outreach that is undertaken by its Community Liaison Team (CLT). The CLT is a small unit with team members located in Brisbane, Melbourne, Sydney, and Perth.[33]

The role of the CLT is to initiate collaborations with Muslim community leaders and agencies. This includes for instance attending Eid events celebrating the end of Ramadan and providing funding to community groups and mosques for local projects. What is particularly important about the work of the CLT is that members never actively seek to illicit information and intelligence from Muslims about terrorist threats or particular "radicalized" individuals—doing so is seen as risking their engagement work and neutrality. Rather, their role is about relationship building and it is here that helping groups access government funds for community initiatives are important. CLT members ensure they have small successes with individuals and mosques, such as helping community members prepare for Hajj and the potential attention and questioning they may attract from airport security when leaving Australia for Saudi Arabia. Efforts are also made to reach out to Muslim youth and listen to their concerns, with CLT members facilitating access to government departments and in some instances politicians to provide opportunities for Muslim youth to voice their concerns to key decision makers. Both examples display *benevolence* that CLT members—and hopefully by default the AFP—have the best interests of Muslims in mind.[34]

Liaison officers are transparent in who they engage with, and are open with community members about the fact that they will engage all Muslims regardless of denomination or religious outlook—this can even involve reaching out to *Salafists* or young Muslims angry with how they are treated by police. This approach projects *neutrality* in the way police deal with different members of the Muslim community. Liaison team members conduct post-resolution meetings with Muslim organizations and mosque leaders following major terrorist arrests to explain the operation and what occurred. This has two purposes. One is to address any rumor and suspicion about the arrests that may begin to circulate within the Muslim community. The second is that it enables questions to be asked about the operation and the process that will be followed post arrest. This demonstrates an opportunity for *voice*—albeit in a limited fashion. Liaison team members also identify intermediaries within the community that can help them reach out to young people or

Muslims who may feel marginalized and thus susceptible to radicalization. By using trusted intermediaries liaison officers are able to build their reputations for being trustworthy among groups who are suspicious of police. Liaison officers also educate counterterrorism investigators about the Islamic religion and practices and the sensitivities of entering a mosque or handling the Koran. Here *respect* for Muslims and Islam is promoted.[35]

It needs to be kept in mind that the AFP have not consciously set out to incorporate elements of procedural justice into their community engagement practices. These practices have simple been analyzed to illustrate how abstract and theoretical concepts (e.g., neutrality, benevolence, respect, and voice), might potentially be operationalized into practice when it comes to counterterrorism policing. The aim has been to provide concrete examples and to interpret these practices in light of the principles that were found in the survey data to increase community cooperation in counterterrorism efforts. The missing piece in the analysis is whether Muslims themselves regard these community engagement practices as reflecting features of procedural justice. Reports in the Australian media do indicate that the AFP has some way to go in building improved relations with sectors of the Australian Muslim community.[36] The literature shows that the fractured nature of the Muslim community does make community engagement a challenging task and that this diversity makes a uniform approach to community-based counterterrorism difficult to identify.[37]

Conclusion

It needs to be recognized there are limitations with the data that have been presented. For example, both the focus group and survey data only reflect the attitudinal views of Muslim respondents. The approach of the AFP to community engagement is not necessarily an exemplar among police services in Australia or abroad. While specific to Australia the results do show that in the context of community-based approaches to counterterrorism there are actions and approaches that police can adopt to improve relations with the Muslim community and increase their cooperation in efforts to tackle terrorism. If designed appropriately these practices can also reduce the degree to which Muslims feel targeted that can result from the broader social and political atmosphere surrounding terrorism. This requires police to build trust with the Muslim community and adopting practices based on procedural justice can help in this regard.

Police need to maximize the opportunities that contact with Muslims can provide for building trust and breaking down barriers to meaningful engagement. This can yield dividends for police counterterrorism efforts (e.g., more trust means greater willingness to work with police), with procedural justice part of the toolkit to build improved relationships with Muslim communities. This comes down to the types of interactions police have with Muslim communities and the quality of those interactions are ultimately in the hands of police to control.

Funding

This research was supported through an Australian Research Council Discovery grant: DP130100392.

Notes

1. Floris Vermeulen and Frank Bovenkerk, *Engaging With Violent Islamic Extremism: Local Policies in West European Cities* (The Hague: Eleven International Publishers, 2012).

2. Cited in Nasreen Suleaman, "Police Chief Calls on Communities," *BBC News* (24 January 2007). Available at http://news.bbc.co.uk/2/hi/uk_news/6296789.stm
3. Personal communication 30 April 2015.
4. Interview with AFP Community Liaison Team Member on the 2 July 2015.
5. For example, see Yahya Birt, "Promoting Virulent Envy: Reconsidering the UK's Terrorist Prevention Strategy," *RUSI Journal* 154(4) (2009), pp. 52–58; Sharon Pickering, Jude McCulloch, and David Wright-Neville, *Counter Terrorism Policing: Community, Cohesion and Security* (New York: Springer, 2008); Basia Spalek, *Terror Crime Prevention With Communities* (London and New York: Bloomsbury Academic, 2013); Vermeulen and Bovenkerk, *Engaging With Violent Islamic Extremism*.
6. Ihsan Alkhatib, "Building Bridges: The Experience of Leaders in Detroit, Michigan," in D. P. Silk, B. Spalek, and M. O'Rawe, eds., *Preventing Ideological Violence: Communities, Police and Case Studies of Success* (New York: Palgrave Macmillan, 2013), pp. 151–169; Deborah Ramirez, Tara L. Quinlan, Sean P. Malloy, and Taylor Shutt, "Community Partnerships Thwart Terrorism," in D. P. Silk, B. Spalek, and M. O'Rawe, eds., *Preventing Ideological Violence: Communities, Police and Case Studies of Success* (New York: Palgrave Macmillan, 2013), pp. 151–169.
7. Robert, A. Lambert, *Countering Al-Qaeda in London: Police and Muslims in Partnerships*. (London: Hurst and Co., 2011); Therese O'Toole, Nasar Meer, Daniel N. DeHanas, Stephen H. Jones, and Tariq Modood, "Governing through Prevent? Regulation and Contested Practice in State–Muslim Engagement," *Sociology* (2015), pp. 1–8. doi:10.1177/0038038514564437; Daniel P. Silk, "The Complexity of Police-Muslim Community Relations in the Shadow of 9/11," *Arches Quarterly* 5(9) (2012), pp. 73–82.
8. Adrian Cherney and Kristina Murphy, "Being a Suspect Community in a Post 9/11 World: The Impact of the War on Terror on Muslim Communities in Australia," *Australian and New Zealand Journal of Criminology* (2015). doi: 10.1177/0004865815585392; Vermeulen and Bovenkerk, *Engaging With Violent Islamic Extremism*.
9. Cherney and Murphy, "Being a Suspect Community in a Post 9/11 World."
10. See Rohan Gunaratna, Jolene Jerard, and Salim M. Nasir, eds., *Countering Extremism: Building Social Resilience through Community Engagement* (London: Imperial College Press, 2013); Daniel P. Silk, Basia Spalek, and Mary O'Rawe, eds., *Preventing Ideological Violence: Communities, Police and Case Studies of Success*. (New York: Palgrave Macmillan, 2013); Vermeulen and Bovenkerk, *Engaging With Violent Islamic Extremism*.
11. For example see Alex P. Schmid, ed., *The Routledge Handbook of Terrorism Research* (New York: Routledge, 2011).
12. See Adrian Cherney and Kristina Murphy, "Being a Suspect Community in a Post 9/11 World."
13. For detail about the methodology and the challenges in conducting the research see Kristina Murphy, Adrian Cherney and Julie Barkworth, *Avoiding Community Backlash in the Fight Against Terrorism*: Research report (Australia Research Council Discovery project DP130100392; 2015).
14. Ibid.
15. The low response rate is not surprising, given the efficacy of finding Muslims using an ethnic naming system, and due to Muslims being cautious about outsiders, particularly for a study focused on counterterrorism policing.
16. For more detail see Murphy, Cherney, and Barkworth, *Avoiding Community Backlash in the Fight Against Terrorism*.
17. International Centre for Muslim and Non-Muslim Understanding, *Australian Muslims: A Demographic, Social and Economic Profile of Muslims In Australia* (International Centre for Muslim and Non-Muslim Understanding, University of South Australia 2015).
18. Anne Aly, "Australian Muslim Responses to the Discourse on Terrorism in the Australian Popular Media, " *Australian Journal of Social Issues* 42(1) (2007), pp. 27–40; Cherney and Murphy, "Being a Suspect Community in a Post 9/11 World."
19. Andrew Lynch, Nicola McGarrity, and George Williams, *Inside Australia's Anti-Terrorism Laws and Trials* (New South Wales: New South Publishing, 2015).
20. Ibid.

21. See Australian Strategic Policy Institute, *Gen Y Jihadists: Preventing Radicalisation in Australia* (Australian Capital Territory, Australian Strategic Policy Institute, June 2015).
22. For example, see Islamic Council of Victoria, *PMs Meeting with Community Leaders* (2014 press release). Available at http://islaminaustralia.com/2014/08/19/islamic-council-of-victoria-to-boycott-meeting-with-tony-abbott/ (accessed 16 September 2014).
23. For example, on 23 February 2015 the Australian prime minister Tony Abbott, during a national security statement, made the comment that: "I've often heard Western leaders describe Islam as a 'religion of peace'. I wish more Muslim leaders would say that more often, and mean it." This statement was criticized by Muslim leaders and organizations as divisive and ignoring local efforts to counter extremism (see Shalailah Medhora and Michael Safi, "Muslim Leaders Outraged by Tony Abbott's Chiding over Extremism," *The Guardian, Australian Edition* 23 February 2015. Available at http://www.theguardian.com/australia-news/2015/feb/23/muslim-leaders-outraged-by-tony-abbotts-admonishment-over-extremism (accessed 2 February 2015).
24. For example see "Hundreds Protest in Sydney about Counter-Terrorism Raids," *The Guardian, Australian Edition* 18 September 2014. Available at http://www.sbs.com.au/news/article/2014/09/18/stop-terrorising-muslims-hundreds-join-sydney-protest-against-terror-raids (accessed 26 August 2015).
25. Leda Blackwood, Nick Hopkins, and Steve Reicher, "Turning the Analytic Gaze on 'Us': The Role of Authorities in the Alienation of Minorities," *European Psychologist* 18(4)(2013), pp. 245–252; Cherney and Murphy, "Being a Suspect Community in a Post 9/11 World."
26. Ibid.
27. The specific seven questions used to construct the targeted scale can be found in the Appendix.
28. Blackwood, Hopkins, and Reicher, "Turning the Analytic Gaze on 'us'"; Masi Noor, Nurit Shnabel, Samer Halabi, and Arie Nadler, "When Suffering Begets Suffering the Psychology of Competitive Victimhood between Adversarial Groups in Violent Conflicts," *Personality and Social Psychology Review* 16(4) (2012), pp. 351–374.
29. For example, see Lorraine Mazerolle, Elise Sargeant, Adrian Cherney, Kristina Murphy, Sarah Bennett, Emma Antrobus, and Peter Martin, *Procedural Justice and Legitimacy in Policing* (New York: Springer, 2014).
30. See Leda Black, "Policing Airport Spaces: The Muslim Experience of Scrutiny," *Policing* 9(3) (2015), pp. 255–264; Badi Hasisi and David Weisburd, "Policing Terrorism and Police–Community Relations: Views of the Arab Minority in Israel," *Police Practice and Research* 15(2) (2014), pp. 158–172.
31. Adrian Cherney and Kristine Murphy, "Policing Terrorism with Procedural Justice: The Role of Police Legitimacy and Law Legitimacy," *Australian & New Zealand Journal of Criminology* 46(3) (2013), pp 403–421; Aziz Z. Huq, Tom R. Tyler, and Steven Schulhofer, "Mechanisms for Eliciting Cooperation in Counterterrorism Policing: Evidence from the United Kingdom," *Journal of Empirical Legal Studies* 8(4) (2011), pp. 728–761; Tom R. Tyler, Steven Schulhofer, and Aziz Z. Huq, "Legitimacy and Deterrence Effects in Counterterrorism Policing: A Study of Muslim Americans," *Law and Society Review* 44 (2010), pp. 365–402.
32. See Mazerolle et al., *Procedural Justice and Legitimacy in Policing*.
33. See http://www.afp.gov.au/ for more detail about the AFP. State police in Australia also have designated Community Liaison Officers, with the AFP and state police liaison officers collaborating and exchanging information when necessary. State police liaison officers have a broader remit beyond counterterrorism and wear a distinct uniform that distinguishes them from other police. For example, in Queensland Police Community Liaison Officers have yellow epilates on their uniform. While AFP officers wear a uniform, AFP liaison officers can and often work in plain clothes and can comprise sworn and unsworn officers. It is difficult to know exactly whether when making assessments of the police Australian Muslims distinguish between State and Federal police, although in a focus group with Muslim youth, participants stated they had no problems with the State police and were critical of the AFP and their dealings with Muslim communities. However, it is unknown whether this sentiment is widespread throughout the Australian Muslim community.
34. These data are derived from interviews the first author undertook with AFP community liaison team members. At the time of writing there were a total of eight members in the unit, all of whom were interviewed face-to-face in July and August 2015. The sample comprised four men

and four women and a mix of five sworn and three unsworn officers. Interviews focused on how AFP liaison team members engage the Muslim community in their respective jurisdictions.
35. Ibid.
36. For example, see Rachel Olding, "Australian Federal Police Cancel Eid Dinner after Backlash from Muslim Community," *The Sydney Morning Herald* 13 July 2015. Available at http://www.smh.com.au/nsw/australian-federal-police-cancel-eid-dinner-after-backlash-from-muslim-community-20150713-gib4ps.html (accessed 13 July 2015).
37. Vermeulen and Bovenkerk, *Engaging With Violent Islamic Extremism*.

Appendix

The Appendix lists the survey questions used to construct the scales reported in this article. * denotes reverse coding of item.

Feeling Targeted

Cronbach's alpha = 0.92; scores on a 1 = strongly disagree to 5 = strongly agree scale. A higher score indicates a greater feeling of being targeted.
- I feel at risk of being accused of terrorist activities because of my faith
- Others in my community feel at risk of being accused of terrorism because of their faith
- I feel under more scrutiny by police and authorities because of my faith
- I feel under more scrutiny by the media and the public because of my faith
- The War on Terror disproportionately targets Muslims
- I sometimes feel police view me as a potential terrorist because of my faith
- I sometimes feel the Australian public views me as a potential terrorist because of my faith

Trust in Police to Combat Terrorism

Cronbach's alpha = 0.90; scores on a 1 = strongly disagree to 5 = strongly agree scale. A higher score indicates greater trust and confidence in police in their efforts to fight terrorism.
- You trust police to make decisions that are good for everyone when they are investigating and prosecuting terrorism
- People's rights are generally well protected by police when they are investigating and prosecuting terrorism
- You have confidence in police to effectively deal with terrorism
- You have confidence in police when they investigate and prosecute terrorism
- When the police fight terrorism they gain respect
- Policing terrorism negatively affects police–citizen relations*
- Police activities in fighting terrorism impair their relationships with Muslim communities in Australia*

Willingness to Work with Police to Combat Terrorism

Cronbach's alpha = 0.92; scores on a 1 = very unlikely to 5 = very likely scale. A higher score indicates greater willingness to work with police to educate members in their community about the threats of terrorism.

If the situation arose, how likely would you be to...
- Work with police to educate people in your community about the dangers of terrorism and terrorists
- Encourage members of your community to generally cooperate with police efforts to fight terrorism
- Attend a community forum held at your local Mosque to discuss with police how terrorism can be prevented

Report Terrorism Related Information

Cronbach's alpha = 0.96; scores on a 1 = very unlikely to 5 = very likely scale. A higher score indicates greater willingness to report terrorism related information to police.
   If you saw or heard about the following, how likely would you be to report it to police.
- A person saying he or she had joined a group you consider politically radical
- A person overheard discussing their decision to help plant explosives in a terrorist attack
- A person visiting Internet chat rooms or websites in which there is material posted that supports Al Qaeda
- A person reading religious literature you believe to be extremist
- A person giving money to organizations that people say are associated with terrorists
- A person talking about traveling overseas to fight for Muslims
- A person distributing material expressing support for Al Qaeda

Procedural Justice

Cronbach's alpha = 0.95; scores on a 1 = strongly disagree to 5 = strongly agree scale. A higher score indicates greater perceptions of procedural justice being used by police when dealing with Muslims regarding counterterrorism (Mean = 3.93; $SD = 0.74$).
   When dealing with people in your community concerning issues of terrorism, the police...
- Give people a chance to express their views before making decisions
- Make their decisions based upon facts, not their personal opinions
- Apply the law consistently to everyone, regardless of who they are
- Consider people's views when deciding what to do
- Take account of the needs and concerns of the people they deal with
- Respect people's rights
- Treat people with dignity and respect
- Treat people fairly
- Try to be fair when making decisions
- Are polite when dealing with people

Community-Led Counterterrorism

Aziz Z. Huq

ABSTRACT
This article explores the idea that nonstate actors embedded in geographically and religiously defined communities have a distinctive role to play in responding to growing terrorist recruitment efforts in Europe and North America. The resulting "community-led counterterrorism" works through at least two causal channels, which I label "ideological competition" and "ethical anchoring." Existing counterterrorism policing strategies do not harness these mechanisms and may well undermine them. Community-led counterterrorism thus presents an untapped opportunity, even as it raises new and difficult ethical questions for both Muslim minority communities in the West, as well as liberal democracies.

On 17 February 2015, three teenage girls from the Bethnal Green neighborhood of east London—Kadiza Sultana, Shamima Begum, and Amira Abase—boarded a Turkish Airlines flight from London's Gatwick airport for Istanbul, Turkey. The trio allegedly were on their way to Syria, with the aim of joining the Islamic State (IS).[1] Distraught at the girls' sudden and unexpected departure, their families appealed to them to come home. At the same time, though, family members also sharply criticized London's Metropolitan Police for failing to share information that might have allowed parents and close friends to have intervened and prevented the girls' departure. Even if the state would have lacked the authority to act coercively against the girls, family members implied, persuasion and appeals from close relations could have mitigated IS's allure and blunted the force of propaganda disseminated through social media.

On both sides of the Atlantic today, the idea that nonstate actors, who are embedded in geographically and religiously defined communities, have a distinctive and important role to play in responding to terrorist recruitment efforts finds increasing resonance in official policy and practice. Little more than a month after Sultana, Begum, and Abase departed for Syria, American authorities flagged two Somali Americans, Abdi Nur and Abdullahi Yusuf, planning the same journey together. The Federal Bureau of Investigation (FBI) was able to prevent only Yusuf from reaching the IS capital of Raqaa in Syria. They failed to interdict Nur even though his social media postings had reflected his intentions. Perhaps cognizant of their epistemic deficiencies, American law enforcement confessed that their investigation was stymied by the fact that there was "no clear pattern" predicting travel to Syria. IS recruits, the FBI found, varied in age, religiosity, and even prior identification with Islam.[2]

Recognizing this difficulty, the U.S. government has conceded that nonstate action will often be crucial to identifying and mitigating terrorist recruitment efforts, especially given the IS's increasingly sophisticated and effective use of social media.[3] In late 2014 the U.S. Department of Justice, and the Department of Homeland Security (DHS) thus launched a series of pilot programs in Boston, Los Angeles, and the twin cities of Minneapolis and St. Paul, all aimed at reaching out to community leaders, teachers, and mental health and social services professionals to help identify and address terrorist recruitment efforts. Although not formally aimed at Muslim-Americans, it appears only those communities are targeted. Speaking at a February 2015 White House summit on this program of "Countering Violent Extremism" (CVE), President Barack Obama expressly picked out Muslim-Americans. He explained the CVE initiative by arguing that private action was needed to "discredit violent ideologies" by supporting "moderate" Muslims and bolstering their ability to compete with IS on social media.[4]

The United States, though, is a relative latecomer to the use of social action against terrorism. The United Kingdom and other European nations have for several years attempted to harness in one way of another community action against terrorism risk. The United Kingdom's Prevent program, in particular, has been a source of much controversy and debate.

This article examines the concept of *community-led counterterrorism* that is implicit in claims, offered by British relatives of IS recruits and President Obama alike, that coreligionist members of (usually Muslim) communities in a given geographic locale have a comparative advantage in thwarting terrorist recruitment. I have three aims here. My first is to help define community-led counterterrorism as a distinct object of academic study. I argue that community-led counterterrorism is distinct and different from the more familiar concept of *community policing for counterterrorism*. The latter has already been extensively analyzed by scholars.[5] It is important to distinguish these two strategies because they depend on distinct causal mechanisms. They also point toward different forms of policing strategy and security-related investments.

My second aim is to specify an agenda for academic study by positing two possible causal mechanisms that might underwrite community-led counterterrorism. My ambition in setting forth these two mechanisms—which I label *ideological competition* and *ethical anchoring*—is not to answer definitively questions about the causal channels through which community-led counterterrorism might (or might not) flow. It is instead to offer a simple and tractable analytic framework for examining the potential efficacy, and potential costs, of an emergent counterterrorism strategy.

My final aim is normative. Both CVE and Prevent seem to target Muslim minorities alone. Given its focus on a discrete and insular minority, community-led counterterrorism raises normative questions about the relationship between minority religious communities and the coercive parts of the state, including the police and security services such as the Security Service (MI5) in the United Kingdom and the FBI and Central Intelligence Agency (CIA) in the United States. This relationship is especially fraught in both American and European contexts because Muslim minority communities have been objects of much private animus and violence over the past decade,[6] which builds on a longstanding ideological framework in which Islam is a systemic antinomy to liberalism.[7] On both sides of the Atlantic, this animus has intensified in the past few years, with increasing public support for openly nativist politicians apparently motivated by diffuse anxieties about economic fragility and mass migration. Community-led counterterrorism's effects cannot be understood without taking account of this historical context and these evolving forms of social contestation over the status of Muslims in European and American societies.

This inquiry into community-led counterterrorism is even more timely because of the rise of the IS, and its apparently successful appeals across Europe and the United States. A 2013 analysis by Thomas Hegghammer found that the number of European fighters in Syria exceeded the total number of Muslim foreign fighters from all Western countries to all conflicts between 1990 and 2010. As of January 2015, one reliable estimate placed the number of Western European IS fighters at 4,000, with 1,200 coming from France, and 500–600 from both Germany and the United Kingdom.[8] The IS has employed social media technologies, including Twitter and Facebook, far more effectively than Al Qaeda ever had to disseminate its perspective on the Syrian conflict and to engage in targeted recruitment in Europe and America, as well as the Gulf states, North Africa, and Asia.[9] This new front in counterterrorism's many wars only makes the question of how private action can respond to *jihadist* groups all the more pressing.

What is Community-Led Counterterrorism?

This section explores the concept of community-led counterterrorism. I also distinguish it from community policing against terrorism. It then offers the U.S. "Countering Violent Extremism" program announced by President Obama as an example of what it might entail. The premise of such programs is that private actions, as well as state policies, are a friction on terrorist recruitment and violence. That premise, however, is controversial. Accordingly, I start by defending the premise, and then go on to address how CVE and its ilk try to harness private action.

Writing in 2011, the sociologist Charles Kurzman pointed out that there are somewhere between 1.1 million to 7 million Muslim Americans in the United States. Yet "in the five years after 9/11 … fewer than 40 Muslim-Americans planned or carried out acts of domestic terrorism. …"[10] From this estimate, Kurzman drew the inference that Al Qaeda had been largely unsuccessful in respect to its one strategic ambitions for the 9/11 attacks. Beyond the massive human and social cost of those attacks, Kurzman explained, their spectacular nature aimed in the long term to accelerate recruitment to Al Qaeda's cause in the United States—a goal that had failed. Kurzman specifically focused on the resistance of American Muslims to the corrosive discourses of victimization tendered by Al Qaeda. Kurzman's point gains more force when set against studies that show that this Islamist discourse, and a concomitant transnational flow in foreign fighters to localized civil conflicts, had been available in one form or another since the late 1970s.[11] If 9/11 could not make it catch on, what could?

Kurzman's analysis points toward a causal link between private behavior within the communities targeted for recruitment by terrorist groups and the volume of terrorist recruitment flows and hence the ultimate rate of terrorist incidents. His argument, moreover, cannot be parried by the counterclaim that, in fact, it is the state that has effectively deterred terrorist recruitment by threatening heavy punishments. Deterrence has been show to yield limited payoffs in the terrorism context,[12] especially when nonpecuniary, ideological motives drive recruitment. It is quite implausible, in other words to think that fear generates this level of nonaction. Nevertheless, Kurzman's focus on the dearth of terrorist recruits may define too narrowly the contribution made by private action on the part of minority religious communities that are in the sights of terrorist recruitment. For Kurzman does not probe the ways in which *action* by private individuals conduces to security. He offers, that is, no theory of security's social production.

Private action mitigates terrorist recruitment and terrorist violence in a range of ways. We might organize these contributions into two categories: community policing for counterterrorism and community-led counterterrorism. These two strategies can usefully be distinguished because they reflect different causal theories of counterterrorism. They also imply different divisions of labor between the state and relevant communities.

To begin with, several scholars have observed that community policing strategies developed in the ordinary crime control context can be transferred, *mutatis mutandi*, into the terrorism context.[13] Although the scope and ambitions of ordinary community policing are hotly contested,[14] one strand of that strategy focuses on police measures to encourage members of a pertinent community (defined in geographic terms) to share information with the police, and to participate in collaborative problem-solving exercises.[15] Analogously, community policing against terrorism focuses on the epistemic "feed" from local contact with police, and then examines the tactical and strategic predicates for such gains. Empirical evidence suggests that members of Muslim communities in both the United States and the United Kingdom are more willing to share information with police, and to engage in participatory activities with police aimed at reducing terrorism risk, if they view the police as legitimate[16] and worthy of trust.[17]

Community policing for counterterrorism has various implications for policing strategy. Spalek and MacDonald begin by underscoring the importance of trust, and observe that levels of trust in the state within British Muslim communities are likely to be low.[18] Spalek argues for the fostering of implicit trust through long-term interaction and trust-building investments by specialist counterterrorism units underpinned specifically by principles of community policing.[19] Lambert provides a case study of the Muslim Contact Unit, which conforms in large measure to Spalek's model, and which claims some success in the British context.[20] Innes, by contrast, favors integrating local police into a national organizational structure.[21] Rather than focusing on the organization of police, Huq, Schulhofer, and Tyler identify specific tactics—such as singling out individuals for public investigative searches on the basis of perceived faith or ethnicity—as likely to undermine legitimacy and hence cooperation.[22] They urge police to act in more transparent and even-handed ways. None of these analyses question the primacy of the state (usually in the form of the police) in acquiring and then acting on, information concerning terrorism risk. Rather, they generate recommendations about how police should be organized or should behave.

Community-led counterterrorism is distinct from community policing against terrorism. As illustrated by the introductory examples, it lacks a guiding text or theoretical framework. But an account might perhaps be synthesized from certain elements of the U.S. CVE program and the U.K. Prevent program, albeit with some effort and imagination. The central way in which it differs from community policing against terrorism is the primacy of nonstate actors over state actors. It is first and foremost *private* behavior that mitigates rates of terrorist recruitment and violence. Rather than serving as a conduit for information or agenda-setting, community-led counterterrorism focuses on the possibility that private individuals—typically enmeshed in a social network that includes potential recruits for terrorism—can take steps to reduce the expected success rate of recruiting tactics. A useful motivating example involves the Florida and California mosques that identified individuals as potential terrorist recruiters, and then expelled them.[23] Self-help measures of this kind, which may be available even absent sufficient evidence to motivate law enforcement, raise the expected cost of terrorist recruiting. Critically, these actions were self-directed, rather than being done at the behest of law enforcement. Hence the label "community-*led*" counterterrorism, which captures an essential difference between this strategy and the more state-centric community policing against terrorism.

At the same time, both concepts of community-led counterterrorism and community policing against terrorism rely in some measure on an extant "community." But matters are rarely that simple. "Communities," especially in minority religious enclaves, are usually fissiparous and inexact entities. While there exist geographic concentrations of American and British Muslims, there are also segments of those subgroups diffused through the general population due to residential segregation by class and wealth. Spatial, as well as social, separation may render the term "community" more euphemistic and ambiguous in the counterterrorism context than in the ordinary crime control context. The high rate of converts among those indicted on terrorism-related charges connected to the IS, moreover, suggests that a large measure of recruitment occurs outside established religious and ethnic enclaves. The underlying fragmentation of community might influence community-led counterterrorism and community policing against terrorism in different ways.

Although it is autochthonic, community-led counterterrorism can be the object of government cultivation (successfully or not is another question). The Obama administration's CVE strategy illustrates one way in which government can try to do this. The policy has percolated in the U.S. government since the first term of the Obama presidency, but received the powerful imprimatur of presidential endorsement in the form of a February 2015 "summit" at the White House devoted to the topic. At least rhetorically, CVE seems aimed at catalyzing community-led counterterrorism. In May 2010, the White House published its National Security Strategy, a global strategy document that in passing flagged "well informed and equipped families, local communities, and institutions" as some of the "best defenses against" terrorism. This hint was elaborated on in an August 2011 policy paper entitled "Empowering Local Partners to Prevent Violent Extremism in the United States." The latter emphasized the state's comparative disadvantage in identifying and speaking to recruiters' targets in ways that mitigate the risk of domestic-source violence, and contrasted the advantage that "[c]ommunities" have. It did not, however, explain precisely what communities would do, or how the government could effectively support their efforts. The February 2015 summit, along with a speech delivered on the occasion by President Obama, marked a significant new level of public commitment to CVE beyond these earlier inchoate policy statements.

Yet it remains to be seen whether the policies that in fact ensue from CVE's three test sites in Boston, Minneapolis-St. Paul, and Los Angeles comprise community-led counterterrorism, as opposed to community policing against terrorism. It appears that these CVE experiments had started to take shape as of early 2016, but early reports suggest that they differ little from the mine run of counterterrorism policies employed since 2001. Thus, a February 2014 press release from the FBI described programs in both Los Angeles and Minneapolis-St. Paul in terms of law enforcement outreach and meetings with "leaders" of local Muslim communities as a way of building "trust and rapport" with local leaders. The same document quotes the Minneapolis deputy assistant director as saying that he had "limited resources" for counterterrorism. Earlier outreach efforts by the FBI have engendered controversy and outright hostility because government agents were perceived as portraying Muslim world leaders in a negative light.[24] At least to date, therefore, the relatively sparse accounts of CVE do not clearly signal an effort to fashion community-*led* counterterrorism efforts that are conceptually, practically, and institutionally distinct from the kind of information-gathering familiar from community policing against terrorism.

U.S. counterterrorism strategy is not unique in praising private diligence against terrorism, and would not be the first to be derailed before fully exploiting the potential for such action. The United Kingdom's counterterrorism strategy, called "Contest," also was based on the premise that that "faith institutions and organizations can play a very important role in preventative activity." The Prevent strand of the Contest strategy that sought to leverage this possibility, however, was not universally acclaimed. Rather, it engendered a long and contentious debate about its mix of intelligence gathering and outreach, the manner in which funds were allocated among different groups, and the theoretical underpinnings of its controversial identification of "vulnerability indicators" to "radicalization."[25] Even without sorting through these debates, it is apparent that Prevent does not represent a pure endorsement of community-led counterterrorism.

How Does Community-Led Counterterrorism Work?

The potential promise of community-led counterterrorism turns on the existence of causal mechanisms linking private action to the reduction of terrorism recruitment rates (and thereby to the reduction of terrorist violence). This section introduces two such causal mechanisms, which I label *ideological competition* and *ethical anchoring* in earlier work.[26] In describing these mechanisms, I make no claim that they are, in fact, always or generally effective. Indeed, in each case, large-N empirical support for their effects is to date lacking (although in each case there is substantial anecdotal evidence that provides cause for optimism). These mechanisms, moreover, may not be exclusive.[27]

Ideological Competition

First, ideological competition is a form of private action that raises the costs of terrorist groups' personnel policies by providing substitute forms of social solidarity and vehicles of collective political action for those targeted by terrorist groups. At its core, it operates through the disciplining effect of competition, which creates higher operating costs (and hence smaller returns) for resource-constrained terrorist groups.

Ideological competition in this vein has been identified in a recent account of political struggles in the Palestinian refugee camp of Ain al-Helweh, where a violent Salafist groups struggles for influence with nationalist and other groups.[28] Similarly, a terrorist organization seeking to appeal via social media to U.S. or U.K. nationals on the basis of putatively shared grievances about foreign policy would, in a situation of real competition, have to expend more resources to remain competitive.[29] Other groups pursuing the same policy goals, albeit without violence, may be more appealing because they provide a vehicle for antiauthoritarian preferences without the severe costs of social outcasting and legal sanctions. All things being equal, it seems plausible to think that the terrorist organization facing a more crowded ideological marketplace must expand more resources attracting recruits, leaving fewer resources for the commission of violence.

Ideological competition by private groups accomplishes a goal that the state acting alone cannot always reach. Starting with Olivier Roy, many analysts have emphasized the extent to which the allure of Al Qaeda, IS, and like groups does not hinge on the consonance of their positions with long-held, well-pedigreed religious dogma.[30] Rather, they appeal as a powerful counterculture in opposition to widely held social views. As a result, the range of groups that engender competition may be quite large: Kurzman thus argues that it is not just politically radical, but also "liberal" Muslim groups that create damaging competition for violent Islamist groups.[31] Kurzman also contends that Tablighi Jamaat, a group sometimes criticized as a conveyer belt organization, should be "seen as part of the crowded ideological field that terrorists face as they compete for Muslims' support."[32] And it is possible to imagine that non-religious sources also supply additional competition. Nevertheless, on the assumption that voices internal to a faith have a distinctive role to play, the ideological competition mechanism implies it is desirable to have a plurality of ideologically proximate alternatives to violent social movements. Rather than denouncing marginal political voices within domestic Islam, the state might, if not cultivate them, then at least tolerate them for their net positive security externalities.

The uses of ideological competition have not completely escaped government attention. In the United Kingdom, the Special Branch of London's Metropolitan Police has created a unit called the Muslim Contact Unit (MCU) for cultivating relations with the London Salafist and Islamist communities, precisely in order to help them identify and dissuade potential recruits to violence early.[33] The MCU was established in the days immediately after Richard Reid's arrest as a way to "enter into dialogue on a partnership footing" with Salafist and other politically extreme groups so as to ensure that police did not "lose their critical support in combating al-Qaeda's established influence in the capital."[34] Accounts of the MCU emphasize Salafist successes in competing with Al Qaeda proxies such as the clerics Abdullah el-Faisal and Abu Hamza.

The theory of ideological competition offered here can be resisted on a number of grounds, First, it may be that a plurality of private associations that share the liminal political views—but not the inclination toward violence—of terrorist organizations might hinder efforts to minimize terrorism risk because they provide ideological "cover" for the grievances cited by terrorist groups. Spinzak has explained the evolution of violent splinter groups within the Israeli settler milieu in the 1980s in roughly these terms.[35] Second, it could be argued that ideological fellow travelers serve as "conveyer belts," by lowering the cost of terrorist recruitment.[36] As Lynch's careful study of the Egyptian Muslim Brotherhood demonstrates, determining whether the existence of a competitor group tends to operate as a "firewall" or a "conveyer belt" to terrorist recruitment is a difficult empirical question. Critiques of governmental tolerance of quietist Islamist groups, at a minimum, must avoid the trap of attributing too much significance to a small number of highly salient cases of the "conveyer belt" mechanism at work without at the same time taking careful measure of the (perhaps much larger) number of instances in which the firewall prevailed.

Moreover, the "conveyor belt" metaphor contains a hidden assumption that its advocates rarely recognize. The metaphor suggests that groups close to a terrorist organization in policy preferences (but not in the use of violence) have an undesirable *causal* effect on the development of terrorist recruits. The causal effect is inferred from the fact that individuals move from a nonviolent but extreme organization to a violent organization. But the inference does not follow: Those individuals may have moved directly to terrorism in the absence of the nonviolent organization, while other individuals who would have adopted terrorist means may have chosen not to do so because they found an ideologically sympathetic environment. It is fallacious to move from observation of individual migrations into terrorism to the conclusion that extremist but nonviolent groups increase the rate of terrorism. Moreover, the conveyer belt model assumes there is a morphological parallel or homology between quietist and politicized extremist groups. But this may not be so: There may instead be importantly divergent readings of religious texts, even between quietist and political Salafists.

Ethical Anchoring

The second mechanism by which private action without direction from the state can preclude terrorist recruitment is through the psychological anchoring effect of close affiliations. Political violence necessitates the violation of generally shared ethical commitments, which in turn leads to breaches with otherwise close members of familial and social networks.[37] Radicalization can involve a "crisis" that induces an individual to reevaluate "existing ways of interpreting experience."[38] To the extent the members of tight social networks reiterate and reinforce existing ethical norms by persuasion or the implicit threat of social sanction, recruitment costs will be higher. On this account, family members and other participants in immediate social networks impose a baseline set of ethical claims on potential recruits. The stronger these claims are, the less likely recruiting propaganda is to be successful.

The basic concept of ethical anchoring, in effect, lay behind the complaints of Sultana, Begum, and Abase's parents, that they were never given an opportunity to dissuade their daughters from the flight to Syria. Gerges provides another example of the phenomenon: A 19-year-old Somali American called Mohammed Osman, who was alleged to have planned a car bomb attack against public holiday celebrations in Portland, Oregon, and who later acknowledged that his "parents held [him] back from jihad in the cause of Allah," at least until they divorced, leaving him to drift toward violence.[39]

To the extent social networks furnish affirmative role-models, there is less cause to seek out violent forms of social action in the first place. An important part of the appeal of certain Al Qaeda figures has been their capacity to act as a kind of role model. Brachtman and Levine, for example, proffer the example of Anwar al-Awlaqi, who became an attractive role model for youth wanting "someone who is easier to emulate, a figure that they can become without too much work or thought, and who makes them feel as it they are producing something meaningful and relevant."[40] Social networks can provide alternative role-models. For example, a potential example of ethical anchoring is the Active Change Foundation (ACF) in North London, founded by a former Al Qaeda sympathizer, which "encourages youth to express their rage about the mistreatment of Muslims in Iraq, Palestine, and elsewhere and channel it into peaceful political action."[41] ACF also provides social services and engages in outreach, in part to identify those targeted for Al Qaeda recruitment, and then engages in "targeted interventions" to challenge that process.

There is some empirical support to suggest that ethical anchoring is a substantial phenomenon. Horgan's case studies of individuals who have left terrorist groups hence emphasize the "role of civil society" in promoting "psychological disengagement."[42] His studies suggest that even individuals who appeared to be committed to a terrorist organization could be swayed, but that "people tend generally to be more trusting of the communicator if they do not perceive that the communicator has something to gain or has the explicit intention to persuade." For obvious reasons, this rules out the state as an effective anchoring voice. The same study found that interlocutors who are similar in social background, but who are older and perceived as more "experience[d]," are also more likely to be effective. These voices are most likely to be drawn from the immediate social context in which a potential recruit is embedded. Providing some confirmatory evidence on this score, van San et al. use a case study approach to identify ways in which educators, social workers, and family members can buffer terrorist recruitment efforts. They caution, however, of the pervasive ignorance of such risks within larger social networks.[43]

Like ideological competition, ethical anchoring can be challenged as a causal predicate of reduced terrorist radicalization rates. Consider again Roy's argument that recent Islamist terrorism has been a countercultural movement animated by a desire to position oneself in opposition to the political and cultural mainstream.[44] Ethical anchoring by family or community leaders will by hypothesis fail because most potential recruits have already broken with their immediate social networks before any tipping point is reached (although not, by all accounts, in many instances of recent recruitment by IS). Alternatively, efforts at ethical anchoring by traditional authority figures (e.g., parents, teachers) might have a perverse effect on individuals who turn to terrorist groups as the most salient and attractive counter-culture on display. It is not hard to imagine, that is, such efforts backfiring by confirming that the IS or Al Qaeda is the paradigmatic form of offensive revolt from parental (or social) authority. If this is so, state efforts to consult with official representatives of a Muslim community may well have the effect of legitimating terrorist recruiting efforts. Another risk is that informal interventions that initially develop within a community can be distorted by the state, either intentionally or inadvertently. Governments, for example, may offer funding that influences the kinds of activities undertaken through informal initiatives. Funding can also delegitimize informal interlocutors in the eyes of their intended audience.

The Utility of Community-Led Counterterrorism

The evaluation of community-led counterterrorism from a strategic perspective turns primarily on its comparative efficacy: Which, if any, of the two mechanisms outlined above is plausible? And how effective are alternative methods of either prophylaxis against recruitment or alternative interdiction? Because there is only anecdotal evidence of ideological competition and ethical anchoring to date, it is not possible to provide a firm answer to these questions. Nevertheless, the anecdotal evidence alluded to above suggests that private action plays some role in deterring recruitment. This section starts from the premise that that there is at least some evidence of efficacy, and then considers whether policymaking under current conditions would benefit from the more clear-eyed recognition of community-led counterterrorism.

The potential efficacy of community-led counterterrorism in part is a function of the set of recruiting strategies employed by terrorism groups such as IS and Al Qaeda. In particular, it must be analyzed in the context of an accelerating deployment of social media technologies such as YouTube, Facebook, and Twitter to disseminate propaganda, as well as the use of messaging apps such as Telegram and Kik to reach potential recruits. These technologies raise complex questions for the utility of community-led counterterrorism. For example, offshoots from the banned British organization al Mujahiroun had, as of 2011, created 41 YouTube channels to disseminate *jihadist* content.[45] Twitter feeds from the Syrian front lines create the impression of urgency and spontaneity, although Europe-based organizational accounts associated with the banned British organization, Al Muhajiroun, and in particular the London-based preacher, Anjem Choudary, also play a role in disseminating "battlefield" information.[46]

But does increasingly successful *jihadist* recruitment via social media technologies call for an enlarged or a diminished role for community-led counterterrorism? The question is difficult to answer. On the one hand, a potential counterweight to terrorist use of social media is the increasing power of states (and in particular the United States in collaboration with its Five Eyes partners the United Kingdom, Canada, New Zealand, and Australia) to conduct electronic surveillance both within and beyond national borders.[47] The United States, for example, collects both content and metadata from electronic communications both inside and outside the United States. Extraterritorial collection, allegedly pursuant to Executive Order 12,333, permits the National Security Agency (NSA) to engage in collection overseas, and simultaneously "incidentally" collect communications and metadata generated inside the United States.[48] Both content and metadata are held for at least five years. Hence, intelligence agencies not only have the capacity to contemporaneously track online communications, but can use algorithmic path-analysis tools to exploit historical data. In effect, once a suspect is identified, intelligence agencies can backfill his (or her) communications history, identifying all those he (or she) has contacted, and who they in turn have contacted. This data can then be cross-referenced with other sources to pin-point potential common sources of recruitment propaganda. Moreover, pace Klausen's concern that U.S. authorities may be overly constrained by free-speech concerns,[49] there is little reason to think that statutory or constitutional rules impede collection efforts. To the contrary, recent U.S. Supreme Court case law permits the governmental regulation of even overtly political speech that notionally lies at the First Amendment's heartland, provided that there is a concern with terrorism at stake.[50]

On the one hand, there are reasons to think that state intelligence and policing agencies will still face severe obstacles when predicting the distribution of terrorist recruitment, as indeed American law enforcement has candidly conceded.[51] Hence, it remains unclear whether even the robust surveillance apparatus that the United States has developed can provide a sufficient response to terrorist groups' new exploitation of social media. At a very minimum, the rate of recruitment to IS implies that current surveillance authorities are no panacea. Self-motivated recruits such as Sultana, Begum, and Abase may act based solely on the consumption of material available on Twitter feeds, chat-forums, and websites. The mere act of visiting such sites or subscribing to such feeds is unlikely to yield a discriminating enough tool for effective risk identification. Moreover, just as states have deepened their surveillance capacities, so private individuals have obtained larger resources for responding to such intrusions. Defensive technologies once exclusively within the domain of experts are now widely available for free download. By encrypting electronic communications—a measure that is increasingly incorporated by default by providers such as Google—and using an anonymizing app, it is quite feasible for a reasonably well-informed teenager in London or Minneapolis to raise dramatically the cost of surveillance. Intrusive measures involving either electronic or human surveillance, accordingly, are unlikely to exhaust responses to post-IS forms of terrorist recruitment.

Hence, even given the increasing power of security agencies to aggregate and analyze massive amounts of communications data, the new wave of *jihadist* propaganda may nonetheless call for even greater reliance on responsive action from within target communities. In the home, parents already have reason to monitor and intervene in respect to minors' use of digital technologies based on concerns about cyberbullying, exposure to harmful or illegal content, and exposure to sexual predators.[52] Efforts to recruit vulnerable teens to the Syrian conflict are but the most recent hazard that the online world presents. Parental monitoring is hardly straightforward given that many minors have smart phones (and, perhaps more to the point, friends with smart phones). But there is no categorical difference between the kinds of prophylactic actions that a parent or caregiver can take in respect to online recruitment than to other online perils.

More generally, even if parents and guardians cannot prevent exposure to IS Twitter feeds and the like, there is still no reason to think that ideological competition and ethical anchoring that occurs offline would be ineffective. To the contrary, it may well be that these are the only measures that have a chance of gaining traction. On this view, the increasingly effective penetration of terrorist groups into the consciousness of Western teens and young adults might be taken to present an opportunity for the development of community-led counterterrorism measures, not a reason for retiring it.

Should Community-Led Counterterrorism be Encouraged?

Even if effective, there are ethical and normative reasons to hesitate before embracing community-led terrorism. The force of these reasons turns on specific historical and contemporary circumstances. Rather than trying to assign weights to them conclusively, my goal in this final section is to identify a series of grounds for normative concern about community-led counterterrorism. Even if it is a necessary element of counterterrorism strategy, that is, the latter may have serious costs that are unevenly, and inequitably, distributed between different communities.

The most important concern arises from the singular focus of community-led counterterrorism on Muslim communities in the United States and the United Kingdom. For the purposes of this section, I will focus on the United States. There, advocacy organizations such as Muslim Advocates have argued that such a focus is unwarranted because an analysis of historical terrorism trends suggests that Muslims are not responsible for even a majority of terrorism incidents in the United States. The empirical predicate for statistical discrimination in counterterrorism efforts, therefore, is unavailable. One possible riposte to this position would focus on the difference in expected cost of a terrorist event committed by Al Qaeda and one committed by a domestic (say, right-wing militia) organization. Al Qaeda and the IS arguably have a unique focus on mass casualty attacks on civilian targets, as well as a capacity for indiscriminate violence that other organizations lack.

Perhaps the more substantial ethnical concern with community-led counterterrorism focuses on its dynamic effects on social attitudes toward Muslims. In other work, I have documented the fluctuating tide of anti-Muslim discrimination in the United States as manifested by employment discrimination, hate crimes, and attacks on mosques.[53] A recent quantitative sociological analysis by Bail identifies and analyzes the emergence of an infrastructure of anti-Muslim grassroots groups, lobbying organizations, and think tanks, and shows how these groups have had a tangible (and deleterious) effect on the content of public discussions of Islam and terrorism in the United States.[54] Against that background, a community-led counterterrorism programs such as CVE that focuses solely on Muslims may have the expressive effect of confirming the public's beliefs that Muslims generally are a source of terrorism risk.[55] Such programs thus have the dynamic effect of exacerbating ambient prejudices. Bail also cautions that anti-Muslim groups have used government antiterrorism efforts as platforms to inject their ideas into public discourse, for example by training police and FBI agents with materials that endorse categorically negative views about all Muslims.[56] This in turn is likely to undermine the efficacy of state-sponsored efforts to facilitate community-led counterterrorism.

Consistent with these concerns, Spalek and McDonald suggest that religiously targeted counterterrorism strategy articulated in a political context in which Muslim religious and political practice is stigmatized as outside the mainstream can have deleterious effects.[57] Even where the range of "legitimate" forms of Islam is broad, Spalek and Imtoual point out, some are stigmatized and excluded on the basis of beliefs that might be quietist in orientation; ironically, these groups may be the most important and valuable contributors to ideological competition.[58]

There are two other normative puzzles raised by state endorsement of community-led counterterrorism that merit attention. First, is it proper to impose a heightened burden (whether enforced by law or not) on certain groups to aid in the production of counterterrorism that do not apply to the general population? In other domains, Anglo-American law tends not to impose a duty to act on persons who are uniquely situated to prevent harms (e.g., there is no duty to rescue a drowning person), while European law does sometimes impose such a duty.[59] The U.S. position has been cogently defended in terms of a concern about the perverse effects of such a duty.[60] In the terrorism context, although behavioral effects may be weaker, a distributive concern may motivate a refusal to extend duties to aid: As noted, Muslim communities in North America and Europe are already subject to heightened levels of scrutiny and intrusion, as well as elevated levels of private discrimination. These groups are then asked to shoulder a particularized responsibility for national security that is not shared by other groups—not as a consequence of what all members of those communities have done, but as a consequence of coreligionists' actions. Burdens of suspicion are thus compounded by obligations to organize communal life in a way that benefits the larger society even as it compromises shared confessional life.[61] What might have been an autonomous domain of civil society can be corrupted by distrust that others are informants *or agents provocateurs*.[62] Alternatively, it may become a grossly functional appendage of the state. In this fashion, religious communities already stigmatized and corroded by suspicion undergo a second, additional kind of loss, which this time sounds in autonomy and equality. This form of collective responsibility, in short, may be iniquitous and unjust—at least without some positive effort at contemporaneous restitution by the state.

Second, state efforts to encourage community-led counterterrorism can have untoward effects. To begin with, the state may co-opt private initiatives in ways that distort and ultimately undermine those initiatives. As noted, in the British context programs such as Prevent and Channel have been indicted not only as stigmatizing but also as *sub rosa* means of gathering intelligence, rather than genuine partnerships between Muslim communities and the state.[63] Private associations that allow ethical and social life independent of the state have an important role to play in a free society. To selectively deprive one ethnic or religious group of the opportunity to develop such associations is arguably a form of invidious discrimination. Even if the state does not capture private initiatives, it nonetheless may distort the play of social forces within a community. It is a mistake, that is, to view ethnic or religious communities as homogenous. Rather, they are inevitably comprised of divergent factions. By subsidizing one faction with material resources or moral support, the state influences the development of that community. Such distortion raises concerns once more about liberal entitlements to religious and ideological freedom being compromised.

Conclusion

This article has defined and explored the casual predicates and normative implications of community-led counterterrorism. To this end, I have focused on two mechanisms—ideological competition and ethnical anchoring. Empirical and theoretical studies of terrorist recruitment processes provide some reason to believe that both mechanisms, equally dependent on the existence of robust ideological debate and position-taking within relevant communities, can have the effect of at least slowing terrorist recruitment. Especially given the increasingly sophisticated use by IS of social media as a means of outreach; however, it is important to stress that neither is a panacea. Because community-led counterterrorism is at best a partial response to terrorist recruitment efforts, it follows that it cannot fully displace other, more traditional tools. Equally, it follows that failures to prevent radicalization cannot be set at the doorstep of any specific segment of society.

British and American security agencies have to date gestured with increasing frequency toward this strategy, which may have particular force in the context of increasing use of social media to target minors and young adults for recruitment. But they have yet to disaggregate it crisply from community policing against terrorism. Even when that distinction is drawn, however, difficult positive and normative questions remain about the role that community-led counterterrorism should play. Community-led counterterrorism risks engendering a perception of collective responsibility for terrorism. Although the grounds of that attribution of blame are false—a good Samaritan is not to be blamed if her well-meant rescue effort fails—the risks of stigmatization and distortion of the religious and political lives of relevant communities are not to be lightly discounted. Like many other elements of counterterrorism policy, in short, the community-led variant presents delicate normative challenges and risks large potential costs. Perhaps it is only because the failure to pursue it has such serious consequences that it warrants such serious consideration.

Funding

The Frank Cicero Jr. Fund of the University of Chicago Law School provided support for this research.

Notes

1. Kimiko De Freytas-Tamura, "Teenage Girl Leaves for ISIS, and Others Follow," *The New York Times*, 24 February 2015.
2. Scott Shane, "From Minneapolis to ISIS: An American's Path to Jihad," *The New York Times*, 21 March 2015.
3. Jytte Klausen, "Tweeting the Jihad: Social Media Networks of Western Foreign Fighters in Syria and Iraq," *Studies in Conflict & Terrorism* 38(1) (2015), pp. 1–22.

4. Juliet Eilperin, "Obama Announces Initiatives to Curb Recruitment of Terrorist Groups," *The Washington Post*, 18 February 2015.
5. Aziz Z. Huq, Tom R. Tyler, and Stephen J. Schulhofer, "Mechanisms for Eliciting Cooperation in Counterterrorism Policing: Evidence from the United Kingdom," *Journal of Empirical Legal Studies* 8(4) (2011), pp. 728–761; Aziz Z. Huq, Tom R. Tyler, and Stephen J. Schulhofer, "Why Does the Public Cooperate with Law Enforcement? The Influence of the Purposes and Targets of Policing," *Psychology, Public Policy, and Law* 17, no. 3 (2011), pp. 419–450; Martin Innes, "Policing Uncertainty: Countering Terror through Community Intelligence and Democratic Policing," *Annals of the American Academy of Political and Social Science* 605, no. 1 (2006), pp. 222–241; Jytte Klausen, "British Counter-Terrorism After 7/7: Adapting Community Policing to the Fight Against Domestic Terrorism," *Journal of Ethnic and Migration Studies* 35(3) (2009), pp. 403–420.
6. Christopher Bail, *Terrified: How Anti-Muslim Fringe Organizations Became Mainstream* (Princeton, NJ: Princeton University Press, 2014); Jocelyne Cesari, *Why the West Fears Islam: An Exploration of Muslims in Liberal Democracies* (New York: Palgrave Macmillan, 2013).
7. Joseph A. Massad, *Islam in Liberalism* (Chicago; London: University of Chicago Press, 2015).
8. Peter R. Neumann, "Foreign Fighter Total in Syria/Iraq Now Exceeds 20,000; Surpasses Afghanistan Conflict in the 1980s," *ICSR*. Available at http://icsr.info/2015/01/foreign-fighter-total-syriairaq-now-exceeds-20000-surpasses-afghanistan-conflict-1980s/ (accessed 22 April 2015).
9. Klausen, "Tweeting the Jihad," pp. 1–22. For a summary of analytic approaches to European radicalization, see Mohammed Hafez and Creighton Mullins, "The Radicalization Puzzle: A Theoretical Synthesis of Empirical Approaches to Homegrown Extremism," *Studies in Conflict & Terrorism* 38(11) (2015), pp. 958–975, and Anja Dalgaard-Nielsen, "Violent Radicalization in Europe: What We Know and What We Do Not Know," *Studies in Conflict & Terrorism* 33(9) (2010), pp. 797–814.
10. Charles Kurzman, *The Missing Martyrs: Why There Are So Few Muslim Terrorists* (Oxford; New York: Oxford University Press, 2011), p. 11.
11. Thomas Hegghammer, "The Rise of Muslim Foreign Fighters: Islam and the Globalization of Jihad," *International Security* 35(3) (2010), pp. 53–94.
12. Bruno S. Frey and Simon Luechinger, "How to Fight Terrorism: Alternatives to Deterrence," *Defence and Peace Economics* 14(4) (2003), pp. 237–249.
13. Innes, "Policing Uncertainty," p. 222.
14. Wesley G. Skogan, *Police and Community in Chicago: A Tale of Three Cities* (Oxford; New York: Oxford University Press, 2006).
15. William Lyons, "Partnerships, Information and Public Safety," *Policing: An International Journal of Police Strategies & Management* 25(3) (2002), pp. 530–542.
16. Huq, Schulhofer, and Tyler, "Mechanisms for Eliciting Cooperation"; Huq, Schulhofer, and Tyler, "Why Does the Public Cooperate with Law Enforcement?"; see also Tom R. Tyler, Stephen Schulhofer, and Aziz Z. Huq, "Legitimacy and Deterrence Effects in Counterterrorism Policing: A Study of Muslim Americans," *Law & Society Review* 44(2) (2010), pp. 365–402.
17. Basia Spalek, "Community Policing, Trust, and Muslim Communities in Relation to 'New Terrorism,'" *Politics & Policy* 38(4) (2010), pp. 789–815.
18. Basia Spalek and Laura Zahra McDonald, "Terror Crime Prevention: Constructing Muslim Practices and Beliefs as 'Anti-Social' and 'Extreme' through CONTEST 2," *Social Policy and Society* 9(1) (2010), pp. 123–132.
19. Spalek, "Community Policing, Trust, and Muslim Communities in Relation to 'New Terrorism,'" pp. 789–815.
20. Robert Lambert, "Empowering Salafis and Islamists against Al-Qaeda: A London Counterterrorism Case Study," *PS: Political Science and Politics* 41(1) (2008), pp. 31–35; Robert Lambert, *Countering Al Qaeda in London* (London: Hurst, 2012).
21. Innes, "Policing Uncertainty," p. 222.
22. Huq, Schulhofer, and Tyler, "Mechanisms for Eliciting Cooperation"; Huq, Schulhofer, and Tyler, "Why Does the Public Cooperate with Law Enforcement?"
23. Sunaina Maira, "Deporting Radicals, Deporting La Migra The Hayat Case in Lodi," *Cultural Dynamics* 19(1) (2007) pp. 39–66; William R. Levesque and Jamal Thalji, "Feds Accuse Man of

Planning Bomb and Gun Attacks in South Tampa and Ybor City," *Tampa Bay Times*, 12 January 2012.
24. Emily Heffter, "FBI Ends up Offending Muslims at Outreach Workshop," *The Seattle Times*, 10 September 2011.
25. Charlotte Heath-Kelly, "Counter-Terrorism and the Counterfactual: Producing the 'Radicalisation' Discourse and the UK PREVENT Strategy," *British Journal of Politics & International Relations* 15(3) (2013), pp. 394–415; Arun Kundnani, *Spooked! How Not to Prevent Violent Extremism* (London: Institute of Race Relations 2009).
26. Aziz Z. Huq, "The Social Production of National Security," *Cornell Law Review* 98 (2013), p. 637.
27. For examples of other mechanisms, see Huq, "Social Production"; Lasse Lindekindle, "A Typology of Backfire Mechanisms," in L. Bosi (Ed.), *Dynamics of Political Violence: A Process-oriented Perspective on Radicalization and the Escalation of Political Conflict* (London: Ashgate 2009).
28. Bernard Rougier, *Everyday Jihad: The Rise of Militant Islam among Palestinians in Lebanon*, trans. Pascale Ghazaleh (Cambridge, MA: Harvard University Press, 2009).
29. Scott Atran, *Talking to the Enemy: Religion, Brotherhood, and the (Un)Making of Terrorists* (New York: Ecco, 2011), p. 421.
30. Olivier Roy, *Globalized Islam: The Search for a New Ummah* (New York: Columbia University Press, 2006).
31. Kurzman, *Missing Martyrs*, p. 15.
32. Ibid., pp. 30–31.
33. Lambert, "Empowering Salafis," pp. 31–34.
34. Lambert, *Countering*, p. 59.
35. Ehud Spinzak, "The Genesis of Zionist Fundamentalism: The Case of Gush Emunim," *Orim* 3(1) (1987), p. 15.
36. Marc Lynch, "Islam Divided Between Salafi-Jihad and the Ikhwan," *Studies in Conflict & Terrorism* 33(6) (2010), pp. 467–487.
37. Aziz Z. Huq, "Private Religious Discrimination, National Security, and the First Amendment," *Harvard Law & Policy Review* 5 (2011), pp. 347–374.
38. Alex S. Wilner and Claire-Jehanne Dubouloz, "Homegrown Terrorism and Transformative Learning: An Interdisciplinary Approach to Understanding Radicalization," *Global Change, Peace & Security* 22(1) (2010), pp. 33–51, and Alex S. Wilner and Claire-Jehanne Dubouloz, "Transformative Radicalization: Applying Learning Theory to Islamist Radicalization," *Studies in Conflict & Terrorism* 34(5) (2011), pp. 418–438.
39. Fawaz A. Gerges, *The Rise and Fall of Al-Qaeda*, Reprint edition (Oxford; New York: Oxford University Press, 2014), pp. 163–165.
40. Jarret M. Brachman and Alix N. Levine, "You Too Can Be Awlaki," *Fletcher Forum of World Affairs* 35 (2011), pp. 25–46.
41. Jessica Stern, "Mind Over Martyr: How to Deradicalize Islamist Extremists," *Foreign Affairs* 89(1) (1 January 2010), pp. 95–108.
42. John Horgan, *Walking Away from Terrorism: Accounts of Disengagement from Radical and Extremist Movements* (Milton Park, Abingdon, Oxon; New York: Routledge, 2009), p. 149.
43. Marion van San, Stijn Sieckelinck, and Micha de Winter, "Ideals Adrift: An Educational Approach to Radicalization," *Ethics and Education* 8(3) (2013), pp. 276–289.
44. Roy, *Globalized Islam*.
45. Jytte Klausen et al., "The YouTube Jihadists: A Social Network Analysis of Al-Muhajiroun's Propaganda Campaign," *Perspectives on Terrorism* 6(1) (2012), pp. 36–53.
46. Klausen, "Tweeting the Jihad," pp. 1–22.
47. Luke Harding, *The Snowden Files: The Inside Story of the World's Most Wanted Man* (New York: Vintage, 2014).
48. John Napier Tye, "Meet Executive Order 12333: The Reagan Rule That Lets the NSA Spy on Americans," *The Washington Post*, 18 July 2014.
49. Klausen, "Tweeting the Jihad," p. 22.
50. Aziz Z. Huq, "The Signaling Function of Religious Speech in Domestic Counterterrorism," *Texas Law Review* 89 (2010), pp. 833–900.

51. Shane, "From Minneapolis to ISIS."
52. David Buckingham and Rebekah Willett, *Digital Generations: Children, Young People, and the New Media* (New York: Routledge, 2013).
53. Huq, "Private Religious Discrimination," pp. 347–374.
54. Bail, *Terrified*.
55. Richard H. McAdams, *The Expressive Powers of Law: Theories and Limits* (Cambridge, MA: Harvard University Press, 2015).
56. Bail, *Terrified*.
57. Spalek and MacDonald, "Terror Crime Prevention."
58. Basia Spalek and Alia Imtoual, "Muslim Communities and Counter-Terror Responses: 'Hard' Approaches to Community Engagement in the UK and Australia," *Journal of Muslim Minority Affairs* 27(2) (2007), pp. 185–202.
59. Alison McIntyre, "Guilty Bystanders? On the Legitimacy of Duty to Rescue Statutes," *Philosophy & Public Affairs* 23(2) (1994), pp. 157–191.
60. Saul Levmore, "Waiting for Rescue: An Essay on the Evolution and Incentive Structure of the Law of Affirmative Obligations," *Virginia Law Review* 72(5) (1986), pp. 879–941.
61. See Spalek and MacDonald, "Terror Crime Prevention."
62. Wadie E. Said, "The Terrorist Informant," *Washington Law Review* 85 (2010), pp. 687–738.
63. Kundnani, *Spooked!*

Community-Based Counterterrorism Policing: Recommendations for Practitioners

Robert Lambert and Tim Parsons

> **ABSTRACT**
> This article presents recommendations for practitioners of community-based counterterrorism policing. The recommendations are located and explained within two broad propositions: *recognize the implications and limitations of policing by consent*, and *respect the legitimate religious beliefs of all communities*. Highlighting tensions between high and low policing and between policing and government imperatives, the article helps illustrate how different aspects of counterterrorism policy and practice may sometimes be at odds with one another. The recommendations are aimed at recognizing and, where practicable, reconciling such tensions. They arise from the authors' engagement with the issues in London and are understood to have application in other towns and cities in the United Kingdom and the West, particularly in communities and neighborhoods where Muslim citizens are the principal recipients of this form of policing.

Recommendations for Community-Based Counterterrorism Policing: Background and Context

This article presents recommendations for practitioners of community-based counterterrorism policing. The recommendations are located and explained within two broad propositions: *recognize the implications and limitations of policing by consent*, and *respect the legitimate religious beliefs of all communities*. Both recommendations are grounded in the authors' London-based academic research, teaching, and prior careers in policing.[1] As such, the authors' police practitioner experience has been subject to critical reflection during the course of subsequent academic research and teaching. At the heart of this reflection on a cumulative and combined experience is a recognition that individuals in communities and neighborhoods where terrorist movements seek recruits and supporters are often more likely to help police identify and disrupt terrorist conspiracies if they are treated fairly. Fair treatment, in this context, entails maintaining a tight focus on the actual terrorist threat. To the extent that Contest, and Prevent in particular, has shifted from such a tight focus on terrorism and violent extremism to a wider target of "extremism"[2] it risks alienating potential allies in Muslim communities and affords opportunities to terrorist recruiters and radicalizers.[3]

Moreover, with suicide terrorist attacks in Brussels on 22 March 2016 echoing many of the features of the attacks in London on 7 July 2005 it is clear that London experience continues to have export potential. This is not to suggest that all such experience is positive but simply that negative as well as positive experience provides opportunities for learning. Nor is it to suggest that the arguments underpinning the recommendations in this article are beyond challenge. To the contrary, it is to recognize that the article represents perspectives that have largely been rejected by U.K. policymakers, security and police chiefs, and many influential commentators. In such circumstances it has the modest ambition of prompting a constructive debate among policymakers, practitioners, and academics.

At the outset it might help to ask the question: *who are the practitioners of community-based counterterrorism policing for whom the recommendations are intended?* Crucially, as a result of government policy the answer is *not just police officers* but also *civil servants operating at both national and local levels, teachers, and nongovernmental organizations (NGOs)*. Consequently, this is to include practitioners operating under the auspices of the Prevent program,[4] a key part of the government's counterterrorism strategy known as Contest.[5] While some NGOs employ full-time practitioners who have a sole focus on Prevent business, others, most notably teachers, are asked to perform a part-time policing role alongside their many other responsibilities. In both instances individuals with no police training are enforcing government policy that risks conflating authentic terrorist recruiters or radicalizers—and those subject to recruitment and radicalization—with those, such as a fifteen-year-old schoolboy viewing right-wing literature on the Internet,[6] with an innocent interest in politics and religion. That, at least, is the concern expressed in this article that prompts the two recommendations under consideration.

The case of the fifteen-year-old schoolboy is particularly relevant because his apparent interest in the politics of the United Kingdom Independence Party (UKIP) and the English Defence League (EDL) was not the government's prime focus when first drafting the Prevent policy. Nor has it been the prime focus for Prevent practitioners who have instead been largely concerned with cases classified as Islamist radicalization. Instead, the case serves to illustrate how a legitimate, secondary Prevent interest in far right terrorism and political violence (of the kind demonstrated by Pavlo Lapshin in the West Midlands in 2013[7]) might stray beyond a legitimate police interest and into democratic politics. Indeed, how could a teacher be expected to tell the difference between the two? In much the same way, the authors argue, Prevent practitioners risk moving beyond a legitimate policing function when they target politically active or religiously observant Muslims without sufficient focus on their capacity for or susceptibility to terrorism or violent extremism.

Broadly speaking, there are four threads that connect and underpin the recommendations: the first is a recognition that counterterrorism policing is necessarily involved in a competition with terrorist movements for credibility and legitimacy in the same communities[8]; the second is a recognition that since 9/11[9] religiously observant and civic minded Muslim citizens have been the major recipients of this *soft* kind of policing; the third is a recognition that the same citizens have also experienced the impact of *hard* counterterrorism policing during the same period; and the fourth is an understanding that the principle of policing by consent imposes responsibilities on police that are likely to be outside the experience of civil servants and other multi-agency partners increasingly involved in community-based policing.[10] Taken cumulatively, the recommendations are concerned to identify and resolve tensions that arise, in part, as a result of fundamentally different priorities and duties that fall to police, in comparison with the priorities and duties of other public servants and multi-agency partners involved in the same work. By doing so, as well as hoping to assist practitioners, it is intended to stimulate academic debate on an understudied but important aspect of counterterrorism activity.

It is worth illustrating the significance of one key point—a broadening or shifting of police responsibility. When the Provisional Irish Republican Army (PIRA) waged a terrorist bombing campaign in London[11] invariably only police officers engaged with fellow Londoners to elicit support and information.[12] In contrast, since 2006 sole police responsibility for community engagement in respect of counterterrorism has been replaced by a multi-agency engagement, managed by Home Office civil servants,[13] in which police play a significant but much reduced role.[14] Therein lie fundamental tensions that have not been widely addressed in either the academic, policy, or practitioner literature hitherto. For example, at the height of the PIRA bombing campaign in London it was not uncommon for "home beat" community police officers in the Metropolitan Police to work the same beat for between five and ten years—unfettered by performance targets—thereby gaining an intimate knowledge of their "patch" and the people who lived and worked on it. As Sir Ian Blair, when Metropolitan Police Commissioner, and leading criminologist Martin Innes have both noted, it is this kind of neighborhood policing role that often affords the best opportunities for community intelligence in support of counterterrorism policing.[15] Suffice to say, such longevity in this key policing role has become rare, notwithstanding the aspirations of community-based counterterrorism policing and the inclusion of civil servants and multi-agency partners.

In fact, notwithstanding the increased role of the Internet in regard to radicalization, recruitment and terrorism activities more generally, Blair and Innes are wise to focus on the ongoing value of effective neighborhood policing. While significant Internet use is often hidden from family, friends, and neighbors, the fact remains that when a terrorist conspiracy is aimed at mounting a bomb, gun, or knife attack on a target in London, opportunities for alert neighborhood policing will continue to arise. Blair's reference to a terrorist bombmaking scenario in which a well-briefed caretaker might have understood and reported the potential significance of a large quantity of empty hair spray canisters to his local police contact[16] remains relevant. This kind of scenario also serves to distinguish between community intelligence that might disrupt a violent terrorist act and community intelligence aimed at challenging the ideology or beliefs of fellow citizens. Whether community confidence in police is high or low, experience suggests the importance of the former kind of intelligence is more likely to be understood and accepted by existing and potential community partners than the latter.

Blair's scenario also serves as one of several contexts in which the term *community-based counterterrorism policing* might be understood and applied. Without seeking to be exhaustive, it is reasonable to identify two main areas of application. First, in the academic literature, the term can be understood as a relatively new conceptual framework pioneered and articulated by Basia Spalek[17] and which also serves to describe closely related literature that has not used the term explicitly but that is also concerned with the community impact of counterterrorism and the role of communities in counterterrorism.[18] This literature goes some way to bridging the gap between separate literatures on community policing on the one hand[19] and counterterrorism policing on the other.[20] Second, there is an extensive literature that surrounds the Prevent strand of the U.K. Contest counterterrorism: written by policymakers;[21] think tanks;[22] as well as by academic researchers.[23] While there is an overlap between the two literatures, this second strand is more focused on government policy—whether explanatory, supportive, or critical. Indeed, while there is a lively debate in both the think tank and the academic literature[24] that fully articulates opposing perspectives about the merits and demerits of Prevent policy there is an absence of constructive criticism that might serve to enhance the legitimacy and effectiveness of community-based counterterrorism policing. That is a gap in the literature that this article seeks to fill.

To recognize that police officers often perform duties that are not fundamentally influenced by government policy is to illustrate the fourth thread that connects the recommendations: namely, that the principle of policing by consent imposes responsibilities on police that are likely to be outside the experience of civil servants and other multi-agency partners increasingly involved in community-based policing. Perhaps the most obvious manifestation of this comes in the immediate aftermath of a terrorist bombing when all elements of counterterrorism policing are geared toward supporting an emergency response and government policy plays little or no part in it. Only later will counterterrorism policing become embroiled in policy responses that might, for example, include lobbying for or against new antiterrorism measures.[25] Here too, whatever police might think of particular measures, they are duty bound to abide by them and to perform their roles regardless. This is similar to the role of government civil servants but also significantly distinct, in so far as the latter are tied to the implementation of policy and generally have no further remit. Given that government policy has granted increasing responsibilities to civil servants to engage in the field of community-based counterterrorism policing an important and interesting tension with policing has arisen. To help illuminate this tension the recommendations that follow highlight how the notion of policing by consent—an essential and relevant experience in policing—is likely to be alien or remote from the experience of civil servants, teachers, and NGOs drafted in to undertake specific community-based counterterrorism policing roles.[26]

Recognize the Implications and Limitations of Policing by Consent

As Sir Richard Mayne noted in *Principles of Policing* at the founding of the Metropolitan Police in 1829, "the power of the police to fulfill their functions and duties is dependent on public approval of their existence, actions and behavior and on their ability to secure and maintain public respect."[27] Mayne did not suggest that public approval was confined to one particular community in London but rather that the principle of policing by consent was the bedrock of the relationship between the police, who were drawn from the citizens of London, and all their fellow citizens. For sure, either London's wealthiest or its most vocal and well-organized citizens have often had the greatest influence on policing policy in London but it is when the principle of policing by consent has been seen to also take account of the city's poorest and least vocal citizens that it has served the capital best.[28]

Very soon after leaving training school all probationer police officers necessarily encounter situations where they ask for the help of a fellow citizen to enforce or uphold the law. A common example would be where a rookie police officer is the first to arrive at the scene of a street robbery and, having obtained a description of the assailant from the victim, asks a nearby shopkeeper if she saw the attack take place and whether she can add to the assailant's description. This is part of a fundamental policing duty that is not fully replicated in any other public role, least of all in the day to day duties of most civil servants and their multi-agency Prevent partners. It is also what might be called a neutral duty, one that is central to a police officer's sworn oath to uphold the law, and which is impermeable to policy change. The point, for the purposes of this article, is to highlight the extent to which this quintessential and formative policing experience informs police engagement with the communities they police. In this sense policing is always neutral, oriented toward upholding the law. It follows that when a police officer asks a fellow citizen for help in identifying a suspected terrorist, the same basic duty is being invoked. When a fellow citizen assists a police officer in either duty—catching a street robber or catching a terrorist—they become party to the discharge of a police duty designed to uphold the law and to protect the wider community they both belong to. Moreover, Section 3 of the Criminal Law Act 1967 draws on a long established Common Law principle when stating that "a person [not just a police officer] may use such force as is reasonable in the circumstances in the prevention of crime, or in effecting or assisting in the lawful arrest of offenders or suspected offenders or of persons unlawfully at large."[29]

In both scenarios—urgent police–citizen engagement to tackle street crime and terrorism—the identity of the individual police officer and individual citizen is largely immaterial; both are discharging a duty that potentially obligates all citizens. This is the sense in which it is helpful to describe such a fundamental police–citizen engagement as neutral and unique—beyond the reach of policymakers. Notwithstanding policing imperatives that require consideration of the special needs of particular victims (victims of sexual offenses and hate crimes for instance) there remains a strong sense in which policing remains blind when seeking the immediate help of fellow citizens to prevent and detect crime and to apprehend suspected offenders. To be otherwise would be to deny certain citizens a fundamental right they share with police officers—a right to defend themselves against unlawful violence and harm, to defend fellow citizens, and to arrest individuals committing crimes. To be sure, situations will arise where these fundamental rights are exercised improperly by a citizen—just as they might be by a police officer—and sometimes by a citizen who is unsuited to the task but neither eventuality invalidates the general right. The London policing adage "communities defeat terrorism"[30] articulates the aspiration that citizens—either collectively as part of a neighborhood watch, or individually when going about their daily business, will assist police in tackling terrorism (and other kinds of political violence) no less than they might do in regard to more routine crimes.

Without this formative policing experience it is understandable that civil servants, teachers and NGOs entering the burgeoning business of community-based counterterrorism policing should seek to work with Muslim citizens who share the views of the government ministers they represent, about the nature of the terrorist threat to be tackled. Haras Rafiq, managing director of the Quilliam Foundation, provides an example of this kind of alliance in his article "David Cameron is Right to Tackle Extremist Ideas As Well as Behaviour."[31] In contrast, police officers are more inclined to allow community perspectives that differ from government policy, especially when the citizens in question display skill and aptitude for the task at hand. To recognize and appreciate the implications of policing by consent is to begin to address a necessary tension between a fundamental police duty, on the one hand, and a necessary government policy imperative on the other. In turn, this is to encourage police independence where necessary, and also to foster an understanding among civil servants of the importance of adopting a more neutral and even-handed approach to citizens who offer to help with the task of tackling terrorism and violent extremism.

To be sure, a tension—sometimes characterized as arising between hard and soft and between high and low policing[32]—has at times been palpable and significant for London policing during the last five decades[33] and remains so today. For example, when observing attempts by the Metropolitan Police to simultaneously address the terrorist threat to the United Kingdom posed by returning *jihadis* and the need to support London families whose children have left the United Kingdom to join Islamic State it is not unreasonable to suggest that the problem is now more acute than it has ever been. On the one hand, the Met's commander Richard Walton adopts an empathetic and supportive tone when addressing the departure of three London teenage girls suspected of joining Islamic State. "We are extremely concerned for the safety of these young girls," he tells Londoners, "and would urge anyone with information to come forward and speak to police." "Our priority," he explains, "is the safe return of these girls to their families."[34] On the other hand, the Met's commissioner, Sir Bernard Hogan-Howe, adopts a more hard-line approach when addressing the parallel concern that there is a serious risk of "a further rapid influx of dangerous militants into the capital as the battle with Islamic State escalates." He calls on ministers "to respond by considering the return of control orders and new legislation to strip British fighters of their passports to stop them coming back to this country." Speaking in terms of high policing, Hogan-Howe argues that "there should be an automatic legal presumption that anyone returning from Syria or Iraq had been engaged in terrorism" and "requested a major injection of extra funding to help police and intelligence agencies cope with the rise in terror suspects."[35]

Clearly, Walton and Hogan-Howe are providing evidence of a necessary tension between hard and soft policing approaches to a gravely serious problem.[36] It is also worth noting how in this contemporary example of returning Islamic State *jihadis*, London policing might enjoy the support of a majority of its citizens for Hogan-Howe's hard-line high-policing approach while at the same time suffering deficits of trust and legitimacy in sections of the community most likely to be affected where Walton's soft, empathetic low-policing approach is more likely to be welcomed. That said, such a positive welcome may turn sour if it is subsequently deemed necessary by police to arrest family members. For now, these are the kinds of competing demands between high and low policing—and competing perspectives among London citizens—which London policing has to negotiate when seeking to tackle terrorist threats. No doubt it will only take one serious terrorist incident carried out by returning Islamic State *jihadis* in which numerous Londoners are killed to tip the scales firmly in favor of high policing. That certainly has often been the experience after terrorist attacks in London in the past.[37]

The need for London policing to negotiate a path between these two critical imperatives—to police by consent while ensuring the protection of the state and its citizens—is the premise on which this recommendation is based and seems to be crucial to achieving the twin goals of legitimacy and effectiveness that underpin any successful policing endeavor. This is not to claim that London is unique in respect of such a negotiation—it has, for example, been vividly evident in the United States where "the many commissions that investigated why the US policing agencies of every stripe failed to prevent 9/11 came up with findings that stressed the gap between high and low policing."[38] That said, London policing is perhaps an ideal case study given that it has been required to balance the two competing requirements in the face of repeated terrorist bombing campaigns and terrorist threats over a long period.

Neither does the London experience suggest that the notion of policing by consent will always be at odds with the requirements of counterterrorism policing, merely that an important and fundamental tension exists. In fact, on countless occasions during the two centuries since Mayne first enunciated the principle, both London's police and the capital's diverse citizens[39] have been beneficiaries whenever it is has been applied effectively and legitimately. For the authors of this article, the support of Londoners first became significant in a counterterrorism context during the bombing campaigns of the PIRA in the 1970s.[40] "Communities defeat terrorism" became a police maxim, premised on the aspiration that Londoners would provide information to police to help prevent acts of terrorism in the capital and to identify wanted and suspected terrorists.[41] Suffice to say, even strong public approval of police would not necessarily translate into active co-operation of the kind being sought—most typically the reporting of suspicious behavior that might relate to the preparations of an IRA terrorist cell. Put simply, there is case built on extensive experience in London that effective and legitimate counterterrorism policing has to negotiate a pragmatic path between the requirements of the state and the principle of policing by consent.

To help negotiate such a path it is often helpful to recognize the interdependent and holistic nature of policing. In an example from the authors' London research experience, a civil servant was required to inform the managers of a community-based Prevent project[42] that it was being terminated. This gave rise to contrasting responses from the police officers and civil servants involved. For the civil servants, termination signaled an immediate transition from intense daily interaction with a community-based group to an absolute absence of contact. Whereas, on the police side there was a recognition that a relationship with the community-based group would continue on a number of levels—notwithstanding the termination of a Home Office contract. Perhaps the most significant aspect of this recognition on the part of police officers was a realization that the community group would continue to undertake the same kind of work that had been the subject of the Home Office contract, on a voluntary basis, just as they had done prior to receiving state support.

In fact, that anticipation by the police officers in this case proved to be well founded. Voluntary community work aimed at helping young people resist the overtures of terrorist and violent extremist propaganda certainly continued after the cessation of Home Office interest, albeit on a much reduced scale. The fact that this voluntary "counterradicalization" youth work was also bound up with parallel community youth work aimed at helping young people avoid or leave gang crime helps to emphasize how the realities of street experience are inherently "bottom up" and therefore characteristic of police and youth workers' experience and generally less familiar to civil servants concerned to implement "top down" government policy. The same case also talks to other aspects of the interdependent and holistic nature of policing. Police officers have a crucial interest in both kinds of voluntary, community work—especially when it is effective, as in this case. Moreover, police have a responsibility to provide emergency support to community outreach work of this kind, especially when serious incidents arise. The case also helps to highlight the importance of the low policing, or community policing requirement to win the trust and confidence of alienated communities in the long term. It is no coincidence that a long serving local neighborhood police officer was responsible for first introducing the key members of this community group to specialist counterterrorism colleagues.[43] Notwithstanding what Brodeur calls the "problematic integration of high and low policing," during the course of the War on Terror,[44] there are examples, of which this London case is but one, of how high and low policing might work reasonably and effectively in tandem.

To be clear, the imperative to police by consent is not limited to particular citizens or to particular sections of the community. Nor is it conditional, dependant on a community or community representative supporting government policy in regard to counterterrorism or any other issue concerned with crime. This is to recognize that there is often a significant contrast and tension between the fundamental policing imperative to engage with communities as they are, and government strategy to foster significant change in communities, and in doing so to engage with community representatives who offer to help deliver that change. In regard to community-based counterterrorism policy, the first time this contrast came to the authors' attention was in 2006 when Ruth Kelly, minister for the Department of Communities and Local Government, launched a new community engagement strategy with community leaders who shared the government's policy agenda.[45] Two years later, Kelly's successor, Hazel Blears, made clear that this government policy was "designed to change behaviour."[46] In addition, in 2011 the Metropolitan Police ended a ten-year engagement with Muslim community representatives at the Muslim Safety Forum (MSF).[47] This followed the U.K. prime minister David Cameron's address to a security conference in Berlin in which he signaled that the U.K. government would come down hard on "non-violent extremism."[48]

Consequently, there is a reasonable concern on the part of excluded Muslim community representatives that they are being treated unfairly and by a different criteria to that which directs police engagement with minority ethnic communities. This runs the risk that constructive Muslim community partners of police may succumb to the overtures of extremists of two kinds: Either antidemocratic, revolutionary Islamist groups such as Hizb ut Tahrir or antidemocratic, revolutionary left-wing groups such as the Socialist Workers Party. Given that both groups often organize peaceful demonstrations in London this may seem unreasonable. However, both groups—and the types they represent—are anathema to community-based counterterrorism policing for one simple reason: they are emphatically opposed to supporting or working in partnership with police. While they may often campaign legitimately in regard to instances where counterterrorism policing makes errors they are duty bound, ideologically, to diminish or dismiss counterterrorism policing successes. Indeed, in the case of the Socialist Workers Party and other Marxist groups on the far left, a carefully orchestrated antipolice agenda is a central plank of a long-term revolutionary agenda. Moreover, both far left and extremist Islamist groups also make it their business to denigrate groups that do work in partnership with police as "sell outs." In these circumstances, it is very much to the credit of Muslim groups that are simultaneously and wrongly categorized by government as "extremist" and by extremists as "sell outs" when they remain loyal to their local police partners and their principles of pro-active citizenship. It is therefore important that Prevent practitioners learn to distinguish extremist Islamists from moderate or mainsteam Islamists[49]—and extremist or "*takfiri*" Salafis from moderate or authentic Salafis[50]—in the same way that extremist Marxists and anarchists have long been understood to be distinguishable from democratic socialists and thereby located outside the big tent of British democratic politics.

Respect the Legitimate Religious Beliefs of all Communities

At the crux of community-based counterterrorism policing in London is a need to respect the legitimate religious beliefs of all its diverse communities, not least its diverse Muslim communities. This is a vital imperative at a time when London faces a severe terrorist threat from movements including Islamic State (otherwise known as the Islamic State of Iraq and Levant), Al Qaeda, and their many affiliates;[51] movements with a proven ability to recruit, "radicalize," or influence young Muslim Londoners. As such this imperative is particularly important when it comes to respecting the legitimate Islamic beliefs of approximately one million Muslim Londoners.[52] There is one key element to this requirement: if police fail to show respect for the religious beliefs of the communities where they are seeking support in their counterterrorism investigations then a serious trust deficit will arise and inhibit this prime policing purpose. Such a trust deficit not only inhibits effective counterterrorism policing but also offers sophisticated terrorist movement opportunities to exploit it in their propaganda and recruitment material.[53] While significant progress was made during the 10 years of the Muslim Safety Forum (2001–2011) in regard to many important issues of religious respect[54] there remain two recurring problems in need of urgent attention.

The first problem is that legitimate aspects of religious practice continue to be described as pointers toward "radicalization." This problematic account was probably first enunciated to a London Muslim audience by Home Secretary John Reid in 2006.[55] More recently, it has been developed by Mak Chisti, a commander in the Metropolitan Police, who expresses concern about "primary school children defining Christmas as "haram." Chisti explains that "while it may not be a police matter, parents and family needed to ask how children as young as five had come to that view, whether it be from school or their friends." [56] "This is not about us invading private thoughts," he argues, " but acknowledging that it is in these private spaces where this [extremism] first germinates":

> The purpose of private-space intervention is to engage, explore, explain, educate or eradicate. Hate and extremism is not acceptable in our society, and if people cannot be educated, then hate and harmful extremism must be eradicated through all lawful means.[57]

Putting aside the issue of privacy, which has attracted the most media attention, there is also an important issue for policing in terms of religious belief and sectarianism. Chisti is a Muslim—seemingly a liberal Muslim—and appears to be conflating a legitimate school of Islamic belief with extremism and radicalization that leads toward support for Islamic State. At best this is a somewhat reductive analysis and one that sits at odds with a more insightful account provided by Mehmood Naqshbandi, a former advisor to the Metropolitan Police, who is at pains to defend legitimate Islamic beliefs from the simplistic distortions offered by Islamic State and others. Naqshbandi shares Chisti's concern that young Muslim Londoners are joining Islamic State but addresses the problem from a different vantage point in explaining that "all ISIS needs to do, and has done, is to put forward more cogent arguments in their own favour, in a format and with [Islamic] sources that the recipients are familiar with." For "young Muslims especially," he explains "and those who are troubled by the discordant clash between their own lives, the ideals of a simple Muslim way of life, the corruption and decadence of the society they are growing up in, and especially the compromises and hypocrisy of their own parents, the ISIS message offers a resolution."[58] Suffice to say, if Naqshbandi is right and parents are part of the problem, Chisti's approach may have limited application.

In addition, Naqshbandi is acutely conscious of inter-Muslim sectarianism—often exploited by Islamic State—and scrupulously avoids feeding it. This runs counter to a strand of liberal Muslim thinking that often enthusiastically endorses attempts to link extremism to legitimate strands of conservative Islamic belief. Instead, Naqshbandi explained basic Islamic beliefs and practice in a guide book for London police officers—published a decade ago—

which runs counter to the perspective of some liberal Muslims and key parts of government Prevent strategy. This extract dealing with sexual relationships is a case in point: "Like most faiths that have the concept of external, objective morality, Islam is deeply antipathetic to homosexuality."[59] Some liberal, radical Muslims might challenge this, in the same way that liberal, radical Christians and Jews might do in regard to the same issue in their religions, but inevitably socially conservative Muslims, Christians, and Jews may not. What becomes crucial, from the perspective of community-based counterterrorism policing, is whether socially conservative or traditional Muslims (no more and no less than their counterparts in the two other Abrahamic faiths)—and whether from Deobandi, Barelvi, Shi'a, Sufi, Salafi, Islamist, or any other Muslim background[60]—maintain genuinely respectful relationships with gay, lesbian, Christian, Jewish, and all other Londoners. When displays of such respect occur it is noteworthy,[61] not least, given that socially conservative Muslims have an innate advantage over liberal Muslims in achieving a degree of credibility when seeking to counter the narratives of violent extremists.

Two key points arise from Naqshbandi's policing guide: first, the importance of understanding religious belief and practice on its own terms; second, recognizing that major, significant similarities and differences exist between the beliefs and practices of many Muslim Londoners and other faith communities in the capital. For example, on the one hand, many Jewish and Christian Londoners share Muslim concerns about what Naqshbandi terms "overtly sexual or lewd behaviour."[62] On the other hand, many Jewish and Christian Londoners would concur with liberal Muslims who prefer to challenge establish norms in their respective religions. Suffice to say, Islamic State, and other terrorist movements, will be less able to exploit community anger if London policing is seen to respect legitimate religious beliefs—which is not to endorse them—such as the teaching of the fundamental tenets of Islam to children in mosques and gender segregation in certain public settings. As well as denying terrorist movements propaganda opportunities, such an approach also facilitates community initiatives aimed at tackling radicalization.[63] Echoing Ian Blair's point about doing *with* not *to* communities, Naqshbandi, argues that, "… the government must realise that there was no top-down solution to tackling radicalisation and reforming mosques." Instead, he suggests, mosques "are the places where extremism should be debated and examined."[64]

The second urgent problem is closely related and concerns the Prevent strategy where it conflates all strands of political Islam (otherwise referred to as Islamism) and all strands of Salafism as being "extremist" and antithetical to British values.[65] Harras Rafiq, managing director of the Quilliam Foundation, typically makes the government case forcefully when he argues that "Islamist groups such as the Muslim Brotherhood and their offshoots have been indoctrinating our youngsters for decades that they have to join the struggle in the creation of a Utopian Islamist Caliphate and then to expand it across the globe."[66] Readily accepted by governments in the last decade, this blanket characterization unfairly conflates mainstream Muslim organizations with extremist groups such as Hizb ut Tahrir. In addition, it overlooks a significant amount of constructive community work carried out from within this much maligned strand of Muslim London. One well documented case study involves the work of the Muslim Association of Britain and the Muslim Welfare House in regard to the successful reclamation of the Finsbury Park Mosque from the hands of violent extremists.[67] Regrettably, Rafiq's negative blanket assessment appears to have gained currency in the banking sector as well as government, with this success being rewarded with the ignominious withdrawal of the mosque's banking facilities.[68]

Similarly, Reverend Alan Green, chair of the Tower Hamlets Interfaith Forum, has "highlighted the value of the close partnership he has established with the East London Mosque and London Muslim Centre over a long period." Significantly, he recalls that "when the bombs went off in London [7/7], I got the bishop down to the East London Mosque so that there could be immediate joint statements, and Dilwar [Dilwar Hussain, the mosque chairman] on the Sunday was here in St. John's preaching with me about our opposition to bombers." "Now that was entirely unnecessary," he adds, "that wasn't before TV screens, it wasn't to get anything out of it. ..."[69] In the past, Metropolitan Police borough commanders have spoken out in support of their partners at Finsbury Park Mosque, East London Mosque, and at other Muslim institutions, not least when they have been wrongly labeled extremist.[70] Under increased government pressure, and the impact of police training delivered by Quilliam and like-minded institutions, police chiefs currently in post are either seriously constrained or, like Mak Chisti, enthusiastic supporters of government policy and the Quilliam approach.

Once a key player in the delivery of Prevent, Abdul Haqq Baker remains committed to tackling violent extremism and does so on a voluntary basis, despite being excluded from official engagement since 2011. Condemned by the reductive analysis of the Quilliam Foundation as extremist by virtue of being Salafi, he offers a more nuanced and accurate account that helps explain the basis for his outstanding track record in tackling violent extremism in London. "ISIS (along with al-Qaida, from within which it originated)," he explains, "does indeed take much of its theology from Salafism." Crucially, however, he notes, "Salafi Islam is as wide and varied as, say, Sufi Islam is, and there are numerous sub-trends within it, each one of which is at odds with the other sub-trends." Baker continues by explaining:

> [that] there are (as only a partial list of the political sub-trends) apolitical pacifist Salafis; politically engaged yet non-militant Salafis who eschew democracy; Salafis who wish to engage with the democratic system to change it; Salafis who believe jihad is an obligation but not at the current time and in the current circumstances; and, of course jihadi-Salafis who are actively engaged in military conflict.[71]

Baker acknowledges that "empowering one strand of Salafism over another will have its pros and cons" but argues that "the pros" in regard to tackling recruitment and radicalization of young British Muslims into Islamic State or Al Qaeda, "far outweigh any potential cons." For the numerous police officers, civil servants, and other public servants who have worked with Baker in the past this analysis will be familiar and will ring true. They have certainly witnessed the "pros" and may also have been satisfied that the "cons" can be mitigated. Interestingly, the "cons"—a religious understanding that places most of their London neighbors in the category of nonbelievers and thereby destined to Hell—is shared by many socially conservative Muslims across London (and of course by socially conservative Christians and Jews), including many who are excused Quilliam's liberal wrath. When Baker suggests he "would much rather live next to somebody who thinks I will go to Hell but still be polite with me, than someone who actively seeks to kill me" he is capturing a reality of contemporary London life.[72] Several officers involved in community-based counterterrorism policing in London can vouch for Baker—and his colleagues—in terms of their regular engagement with their fellow Londoners with genuine respect and consideration—irrespective of gender, religion, or sexual orientation.[73]

Conflating all London Muslims with affiliations to Islamist and Salafi institutions with extremists such as Anjem Choudhury[74] is also to ignore much positive work they have done to tackle them.[75] This aspect of Prevent strategy is ill-considered and unintentionally sends out a signal to London Muslims that sections of their community are being stigmatized in favor of others. It is also a proven target for terrorist propaganda.[76] Moreover, it has become an entrenched policing position since organizations that promote this approach were given major roles in police training and Prevent delivery.[77] Quite pointedly, while the anti-Islamist, Quilliam organization was given a key role in police training, the majority of voluntary Muslim organizations that dutifully attended the Muslim Safety Forum for a decade have subsequently been excluded from such work. Instead of exclusion, case by case judgments should be made, and individuals who have built up a positive reputation with police re-established as valuable interlocutors and trainers.

Conclusion: Provide Honest Feedback to Policymakers

London policing, as elsewhere, cannot forego a responsibility to explain the requirements and implications of government counterterrorism policy to representatives of the communities it serves. However, when it chooses to adopt a community-based counterterrorism policing model it should ensure that it listens attentively to messages from those communities and provides feedback to policymakers. Speaking truth to power is never a safe route to career advancement in policing—in London or elsewhere—but is clearly necessary on those occasions when government counterterrorism policy is unintentionally proving to be counterproductive, however well-intentioned it may be. This is especially important when terrorist movements are able to exploit weaknesses or mistakes in counterterrorism policy or practice for their benefit in terms of recruitment and support. This is the sense in which these recommendations are aimed at enhancing the legitimacy and effectiveness of counterterrorism responses to formidable and inventive terrorist opponents.

As Ian Blair expresses his learning from extensive experience in regard to counterterrorism policing and Muslim communities: "I just think we have to be incredibly careful, we shouldn't be doing this to the community, we should be doing this with the community."[78] Interestingly, this is an approach the authors first articulated as "partnership policing" with London-based Muslim organizations and groups in 2003 and continue to recommend it to practitioners of community-based counterterrorism policing—whether operating within or outside the government Prevent strategy. To do so is to ensure that an established policing approach, grounded in the notion of policing by consent, is extended to Muslim community representatives. For reasons this article has highlighted, a genuine partnership approach with Muslim community representatives has gained little traction in the last decade. Instead, where police engagement has often been *with* and not *to* Muslim communities—as in the case of the abandoned Muslim Safety Forum—it has been closed down under pressure of government policy.[79] Although that pressure has been more pronounced under David Cameron's leadership, it was certainly evident when Tony Blair was at the helm and not wholly absent during Gordon Brown's premiership. In truth, the partnership approach that underpins the recommendations in this article runs counter to a strand of government policy enacted by Labour, Conservative, and Liberal Democrat Coalition and Conservative administrations during the last decade. Interestingly, in so far as this strand of government policy has sometimes treated Muslims differently than other faith communities, it is not central to the ideologies of any of the three political parties involved. Rather, as the staunch Conservative commentator Peter Oborne observes, government policy in this arena has more to do with transatlantic, neo-conservativism than with mainstream U.K. politics of any stripe.[80] To be sure, individually, the authors of this article differ in their political allegiances, yet neither sees this issue in terms of party politics. Instead, it is respectfully recommended that police chiefs should summon the resolve to speak truth to power on this fundamental policing issue before retirement and to whichever party is in office.

Moreover, the emergence of community-based counterterrorism initiatives aimed at inhibiting London citizens—and citizens of other towns and cities in the United Kingdom—from leaving home to fight for Islamic State in Syria and Iraq highlights the topicality and potential value of the issues raised in this article when seeking to enhance counterterrorism practice in a complex and demanding arena. To the extent that policing plays a reduced role in regard to a problem that extends beyond counterterrorism and increasingly overlaps with counterinsurgency, counterextremism, counterradicalization, and de-radicalization, practitioners should reflect on how to ensure all strands of community opinion are fully understood. To misrepresent or stigmatize the religious beliefs or political opinions of Muslim Londoners either with a track record or with potential of tackling terrorism and violent extremism in the capital is to play into the hands of sophisticated terrorist movements and networks eager to drive a wedge between the communities where they seek recruits and supporters and the authorities employed by the state to disrupt them. Ian Blair argues that "we have to accept there are people who live their lives by fundamentalist rules" and that "fundamentalism in itself is not a matter for the state to interfere with" but that rather "when it slides into violent extremism it is." He is surely right to argue, from his experience, that "if we cut ourselves off from talking to some people whose views we do not like but to whom millions of young people listen that's a very difficult issue for us."[81]

London policing still needs to listen to all strands of Muslim opinion as it previously sought to do at the Muslim Safety Forum. This is to avoid being seen to talk just to John Grieve's "nodding dogs" in the community.[82] Interestingly, in all other areas of London policing the imperative to engage with its most stringent critics appears to be alive and well.[83] The fact that it is less of a priority in relation to counterterrorism may well indicate the level of policing subordination to government policy in this arena. If that is the case, it only increases the duty of police to listen to its critics in the community in regard to counterterrorism issues—Prevent included—in exactly the same way as it does in all other areas of policing. Apart from its own intrinsic value as a method of policing by consent it has the added value of reducing the risk of bolstering sectarian divisions that are regularly exploited by Islamic State, Al Qaeda, and their affiliates. At its best the Muslim Safety Forum achieved this objective and enabled police chiefs to brief government on key areas of concern in regard to counterterrorism policy and practice.[84] To be sure, there is an absence of accessible research that seeks to evaluate success and failure in this field. However, the difficulties inherent in establishing and measuring success in preventative and community policing of all kinds should not deter researchers in the future. Especially those willing and able to engage closely with community perspectives.[85]

It follows that London policing should notify government when the Prevent strategy aimed at tackling extremism is unfairly targeting or stigmatizing Muslim groups and individuals who are not extremist but rather the exact equivalent of groups and individuals in other London faith communities who are recognized as representatives of conservative or radical strands of legitimate religious belief and political opinion. Again, apart from its own intrinsic value as a method of policing by consent this also has the added value of reducing the risk of bolstering sectarian divisions that are regularly exploited by Islamic State, Al Qaeda, and their affiliates. More generally, London policing should reflect on its unique learning, especially over the last two decades, and offer an honest appraisal of the successes and failures of government counterterrorism policy at the community level. This will be especially valuable for the growing number of civil servants and public and voluntary sector employees involved in community intervention strategies in London as well as in towns and cities across the United Kingdom.

Acknowledgment

Robert Lambert is an unaffiliated academic; he was previously a Lecturer at the Handa Centre for the Study of Terrorism and Political Violence (CSTPV), University of St. Andrews (2008–2015) and Senior Lecturer at the John Grieve Policing Centre, London Metropolitan University (2012–2015).

Notes

1. For details see Robert Lambert's *Countering al-Qaeda in London: Police and Muslims in Partnership* (London: Hurst, 2011) and see Parson's staff webpage at http://www.londonmet.ac.uk/faculties/faculty-of-social-sciences-and-humanities/people/surnames-n-to-s/tim-parsons/ (accessed 30 March 2016).
2. Anthony Richards, "From Terrorism to 'Radicalisation' to 'Extremism': Counter-Terrorism Imperative or Loss of Focus?," *International Affairs* 91(2), pp. 371–380.
3. Lambert, *Countering al-Qaeda in London*, pp. 4, 16, 19, 21, 58, 133.
4. *Contest: The United Kingdom's Strategy for Countering Terrorism* (London: Home Office, 2011). Available at https://www.gov.uk/government/uploads/system/uploads/attachment_data/file/97994/contest-summary.pdf (accessed 22 April 2015).
5. *Prevent Strategy* (London: Home Office, 2011). Available at https://www.gov.uk/government/uploads/system/uploads/attachment_data/file/97976/prevent-strategy-review.pdf (accessed 20 March 2015).
6. Alexander Robertson, *Boy, 15, is Quizzed by Anti-Extremist Police after Deputy Headteacher Caught Him Looking Up Ukip's Website at School*, Daily Mail, 28 February 2016. Available at http://www.dailymail.co.uk/news/article-3468162/Furious-father-reveals-son-15-quizzed-police-tracking-extremists-looked-UKip-s-website-school.html#ixzz44O6Lz5be (accessed 15 October 2016).
7. BBC News, "Mosque Bomber Pavlo Lapshyn Given Life for Murder," 25 October, 2013. Available at http://www.bbc.co.uk/news/uk-england-birmingham-24675040 (accessed 30 March 2016).
8. Robert Lambert, "Empowering Salafis and Islamists against Al-Qaeda: A London Counter-terrorism Case Study," *Political Science and Politics* 41(1) (2008), pp. 31–35.
9. 9/11 is recognized shorthand for 11 September 2001, the day on which Al Qaeda operatives carried out terrorist attacks against the World Trade Center in New York and the Pentagon in Washington, DC. For an insight into the immediate impact in London in terms of community-based counterterrorism policing see Lambert, "Empowering Salafis and Islamists against Al-Qaeda," p. 31.
10. Interestingly, in the authors' experience in London, this diversity of individuals involved in community-based counterterrorism policing extends to academics and researchers with think tanks—a fact that adds value to this article's aim of informing and stimulating academic as well as practitioner debate.
11. For details of the PIRA bombing campaign in London, see Richard English, *Armed Struggle: The History of the IRA* (Oxford: Oxford University Press, 2002), for example, pp. 278–279.

12. Bear in mind as well that until 1992 when responsibility was given to the Security Service (MI5), Metropolitan Police Special Branch was responsible for gathering intelligence on the IRA threat to London and the rest of the British mainland. See Frank Foley, *Countering Terrorism in Britain and France: Institutions, Norms and the Shadow of the Past* (Cambridge: CUP, 2014), p. 131.
13. Under the auspices of the Office for Security and Counter-Terrorism (OSCT), an "executive directorat'" of the Home Office, established in 2007.
14. Lambert, *Countering al-Qaeda in London*, p. 252.
15. Ian Blair, *Dimbleby Lecture*, see BBC News, transcript of Sir Ian Blair's speech. 16 November 2005. Available at http://news.bbc.co.uk/1/hi/uk/4443386.stm (accessed 11 September 2015); Martin Innes, "Policing Uncertainty: Countering Terror through Community Intelligence and Democratic Policing," *Annals of the American Academy* 605 (2006), pp. 1–20; see also Lambert, *Countering al-Qaeda in London*, pp. 191–192.
16. Blair, *Dimbleby Lecture*.
17. Basia Spalek, *Terror Crime: Prevention with Communities*. (London: Bloomsbury, 2014); Basia Spalek, ed., *Counter-Terrorism: Community Based Approaches to Preventing Terror Crime* (Hampshire: Palgrave Macmillan, 2012).
18. See, for example, Martin Innes and Darren Thiel, "Policing Terror," in Tim Newburn, ed., *The Handbook of Policing*, 2nd ed. (Cullompton: Willan, 2008), pp. 553–579; Sharon Pickering, Jude McCulloch, and David Neville-Wright, eds., *Counter-Terrorism Policing: Community, Cohesion and Security* (London: Springer, 2010); Lambert, *Countering al-Qaeda in London*.
19. See, for example, Nigel Fielding, *Community Policing* (Oxford: Oxford University Press, 1996); M. Brogden and P. Nijhar, *Community Policing: International Concepts and Practice* (Devon: Willan, 2005).
20. See, for example, Andrew Staniforth, *Blackstone's Counter-Terrorism Handbook* (Oxford: Oxford University Press, 2013); David Lowe, *Policing Terrorism: Research Studies into Police Counter-terrorism Investigations* (London: CRC Press, 2015).
21. See, for example, the following three U.K. government strategy papers: (1) *Contest: The United Kingdom's Strategy for Countering Terrorism* (London: Home Office, 2011). Available athttps://www.gov.uk/government/uploads/system/uploads/attachment_data/file/97994/contest-summary.pdf (accessed 22 April 2015); (2) *Prevent Strategy* (London: Home Office, 2011). Available at https://www.gov.uk/government/uploads/system/uploads/attachment_data/file/97976/prevent-strategy-review.pdf (accessed 20 March 2015); (3) *Contest: The United Kingdom's Strategy for Countering Terrorism: Annual Report for 2014* (London: Home Office, 2015). Available at https://www.gov.uk/government/uploads/system/uploads/attachment_data/file/415708/contest_annual_report_for_2014.pdf (accessed 15 April 2015).
22. See, for example, three competing reports from three distinctively different London think tanks: (1) Jamie Bartlett, Jonathan Birdwell, and Michael King, *The Edge of Violence: A Radical Approach to Extremism* (London: Demos, 2010); (2) Martin Bright, *When Progressives Treat with Reactionaries: The British State's Flirtation with Radical Islam* (London: Policy Exchange, 2005); and (3) Arun Kundnani, *Spooked. How Not to Prevent Violent Extremism* (London: Institute of Race Relations, 2009).
23. See, for example, Tufyal Choudhury and Helen Fenwick, "The Impact of Counter-Terrorism Measures on Muslim Communities," *International Review of Law, Computers and Technology* 25 (3) (2011), pp. 151–181; Martin Innes, Colin Roberts, and Helen Innes with Trudy Lowe and Suraj Lakhani, *Assessing the Effects of Prevent Policing: A Report to the Association of Chief Police Officers* (Cardiff: Universities' Police Science Institute, 2011). Available athttp://www.acpo.police.uk/documents/TAM/2011/PREVENT%20Innes%200311%20Final%20send%202.pdf (accessed 12 March 2015).
24. Of course there is significant overlap between the think tank and academic worlds in terms of personnel, just as there is an overlap between academia and the policy world with several academic researchers being recruited to the Research, Information and Communications Unit (RICU), a cross-departmental strategic communications body based at the Office for Security and Counter-Terrorism (OSCT) at the Home Office in recent years. RICU "aims to coordinate government-wide communication activities to counter the appeal of violent extremism while promoting stronger grass-roots inter-

community relations." Counter-Extremism.org, "Role of Research the Research Information and Communications Unit (RICU)." Available at https://www.counterextremism.org/resources/details/id/413/research-information-and-communications-unit-ricu (accessed 2 June 2015).

25. See, for example, Robert Lambert, "Counter-Terrorism and Its Effectiveness in the UK since 1969: Does It Pay to be Tough on Terrorism?," in Marie Breen-Smyth, ed., *Ashgate Companion to Political Violence* (Aldershot: Ashgate, 2012), p. 742.
26. Here we have in mind roles managed by the Office for Security and Counter-Terrorism (OSCT) that fall under the remit of Prevent (a strand of the UK Contest counterterrorism strategy) including training roles where representatives of think tanks guide the delivery of Prevent programs for police and multi-agency partners.
27. Quoted in Robert Reiner, *The Politics of the Police* (Brighton: Wheatsheaf, 1985), p. 49; also discussed in Lambert, *Countering al-Qaeda in London*, p. 18.
28. See, for example, Lambert, *Countering al-Qaeda in London*, p. 9.
29. Available at http://www.legislation.gov.uk/ukpga/1967/58/section/3 (accessed 9 October 2015).
30. Lambert, *Countering al-Qaeda in London*, pp. 8, 221, 239.
31. Haras Rafiq, "David Cameron is Right to Tackle Extremist Ideas as Well as Behaviour." *The Telegraph* 20 July 2015. Available at http://www.telegraph.co.uk/news/uknews/law-and-order/11751259/David-Cameron-is-right-to-tackle-extremist-ideas-as-well-as-behaviour.html (accessed 11 October 2015).
32. The concepts derive from seminal texts by Jean-Paul Brodeur, in particular see, "High Policing and Low Policing: Remarks about the Policing of Political Activities," *Social Problems* 30 (5) (1983), pp. 507–520; and "High Policing and Low Policing in Post 9/11 Times," *Policing: A Journal of Policy and Practice* 1(1) (2007), pp. 25–37.
33. See, for example, Lambert, "Counter-terrorism and Its Effectiveness in the UK since 1969," pp. 728–754.
34. Martin Evans, "Three Missing London Schoolgirls 'Travelling to Syria to Join Isil," *The Telegraph* (2015). Available at http://www.telegraph.co.uk/news/uknews/crime/11424884/Three-missing-British-schoolgirls-travel-to-Syria.html (accessed 2 June 2015).
35. Martin Bentham, "Met Chief Sir Bernard Hogan-Howe: London is Home to Hundreds of 'Militarised' Jihadi Fighters." *London Evening Standard* (27 August, 2014). Available at http://www.standard.co.uk/news/uk/met-chief-sir-bernard-hoganhowe-warns-of-londons-200-militarised-jihadi-fighters-9693477.html (accessed 2 June 2015).
36. "At least 700 people from the UK have travelled to support or fight for jihadist organisations in Syria and Iraq, British police say. About half have since returned to Britain. Most of those who went to the conflict zone are thought to have joined the militant group that calls itself Islamic State." BBC News, "Who are Britain's Jihadists?" 18 September 2015. Available at http://www.bbc.co.uk/news/uk-32026985 (accessed 11 October 2015).
37. Lambert, *Countering al-Qaeda in London*, pp. 3–28; "Counter-Terrorism and Its Effectiveness in the UK since 1969," pp. 728–754.
38. Brodeur, "High Policing and Low Policing in Post 9/11 Times," p. 29.
39. According to the 2011 census 2,998,264 people or 36.7 percent of London's population were foreign-born. When added to a significant number of Londoners whose parents were foreign born a sense of London's diverse and evolving population emerges. See, for example, Sarah Kyambi, *Beyond Black and White: Mapping New Immigrant Communities* (London: Institute for Public Policy Research, 2005).
40. The PIRA continued to mount bomb attacks in London throughout the 1980s and 1990s. From the 1970s onward Londoners also became familiar with occasional terrorist attacks carried out by organizations from the Middle East such as in June 1982 when three gunmen belonging to the Palestinian Abu Nidal group shot and seriously injured Shlomo Argov, the Israeli Ambassador outside the Dorchester Hotel in London's West End.
41. Lambert, *Countering al-Qaeda in London*, pp. 8, 221, 239.
42. Robert Lambert, "Competing Counter-Radicalisation Models in the UK," in Rik Coolsaet, ed., *Jihadi Terrorism and the Radicalisation Challenge. European and American Experiences* (Ashgate, Aldershot, 2011), pp. 215–225.

43. Lambert, *Countering al-Qaeda in London*, pp. 191–192.
44. Brodeur, "High Policing and Low Policing in Post 9/11 Times," p. 29.
45. Lambert, *Countering al-Qaeda in London*, pp. 252–253.
46. Hazel Blears quoted in ibid., pp. 252–253.
47. Robert Lambert, "Muslim Safety Forum: Senior Police and Muslim Community Engagement during the War on Terror," in P. Daniel Silke, Basia Spalek, and Mary O'Rawe, eds., *Preventing Ideological Violence: Communities, Police and Case Studies of "Success"* (Hampshire: Palgrave Macmillan, 2013), pp. 67–90.
48. See *New Statesman*, full transcript, David Cameron, Speech on radicalisation and Islamic extremism, Munich, 5 February 2011. Available at http://www.newstatesman.com/blogs/the-staggers/2011/02/terrorism-islam-ideology (accessed 22 January 2017).
49. Lambert, *Countering al-Qaeda in London*, pp. 79–134.
50. Lambert, *Countering al-Qaeda in London*, pp. 155–220.
51. MI5, "Current International Terrorism Threat Level: SEVERE (UK-Wide), the Threat Comes Principally from Al Qaida and Related Networks; and the Islamic State of Iraq and Levant (ISIL)." Available at https://www.mi5.gov.uk/home/the-threats/terrorism/threat-levels.html (accessed 8 June 2015).
52. Muslim Council of Britain, *British Muslims in Numbers* (London: MCB, 2015). Available at http://www.mcb.org.uk/wp-content/uploads/2015/02/MCBCensusReport_2015.pdf (accessed 5 October 2015).
53. See, for example, Lambert, *Countering al-Qaeda in London*, pp. 224–225.
54. Lambert, "Muslim Safety Forum," pp. 67–90.
55. Lambert, *Countering al-Qaeda in London*, p. 5.
56. Vikram Dodd, "Jihadi Threat Requires Move into 'Private Space' of UK Muslims, Says Police Chief." *The Guardian* 25 May 2014. Available at http://www.theguardian.com/world/2015/may/24/jihadi-threat-requires-move-into-private-space-of-uk-muslims-says-police-chief (accessed 7 June 2015).
57. Ibid.
58. Mehmood Naqshbandi, "Why a Comprehensive Theological Response to ISIS is Desperately Needed." Muslimsinbritain.org blog. 19 March 2015. Available at http://www.muslimsinbritain.org/blog/ (accessed 7 June 2015).
59. Mehmood Naqshbandi, *Islam and Muslims in Britain: A guide*. Available at http://guide.muslimsinbritain.org/guide1.html (accessed 7 June 2015).
60. For an overview of established strands of Islamic belief and practice in Britain, see Bowen, *Medina in Birmingham, Najaf in Brent* (London: Hurst, 2014).
61. For positive examples involving Salafi Londoners see Lambert, *Countering al-Qaeda in London*, pp. 155–220.
62. Naqshbandi, *Islam and Muslims in Britain*.
63. See, for example, Lambert, *Countering al-Qaeda in London*, pp. 155–220.
64. Laura Pitel, "Out-of-Touch Imams Can't Halt Terrorism, Says Adviser," *The Times* 30 August 2014. Available at http://www.thetimes.co.uk/tto/news/uk/article4199696.ece (accessed [via subscription] 7 June 2015).
65. See, for example, Lambert, *Countering al-Qaeda in London*, pp. 155–158.
66. Haras Rafiq, "London Has Been Primed for Decades by Muslim Brotherhood Extremists," *The Express* 24 August 2014. Available at http://www.express.co.uk/comment/expresscomment/502795/London-has-been-primed-for-decades-by-Muslim-Brotherhood-extremists (assessed 10 October 2015).
67. Lambert, *Countering al-Qaeda in London*, pp. 135–154.
68. Peter Oborne, "HSBC, Muslims and Me." BBC Radio 4 first broadcast 28 July 2015. Available at http://www.bbc.co.uk/programmes/b0639w47 (accessed 10 October 2015).
69. Robert Lambert, "Anti-Muslim Violence in the UK," in Max Taylor, P. M. Currie, and Donald Holbrook, eds., *Extreme Right Political Violence and Terrorism* (London: Bloomsbury, 2013), p. 34.

70. See for example role of Barry Norman, former Islington Borough Commander, in Lambert, *Countering al-Qaeda in London*, pp. 97, 100, 103–114, 285.
71. Abdul Haqq Baker, "Is Quietist Salafism an Alternative to ISIS?" Blog article at Abdul Haqq Baker, Ph.D. website. Available at http://abdulhaqqbaker.com/is-quietist-salafism-an-alternative-to-isis/ (accessed 11 October 2015); for background and context see Abdul Haqq Baker, *Extremists in our Midst* (London: Palgrave, 2011).
72. Baker, "Is Quietist Salafism an Alternative to ISIS?"
73. Lambert, *Countering al-Qaeda in London*, pp. 155–222.
74. Jamie Grearson and Shiv Malik, "Preacher Anjem Choudary Charged with Encouraging Support for Islamic State," *The Guardian* 5 August 2015. Available at http://www.theguardian.com/uk-news/2015/aug/05/cleric-anjem-choudary-charged-with-encouraging-support-for-islamic-state (accessed 5 October 2015).
75. Lambert, *Countering al-Qaeda in London*, pp. 287–288.
76. Ibid., pp. 224–225.
77. See, for example, Quilliam Foundation, "Quilliam Trains over 1,000 Public Sector Workers," Press release, 2009. Available at http://www.quilliamfoundation.org/press/quilliam-trains-over-1000-public-sector-workers/ (accessed 8 June 2015).
78. Ned Simons, "Ex-Police Chief Lord Blair Questions David Cameron's Terror Strategy," *Huffington Post* 1 July 2015. Available at http://www.huffingtonpost.co.uk/2015/07/01/ex-police-chief-questions-camerons-terror-strategy_n_7709882.html (accessed 5 October 2015).
79. Lambert, "Muslim Safety Forum," pp. 80–83.
80. Peter Oborne, "Neoconservatives Ruined David Cameron's Foreign Policy Realism," *Middle East Eye* 7 May 2015. Available at http://www.middleeasteye.net/columns/neoconservatives-ruined-david-camerons-foreign-policy-realism-550147284#sthash.4tSiiqQf.dpuf (accessed 10 October 2015).
81. Simons, "Ex-Police Chief Lord Blair Questions David Cameron's Terror Strategy."
82. In the wake of the Stephen Lawrence Inquiry John Grieve highlighted the importance of listening to challenging community voices and not simply talking to "nodding dogs." See John Grieve and Julie French, "Does Institutional Racism Exist In the Metropolitan Police Service?," in David G. Green, ed., *Institutional Racism and the Police: Fact or Fiction?* (London: Institute for the Study of Civil Society, 2002), p. 19; quoted in Lambert, *Countering al-Qaeda in London*, p. 61.
83. See, for example, Deputy Assistant Commissioner Mark Simmonds of the Metropolitan Police listening to blistering criticism from "community activist" Lee Jasper at a police/community meeting in Brixton in episode 1 of the BBC TV documentary, "The Met: Policing London," first broadcast on BBC1 at 9 p.m. on Monday, 7 June 2015. Available (for a limited period) at http://www.bbc.co.uk/iplayer/episode/b05ztwsj/the-met-policing-london-episode-1 (accessed 8 June 2015).
84. Lambert, "Muslim Safety Forum."
85. Spalek, *Terror Crime: Prevention with Communities*.

"Doing Peace": The Role of Ex-Political Prisoners in Violence Prevention Initiatives in Northern Ireland

Carmel Joyce and Orla Lynch

ABSTRACT
While a considerable amount of research has been conducted on community-based initiatives aimed at preventing violence, including the role of the ex-political prisoner community in preventative and counterterrorism work, little is known about how the ex-prisoners themselves manage their identity transition between the role they occupied during the conflict and their current role in violence prevention. We argue that it is important to consider the perspective of ex-prisoners who are both architects of their own process of desistance from political violence, as well active leaders of bespoke desistance programs. While many researchers have recognized the utility of the role of ex-prisoners in violence prevention work, theoretically, the way in which ex-prisoners *do* violence prevention through their use of language and intergroup contact and other resources, is poorly understood. Ultimately, the aim of the article is twofold: to understand the resources (discursive or otherwise) that the community of ex-political prisoners use in their preventative work and (2) to understand how this community understand their role in desistance programs in the context of their personal involvement in violent conflict, including the ways in which participants manage their identity transition.

In recent years, notions of de-radicalization have become central to discussions around preventing recidivism for those convicted of terrorist offenses as well as a means of preventing violent action among those who are deemed at risk of escalation due to extreme beliefs.[1] Of significant political concern are those individuals who have chosen to participate in Islamic-inspired extremism in theaters of war abroad as well as those supposedly *self-radicalized* individuals in Western countries.

In an effort to counteract this risk, many rehabilitation or de-radicalization programs have been undertaken by governments through formal behavior change initiatives managed by prison, police, and probation services (e.g., Deradicalization program, Saudi Arabia; Hayat, Germany; De-radicalisation—Targeted intervention, Denmark; Channel, UK) via nongovernmental organizations (NGOs) working with families (e.g., Women without Boarders, Austria) through community groups (e.g., Street, UK) and via multi-team initiatives seeking to combine police and community approaches (e.g., EXIT, Sweden). The strategies employed in these initiatives are idiosyncratic, context related, funding dependant, and ideologically diverse. Fundamentally, however, all seek to achieve the same goal: a combination of cognitive and behavioral change to reduce the risk of offending and/or re-offending and thus to prevent further terrorist attacks.

Much has been written about the possibility of encouraging individuals to withdraw from or reject participation in terrorism and political violence. Debates have raged around the necessary individual and group factors that encourage individuals to end the violence, as well as the social and legal measures that can push individuals toward non-offending.[2] Parallel debates surrounding the cognitive processes inherent in radicalization and de-radicalization have similarly been voiced, blurring distinctions between desistance and de-radicalization as explanatory frameworks and obscuring the conceptual peculiarities of both processes. What is important within this debate is the very real possibility that a particular community of individuals—former fighters—can arguably desist from political violence, but by no means de-radicalize from the views that led them to, or guided them through, their choices in the first place.[3]

Within the literature that is generally referred to as terrorism studies, but also reflected in the broad counterterrorism and de-radicalization policies of a number of European and Middle Eastern countries, the notion of de-radicalization has gained significant currency as a key explanatory[4] if not causal construct in the conceptualization of terrorism.[5] Identifying vulnerability to radicalization, and thus presumably terrorism, has become a major policy imperative witnessed in the creation of so-called de-radicalization programs.[6] The assumption inherent in such initiatives is of course that because radicalization is conceived of as somehow linked to terrorism and violence, de-radicalization can then prevent further incidences of offending; there is, however, little evidence for and understanding of such a process.[7]

Outside of the mainstream, discussions on de-radicalization and government-led de-radicalization programs, another sub-strand of preventative and rehabilitative *counterterrorism* work is silently underway in many communities; one that incorporates the role of former perpetrators in preventing future instances of terrorism and political violence. In the United Kingdom, a number of individuals are active in researching and implementing preventative programs (e.g., Quilliam Foundation). Similarly, in Norway, Sweden, and Germany former violent right-wing extremists regularly engage with individuals at risk of engagement with gang and political violence (e.g., EXIT). As unpalatable as it may appear politically, there are many instances of former perpetrators actively working to prevent terrorism and political violence or in other words "doing" de-radicalization; in many instances these groups operate below the radar of security and criminal justice services and would oppose the portrayal of their work as de-radicalization or counterterrorism initiatives[8]; Northern Ireland is a key example.

In Northern Ireland the communities of ex-prisoners were and are an integral element in the 1998 peace process that ultimately led to the disarmament of the main paramilitary groups active during the Troubles (1969–1998/2005); during and after incarceration, prisoners were involved in the design and implementation of the peace process; their buy-in to the process was seen as essential to the success of the entire undertaking. Upon their release, many ex-prisoners mobilized collectively to initially campaign for ex-prisoner rights and later extended their work to include community development and conflict transformation.[9]

The range of work undertaken by ex-prisoners is varied and includes (but is not limited to), practical community development work within and between communities, direct conflict-related work (i.e., working at interfaces), as well as the design and implantation of economic regeneration projects.[10] Many researchers both within Northern Ireland and internationally have recognized the vital role of ex-prisoners in violence prevention and community development initiatives. However, theoretically, the way in which ex-prisoners *do* violence prevention through their use of language, intergroup contact, and other resources, is under-researched. Northern Ireland was chosen as a case study for this research due primarily to the significant involvement of ex-prisoners in violence prevention initiatives, but also due to the fact that these interventions are locally driven and community led; the approach to ideological extremism in the case of Northern Ireland is also an interesting case that challenges assumptions about the need for the de-radicalization of ideas in the case of Terrorism and Political Violence.

Additionally, while researchers have attempted to determine the utility of the role of ex-prisoners in preventative work, in the case of political violence in a society with sharp community divisions such as Northern Ireland, little is known about the psychological function that such preventative work holds for the ex-prisoners themselves (i.e., to process and make meaning out of their role in the conflict and to encourage sustained desistance). Importantly, and somewhat separate from other literature that looks at the role of ex-prisoners[11] in preventing violence, the issues of intergroup social identity, identity complexity, and intergroup contract are central in understanding individual ex-prisoner experience, particularly in the case of Northern Ireland. In this context the ways in which ex-prisoners create meaning of the past in their current role is largely overlooked by academics and policymakers alike, in favor of attending to the needs of other social groups.[12] This is despite the fact that researchers have highlighted a need among this population, particularly in terms of the elevated incidences of interpersonal difficulties, substance abuse, mental health issues, and suicide.[13]

In this article we argue that the ways in which ex-prisoners in Northern Ireland use their current role to make meaning out of their involvement in the conflict (and vice versa) is vital to ensure, not only their own continued support for the peace process, but also that of a younger generation searching for meaning in a post-conflict environment. This article will briefly discuss elements of social identity theory relevant to the work of ex-prisoners in Northern Ireland and subsequently present the results of a study conducted with a sample of over fifty ex-prisoners.

Social Identity Theory

In relation to political violence, achieving desistance involves the ceasing of violent terrorist activities. Importantly, desistance in instances of political violence is complex given the relative rarity of the violent events, the likelihood of parallel *criminal* activity and the role of the group in sustaining support for the violence. In such instances conceptions of de-radicalization are less useful in trying to understand a move away from violence because they simplistically link ideologies to behaviors as well as failing to capture the realities of offending for those involved in political violence. Importantly, in terms of behavioral de-radicalization individuals can and do desist from political violence all the while maintaining their personal and/or group-based ideologies, problematizing the notion that re-radicalization is a precursor to or related to the process of desistance.[14]

While significant conceptual dissimilarities exist, there are important parallels between both gang research on desistance and applying the concept to terrorism research. There are a number of shared foundational issues, particularly the parameters of desistance related to group membership; must all ties be cut or is a termination (even a reduction) in serious crime sufficient?[15] Furthermore the notion of status change is an important factor in the literature on gang desistance. In desisting from gang violence, and as a result terminating relationships with that gang, there is a distinct and identifiable change in status for individuals.[16] In the case of terrorist groups there is a complex interplay between *membership* of the organization and later membership of associated tangential organizations that effectively have the same individuals involved and may even espouse similar ideological positions; therefore, the termination of the group's existence is often not a reality. For example after the Good Friday Agreement (GFA) (and in some cases before) a number of ex-prisoners groups emerged linked to (among others) the Provisional Irish Republican Army (PIRA).[17] For the purpose of group support and thus the group processes of desistance, the issue is whether there was in fact any status shift for desisters or whether the ex-prisoner groups mediated that shift, implying an interesting role for the de-criminalization or *tolerance* of nonviolent organizations linked to the original paramilitary groups. In the case of Northern Ireland, rather than abandon the group, individual members are more likely to redefine the characteristics associated with the group; a process known in the social identity tradition as "identity transformation."

Social identity has been used to explain the processes involved in identity transformation or the reshaping of socially devalued groups. Individuals can engage in a number of different strategies in response to negatively valued group membership.[18] An individual can, for example, choose to dis-identify or leave the socially devalued group. Alternatively, an individual can choose to remain within the group and engage in a process of "social creativity" to redefine the shape and dimensions of the group.[19] Social creativity involves the strategic use of components of identity to shape and redefine aspects of the category. For example, group members may emphasize the variability within the group ("we're bad but we're not all bad"), they can make comparisons over time ("we're bad but we're better than we used to be"), or compare themselves to an alternative outgroup ("we're bad but not as bad as others") to buffer against their subordinate status or the negative associations with the group.[20] In Northern Ireland further complexity exists regarding the perceptions of the group (e. g., the PIRA), and whether it is actually perceived as a negative entity and devoid of social status. The GFA ensured that the PIRA as a violent organization had reduced social support, but given its history, its well-constructed narratives of liberation and justice, and its role as a key representative of community identity, the organization was still able to exist post peace process as a result of its identity transition through demilitarization.

This transition from "paramilitary" to "peacemaker" has perhaps been one of the most controversial attempts to redefine a social category in Northern Ireland.[21] A number of researchers have examined Republican and Loyalist ex-prisoners' explanations for involvement in conflict and their transition to peace.[22] Many ex-prisoners released as part of the GFA now work in the community, promoting nonviolence in the most volatile constituencies in Northern Ireland.[23] Ex-prisoners have educated themselves on the principals of restorative justice during incarceration and have applied these principals in the promotion of community policing upon their release, working closely with the Police Services of Northern Ireland (PSNI) to decriminalize behavior stemming from social and economic disadvantage, trauma, and mental health.[24] However, little is known about how ex-prisoners manage the transition from "paramilitary" to "peace maker" and the practicalities of this transition.

Indeed, while a considerable amount of research has been conducted on the role of ex-prisoner in preventative work, little is known about how individuals themselves manage the identity transition between their role in the conflict and their current role in violence prevention. We argue that it is important to consider the perspective of ex-prisoners who are both architects of their own process of desistance from political violence, as well active leaders of bespoke desistance programs in Northern Ireland. While many researchers have recognized the utility of ex-prisoners role in preventative work, theoretically, the way in which ex-prisoner *do* violence prevention through their use of language and intergroup contact and other resources is much less understood. Ultimately, the aim of the article is twofold: (1) to understand the resources (discursive or otherwise) that participants use in their role in preventative work and (2) to understand how participants understand their role in desistance programs in the context of their previous role in the conflict, including the ways in which participants manage their identity transition.

Method

In order to investigate the role of ex-political prisoners in violence prevention and broader community development initiatives in Northern Ireland, semi-structured interviews were conducted with self-identified Republican ($n = 25$) and Loyalist ($n = 27$) ex-prisoners who are members of ex-prisoner support organizations involved in self-defined restorative justice projects, peace building initiatives, and ex-prisoner support services. In addition to identifying as politically motivated former prisoners, participants also self identified as "community activists," "politicians," and "restorative justice" and "peace practitioners." Participants were not asked in advance of the interview to state their religious or political affiliations (which are assumed to align with their paramilitary affiliations). However, the identity categories participants used in the interview (i.e., Catholic, Protestant, etc.) was noted and informed the analysis. Respondents ranged in age between 37 and 65 years *(Mean age* = 53), all were born in Belfast.

To recruit participants the researchers contacted ex-prisoner organizations in Belfast via e-mail and later organized one-to-one meetings with representatives of the organizations. Interviews were conducted on the premises of the ex-prisoner organizations where participants worked in Northern Ireland between 12 October 2013 and 20 May 2014. The interviews were transcribed verbatim, entered into NVivo text-tagging software, and open-coded into "free nodes" or the smallest unit of meaningful data identified without restriction.[25] When possible, these labels were chosen to reflect "emic" categories that are likely to preexist in the participants' repertoires, used by social actors themselves to explain certain phenomenon.[26]

Three dominant themes were identified in the data: "preventing the transgenerational transmission of political violence," "promoting peace through intra- and intergroup contact," and "promoting restorative principals and capacity building". Each subtheme was considered in relation to the main themes, which related upward to the preceding theme, thus demonstrating the hierarchy of meaning within the data.[27]

Managing transitions:
- Ex-prisoners and identity continuity
- Transferring ownership of community issues

- Addressing issues underpinning criminality

Preventing transgenerational transmission of political violence:
- Dispelling myths and romanticism
- Firefighting and stabilizing interface violence
- Dismantling processes of indigenous learning

Promoting peace through intra- and intergroup contact:
- "Doing" intergroup contact: Constructive engagement with the outgroup
- Challenging intergroup difference: The use of shared experience
- Exporting peace: Creating transferable models of peace building

The development of themes was then used, in part, as a data management tool to organize segments of data for subsequent analysis. The extracts were analyzed using resources from discourse analysis.[28] More specifically, the basis on which participants constructed their own identities (and that of others), as well as how these identities were mobilized to perform different discursive actions, were identified in the text.

Analysis

In the following section, we will outline a three-tiered approach to understanding the role of ex-prisoners in encouraging desistance from violence namely personal, preventative, and symbolic dimensions. At the personal level, we will discuss how their role provides ex-prisoners with a sense of identity continuity between their past and current position in Northern Ireland. In addition, we will also discussion how ex-prisoners use their role to manage accountability for the past and their role in the conflict. At a preventative level, we will discuss how ex-prisoners mobilize their identities in their role in preventative work with youth at risk in Northern Ireland. Finally, at a symbolic level, we will discuss ex-prisoners use of direct interaction with ex-prisoner peers to simulate a vicarious experience of cross-group interaction. Throughout the analysis, particular attention is paid to how participants *do* violence prevention work in Northern Ireland through the mobilization of identities, the use of rhetorical devices to manage accountability, as well their use of legitimizing narratives to bridge the transition from "paramilitary" to self-identified "peace practitioner."

Personal

Managing Identity Transitions

Ex-prisoners interviewed for this research often used their role in preventative work to emphasize the continuity of their role during and post conflict. Many of the ex-prisoners who were involved in violence during the Troubles, consider their current involvement in self defined restorative programs as a natural extension of their motivations for their participation in violence during the conflict.

> P: I have been involved in my community from day one . this is what I've been doing all my life . trying to make my community better . I am still fighting for my community . it's a different fight but it's the same in many ways. (Republican ex-prisoner)

Indeed, it was common for a Republican ex-prisoner to draw parallels between their past and current roles, "fighting" on behalf of their community to end perceived injustices. In the following extract, a Republican ex-prisoner provides a collective narrative of "victims of injustices" and uses this narrative to bridge the transition between past and current roles in the community:

> P: You know and I saw enough of . of trouble on the ground and I saw enough army brutality or whatever to do me a lifetime . and I experienced it then first hand and the thing of it was I suppose I reached the conclusion about 15 years of age you know if you go back to the old adage "turn the other cheek" and when they slapped that one too I thought yea . it's time I slapped someone's cheek back
> I: So umm . then did you feel like you were a victim of injustice
> P: No I didn't feel like I was that . I <u>knew</u> I was a [victim of] injustice
> I: [yeah yeah]
> P: There was no <u>feeling</u> about it . we fought for our communities before and we're still fighting . it's no longer an armed struggle but still a struggle. (Republican ex-prisoner)

At the start of the extract, the participant provided an account of his own observation and direct experience of perceived "brutality" by the British army. By initially positioning himself as an uninvolved observer of "brutality," repeatedly ("to do me a lifetime"), the participant positions himself and others who were subjected to army brutality, as the passive recipients of harm. The participant then adopts the category introduced by the interviewer "I <u>knew</u> I was a victim of injustice," but problematizes the subject nature of the statement "there was no feeling about it." In such a way, the participant works up and adopts the identity of "victim of injustice" as justification for involvement in the conflict and, as indicated in the final line, their continued effort to "fight" for their cause; albeit unarmed. Their role in the community is held constant. The implications of such *identity* continuity is that individuals need not reimagine their violent past in terms of the current peace environment, but can situate their choice to participate in violence in light of the context in which they found themselves. Serving to *save face* allows the ex-prisoners to maintain their status in their community particularly among at risk youth, and provides a platform for the ex-prisoners to continue their community struggle by other means.[29] This attribution of their violent past as an artifact of personal and vicarious victimhood is reinforced by the regular addage of:

> P: "Anyone in their right minds would have done what we did" (Republican ex-prisoner)
> I: Knowing what you know now . would you have done anything differently?
> P: No . we were in a way situation . there was no doing anything differently . you didn't think . you had to defend your community . that's the bottom line. (Loyalist ex-prisoner)

In effect, constructing their involvement in violence as a response to injustice and the response itself as a crusade against this injustice allows ex-prisoners the flexibility to defend their personal history and motivations for violence. It also simultaneously allows ex-prisoners to encourage nonviolence in the contemporary arena through reference to the current lack of discrimination and vicimization on the streets of Belfast. In effect, their argument can be summed up by recalling an ex-prisoner statement

> P: Things are different now. (Republican Ex-prisoner)

However, importantly, and extremely relevant in their conversations with at-risk youth, the ex-prisoners reserve their right to support the role of violence in Northern Ireland (NI) in the future. They outline how in their work with youth who are or have participated in violence on the streets of Belfast, be it as a result of the Flags Protests[30] or violence at the interfaces, that if circumstances were to change in NI society, there may well be a role for paramilitary action in the future. This is less an example of the risk these individuals may pose as violent actors and more relevant in justifying their own use of violence in the past.

> P: I am too old now. (Republican Ex-prisoner)

Furthermore, this reliance on victimization and discrimination as a motivator for violent action allows the ex-prisoners to encourage what may be termed temporary desistance among the youth. The ex-prisoners are not seeking a lifelong commitment to nonviolence but a temporary avoidance of violence unrelated to one's ideological commitment to a cause or fundamental belief in the role of violence in political change. They are encouraging the youth not to engage in violence given the current context they face in NI. This is not to say that peace in NI is fundamentally at risk of collapse but reflects the reality of desistance; as demonstrated in the criminological literature, that all desistance is ultimately temporary.[31]

> P: I wouldn't tell anyone not to take up arms. (Republican Ex Prisoner)

Loyalist ex-prisoners also emphasized the continuity between their past and their current role in the community. It was common for Loyalist participants to bridge the transition between their past and current role using the phrase "from defender to mender." The following extracts are taken from the transcripts of loyalist participants who discuss their role in the conflict, as well as their role in peace building using the phrasing "from defender to mender":

> P: It was a natural progression . all my life I have been fighting for my community . so if . if . if the armed part of fighting for my community is over then I'll fight for my community in another way . "from defender to mender." (Loyalist ex-prisoner)
>
> P: "Defender to mender" is what we say . we were defending our community in the past . now we're mending . you know working with the community . in the past every aspect of life here was dealt with by the organisation but our feeling was . if the conflict is over and the organisation is going to go away then it's important that the capacity of the community is built up . that the community takes that into their own hands. (Loyalist ex-prisoner)

In the above extracts, it is possible the continuity between their past and present role can also demonstrate their commitment to preventative work and community development. As demonstrated by the second extract, it was common for Loyalist ex-prisoners to emphasize their peripheral role in community capacity building, as a facilitator of this process rather than active participants. Toward the end of the extract, the participant shifts footing[32] from the use of "we"—"the organisation"—to speaking about "the community" as an entity with agency "that the community takes it into their own hands." In effect, this can demonstrate the way in which ex-prisoners "do" restorative work by rhetorically distancing themselves from the account and shifting ownership for community issues to "the community" itself. The use of "defender" is one that reflects a common narrative employed by Loyalist ex-prisoners, similar to the exercise by Republicans in their reference to "victimisation and discrimination." In working up a justification of their use of violence, Loyalist ex-prisoners rely heavily on the their construction of the Troubles as Republican-initiated violence that resulted in the need to *protect* Loyalist communities.

Both Loyalist and Republican ex-prisoners used their discussion of restorative principles and practices to highlight the continuity between their role in the conflict and their current role in preventative work. Their role in preventive work allows ex-prisoners to create a sense of identity continuity which, in turn, can serve a variety of functions. According to the Meaning Maintenance Model,[33] individuals strive to parsimoniously integrate beliefs about oneself across time and context. Ex-prisoners' role in preventative work provides them with an opportunity to emphasize the continuity of their identity, post conflict. In a post-conflict environment, it can provide a framework of meaning in which to interpret the past and to use their experiences as a preventative resource. Relatedly, this can, perhaps, be viewed as a strategy to manage accountability for past actions: if the participant has changed as a person, they are open to questions concerning "why," which, inevitably, casts a shadow of doubt over the legitimacy of their individual or group-based narratives for involvement.

Importantly, when discussing their role in preventative work with youth at risk in Belfast, the issue of responsibility and blame were notions that were continually addressed. This was particularly evident in ex-prisoners' retrospective accounts of their reasons for becoming involved in violence, but also in relation to specific acts of violence. As mentioned, quite often, participants attributed blame externally and minimized personal agency. Their actions were, in effect, retaliatory and in response to continual unprovoked attack. The following are examples from both Loyalist and Republican ex-prisoners:

> I: Yea . and what was the justification of umm . for like your involvement (pause) in comparison?
> P: Well the IRA . the IRA were killing everything and anything and you know . we were . we just had to do something . they were killing friends of ours . they were bombing . like like . when the Troubles started I was going into Newry . a small glorious village between Belfast and Lisburn … they had blown up the two bars . they had blown up the hotel . they had blown up two or three shops. (Loyalist ex-prisoner)
> P: If the police stop you . and your name is Peter Robinson . "ah mister Robinson off you go . I know you and your kids go to the same school as my kids . and everything is great and how you doing" . if you're Jerry Adams or Mary O'Neill or some Catholic sounding name and says West Belfast or North . parts of North Belfast . "ah ok just check your registration . do you want to step out of the car" and all of that stop and search they're doing in New York and all . is what we got . that apparatus of the state from helicopters in the sky . undercover soldiers . massive amounts of very visible soldiers . with high end resources . best cars . best technology and all that stuff . unlimited resources directed against us . right and I grew up and that's the world I grew up in . it's almost like Israel with the Palestinians you know . something had to be done you know. (Republican ex-prisoner)

Relatedly, as illustrated in the above extracts, participants in this study often drew heavily on social responsibility repertoires or the notion that it is their responsibility to "step up" and "defend our community." This has long been recognized in the literature on former prisoners in NI.[34] In all instances provocation was seen as the motivator for action. Participants often considered it their role to defend their community from any outside threat. The issue of responsibility for the conflict was thus diverted to those who initiated the provocation in the first instance. The participants also draw on documented international examples of injustice and compare their own experience to well-known instances of oppression and discrimination. The ex-prisoners' construction of their violent past as being related to their willingness to defend their community is further developed by the participants as a tool to construct themselves as victims, having sacrificed their life and their liberty for the sake of their community. Many of the ex-prisoners recall their hardship in prison, their personal sufferings through isolation, divorce, and exclusion, and their oftentimes *pariah* status politically in NI.

As illustrated in the above extracts, for the ex-prisoners in their discussion of their personal histories as well as in their accounts of their methods for dealing with youth at risk of involvement in political violence, the ideas that supported the violence are not called into question; the justification and motivations for the violence remain intact. A key element in encouraging desistance among the youth is the encouragement of a temporary moratorium on violence justified solely on the context—the time is not right. The work that ex-prisoners do with youth at risk of involvement in political violence is based not on a deconstruction of the ideology that is drawn on to explain their violence. Rather, ex-prisoners evoke their personal experience of injury, loss, and self-sacrifice as a deterrent to youth engagement in violence.

By continually referring to the context to their experiences, the ex-prisoners construct a logic that allows a justification for their violent past but at the same time, justifies their current nonviolent activities through the external attribution of their motivation for violence. Being able to establish a continuity between their violent past and their nonviolent present enables the ex-prisoners to create a coherent narrative of identity continuity and effectively attribute their actions entirely to the situation they found themselves in during the Troubles. Ultimately, "de-radicalization" and the abandoning of group-based ideologies were concepts that did not have residence in this context. However, participants were effectively engaging in work that would be termed behavioral "de-radicalization" in their role in preventative work with youth at risk. This is illustrated further in the next section.

Preventative: Preventing the Transgenerational Transmission of Political Violence

Both Republican and Loyalist ex-prisoners identified the superordinate goal of preventing the transgenerational transmission of political violence. Participants were universally concerned with "not wanting the next generation to inherit our experiences and to live with what we faced" (Loyalist ex-prisoner). Many drew on historical accounts of reincarnations of political violence as an illustration of the need to end cyclical violence in NI: "we have been here before" (Republican ex-prisoner). All participants spoke of their sense of social responsibility to end cyclical violence.

Although ex-prisoners did not spontaneously self-identify as "victims," they did provide accounts of victimization as an illustration of the need to end cyclical violence in NI:

I: What motivates the work that you do?
P1: I don't want to see this happen again . I've carried too many of my friends . my relatives down the road in coffins . I don't want to ever do that again . I don't want anyone to ever have to do that . you know what I mean . I don't think anyone here today would. (Republican ex-prisoner)

During one of the interviews for this study, a participant accompanied the researcher to a gallery of images on display in a community center. The images were displayed in order to demonstrate the reality of conflict and the experiences implicit in involvement. The participant referred to the images as a "violence prevention resource." In reference to one image in particular that showed a funeral cortage, including the hearse, and mourners, the participant evoked notions of personal victimization:

I: And this is a photo of?
P2: It's of the funeral yea . I remember that . I was there that day . this is to show young people that it isn't fun . people die . I lost my friends . uncles . every week there was someone . no one wants that. (Loyalist ex-prisoner)

Relatedly, as illustrated in the above extract, participants often evoked victimhood narratives in order to illustrate the "true cost of the conflict" (Republican ex-prisoner). All participants used their identities as a resource to illustrate the realities of conflict: the cost in terms of lives lost, time lost during incarceration, futures lost due to employment restrictions, injuries, and emotional repercussions for family members. Essentially, participants identified their role in "dispelling myths and romanticism" around the conflict.

Indeed, all participants considered their identity as a valuable public resource to "dispel myths and romanticism" surrounding the conflict and importantly, they also mobilized their identities for this strategic purpose. Although ex-prisoners never directly identified as a victim of the conflict, they did evoke notions of personal and collective victimization. However, the indirect claim to victimhood, in this particular context, was not used to absolve responsibility, shift blame, or acquire resources, but was used as a resource in-and-of-itself to illustrate the realities of violent conflict: "this is to show young people that it isn't fun," It was also not uncommon for political ex-prisoners to discuss their creation of victims and their infliction of harm (direct or indirect) as an illustration of the true cost of conflict:

> I: What do you tell the young people you work with about your experiences?
> P3: Well there is nothing glamourous about it to begin with . they think it was all fun and games . it wasn't . lots of people died . I dug bodies out of buildings that were blown up . I saw things no one should ever have seen and did things too . there is nothing sexy about that. (Loyalist ex-prisoner)

It is interesting to note here that the participant inserts himself into the account in the first person pronoun "I dug out bodies," "I saw things," and omits the pronoun "I" with reference to their own actions: "did things too." Also, while the participant "should never have seen" the things he did, there is no indication whether his personal actions were unjustified. We draw attention to these shifts in footing[35] not to suggest that the participants are avoiding responsibility for their actions or to cast value judgments. When individuals shift from first to second person pronouns, also known as footing shifts, it is often when they discuss contentious issues.[36] These shifts can be used to create distance, discursively, from the account being produced. In such a way participants can be seen to manage their identity within their account. We also note the numerous ways in which participants can use victimhood as a resource to illustrate the cost of the conflict, while also managing the issues that may arise from its use (i.e., issue of blame for the past).

In addition to evoking notions of personal victimization as a conflict transformation resource, political ex-prisoners also mobilize "class identities" as a superordinate identity highlighting similarities between subgroups:

> P4: I tell them all the time . there is more you have in common than separate you . we are working class people in Belfast . there kids are struggling with the same issues . employment . getting a job . trying to get ahead in life. (Republican ex-prisoner)

Ex-prisoners use the superordinate identity "we are working class people." The Common Ingroup Identity Model[37] would suggest that intergroup prejudice and hostilities can be reduced through the creative redefining of category boundaries to include superordinate categorizations. While other models of subgroup-superordinate categorization have been developed and suggest that superordinate categorization can exacerbate intergroup differences,[38] what is interesting here is that participants use superordinate categorization spontaneously in their work, perhaps as a resource to reduce intergroup hostilities.

As mentioned, the participants in this study continually drew on their ex-prisoner identity during the process of engaging with youth in preventative work. The ex-prisoners were acutely aware of the prestige accorded to this personal history among the youth in question:

> I was on hunger strike twice . and the young people we work with . you know they know that . they heard stories . and you know that gives us a certain amount of umm (pause) say respect. (Loyalist ex-prisoner)

A romanticism around the community spirit during the Troubles and the comradery among the paramilitaries in the prisons is commonplace for the youth. In many accounts, the participants in this study acknowledge that they are seen as heroes, a part of a folklore that glorifies the Troubles. In an effort to refocus the youth on the reality of the Troubles, very personal accounts of loss are drawn on to de-mystify the experience of prison and the violence on the streets. Participants would also explain how their incarceration was made bearable due to the existence of effective political status within the prisons, a comradery among inmates and a very vocal support network on the outside. This, they would explain, is why you must not be imprisoned now… "times have changed, the context is different."

Symbolic: Promoting Peace Through Intra- and Intergroup Contact

Loyalist and Republican ex-prisoners are involved in collaborative work across interfaces in NI. This work, we argue, is particularly important on a symbolic level and represent an "imagined interaction" in the absence of intergroup contact.

> I: How would you introduce yourself . like in a classroom like that . how would you introduce yourself to the young people in the room
> P8: Well I would say I'm a former member of the UDA . and there would be someone with me . and Republican . Provo or whatever and they'd say who they are . it's important that they see we work together. (Loyalist ex-prisoner)

Often, and particularly in classroom contexts where ex-prisoners are asked to speak to young people about the dangers of intergroup violence, participants will use their "ex-prisoner" identities (i.e., paramilitary affiliations) to illustrate their willingness to engage collaboratively with members of the other community, their former enemies: "it's important that they see that we work together." Indeed, the importance of "being seen" to engage with their ex-prisoner counterpart appeared consistently across ex-prisoner transcripts:

> P6: If myself and . and ah (pause) my peers . my ex- . my combatants at that time . um could go down to the interface and walk across the street and start talking to people from the other side of the street who were ex-combatants from the other side . um that sent a message out into the community . we don't "just talk the talk" . that's what they say isn't it . they think if those guys can cross over and talk to each other . you know . you know . what's this all about . so it's getting that message across. (Loyalist ex-prisoner)
> P7: … they knew that we were able to go there and speak to each other and basically what people were saying was "well if it's good enough for them to be doing that surely it would be alright for us to do it." (Republican ex-prisoner)

Participants also mobilized their conflict-related "community" identity to demonstrate their willingness to engage in intergroup contact with the "other community." This (often spontaneous) display of intergroup contact and cooperation could be particularly powerful in certain areas of NI where mixed group interaction (between Nationalist/Catholic and Unionist/Protestant) is minimal. Participants demonstrate an awareness of the utility of their direct contact with the other community and their use of direct contact as a resource: "its' showing that we all work together." This "showing" or "having been seen" to engage with the other community is an indicator of the performative function of direct contact, over-and-above what it is offering to participants (in terms of possible prejudice reduction); it is being used to provide a vicarious experience of cross-group interaction.

Additionally, we argue, participants' display of intergroup interaction is being used as a discursive resource to demonstrate the legitimacy or credibility of their role. This is somewhat reminiscent of literature on community-based approaches to counterterrorism where the focus is on identifying members of particular communities who act as leaders and have the ability to represent as well as alter community views. In these instances it is also necessary for such individuals to first demonstrate their credibility as ingroup members.[39] There are various ways in which participants can use their account of intergroup interaction to work up their credibility. For example, in the first extract, the Loyalist participant introduces their partners in the interaction as "peer," which suggests an equal interaction and is temporally distinct from "combatants at the time." This equal interaction between ex-prisoner "peers" is communicating the message that they do not just "talk the talk," allowing the listener to finish the phrase—they also "walk the walk." The rhetorical commonplace—"talk the talk"—is a device to manage accountability and build credibility by appealing to sentiments that are assumed to be commonly held "that's what they say isn't it."[40] In such a way, their direct interaction with ex-prisoner peers can be used as a rhetorical resource to demonstrate their credibility of the message being sold and of themselves as messengers.

Participants often discuss the symbolic aspect of their role in preventative work. In particular, as illustrated in the above extracts, participants emphasized the importance of "being seen" to interact with members of the other community and the symbolic connotations for those who witness the interaction "that sent a message." The interaction between ex-prisoners across the interface is a marker of their ability and willingness to engage in collaborative work to meet superordinate goals. This can be seen as a working example of the notion of Contact Hypothesis first developed by Alport,[41] which states that, theoretically, positive intergroup contact under certain conditions can reduce prejudice and hostility between groups. In terms of the Contact Hypothesis participants are "doing" positive intergroup interaction. However, in addition, we argue that participants are using their interaction with known outgroup members as a conflict transformation resource. More specifically, their interaction with the outgroup is being used strategically as "symbolic contact" to "carry a message" to fellow ingroup members that positive interaction with the other community is possible. This simulated interaction is in some ways, we argue, a hybrid of "extended" and "imagined" contact but with a performative, strategic function.

All participants engaged in the collaborative activity of "humanizing the ingroup" and used counternarratives for this strategic purpose. This role, for the most part, occurred on an intragroup level of interaction in which group members spoke to those in the other community—generally young people in a classroom context. Again, in addition to their identities as "political ex-prisoners," participants' conflict-related identities also played an important role. In the following extracts, participants discuss their engagement with young people in classroom settings:

I: Why do you think this work is important?
P9: Well I tell them I'm so and so . tell them a bit about myself the work I do . that I'm an ex-prisoner . some of these kids would never have met anyone from the other community . you know what I mean . let alone an ex-prisoner . so I tell them about life during the conflict and I think they say "I heard me ma say that or me da say that . they had those experiences too . maybe they're not monsters. " (Loyalist ex-prisoner)
I: Yea of course . but when it comes to talking to young people there is a certain advantage to saying you're an ex-prisoner
P11: Yea it can be … it's about breaking that down for young people . giving them the chance to understand . 'He's just like the person in my community who done that and experienced this' . so it's about . see when we talk to young people and I would go to different Catholic schools and stuff like that . umm (pause) you can surprise them . you know you can shock them sometimes . you know it's not what they're expecting to hear . you were the enemy you have to remember for some people in their community but I don't think they got the same baggage as us. (Republican ex-prisoner)

All participants use their identities as members of the "other community" in their interaction with young people in a classroom context. In certain communities in NI where direct interaction with members of the "other community" are rare, participants, as representatives of the other community, can challenge stereotypes that maintain intergroup differences: "maybe they're not monsters." Within these accounts, participants are also managing their identities as individuals involved in preventive work. Take the first extract—the participant's identity as an "ex-prisoner" is not introduced immediately, rather it follows a general introduction: "I tell them a little about myself." This introduces the notion of identity complexity, or that individuals can occupy different roles simultaneously and that their identity as "ex-prisoner" is not necessarily the most salient. This works to both manage their dual positions as "ex-prisoners" and "peace practitioners" and also, on a symbolic level, communicates the message to the audience that identities are complex and not always consistent with stereotyped notions of the "other community." Ultimately, participants evoke shared experience with the other community, which could, theoretically, function as a symbolic interaction, reducing intergroup differences.

Discussion

There is a considerable amount of research on the role of former political prisoners in preventing political violence.[42] While we have provided corroborative evidence for some of the roles identified in the literature (i.e., stabilizing interface violence), we have also drawn attention to the resources participants use to perform these roles. In particular, we have illustrated in the analysis the ways participants *do* preventative work, through their use of their own identities, superordinate categorizations, "symbolic contact" and simulated interaction, as well as the active use of restorative principals. These findings highlighted the unique role of political ex-prisoners in conflict prevention by drawing attention to their use of their identities and that of others (i.e., their ex-prisoner counterparts) in their work. In doing so, we have not only provided thematic categorization of the role former political prisoners play in preventing political violence, but we have illustrated the various resources (discursive and otherwise) that participants mobilize to perform these roles. Importantly this categorization demonstrates the necessary complexity of so-called de-radicalization programs, the importance of personal and community identity within this process, the necessity of grass-roots initiatives in this area. It also demonstrates the importance, palatable or not, of encouraging and enabling ex-prisoners to remain committed to nonviolence.

These findings also contribute to our understanding of the utility of superordinate goals in the process of preventing political violence among at-risk youth. In order to reduce prejudice and intergroup hostility, according to the Contact Hypothesis, the interaction between groups must be frequent and long term, each group should have equal status (within the interaction) and the interaction should facilitate superordinate goals that require collaborative engagement by both parties. The superordinate goal of "preventing transgenerational transmission of political violence" or in participants' own words "not wanting young people to live with what I faced," provides participants with a meaningful framework to engage collaboratively in pursuit of superordinate goals.

The analysis presented here also contributes to the literature on forms of simulated contact. In particular, the analysis speaks to the notion of "Symbolic contact" as a simulated interaction and how "being seen" to interact with the "other community" has a performative and strategic function to "send a message" to ingroup members that positive interaction is possible. In divided societies such as NI where direct contact is not always possible and other forms of simulated contact (i.e., "extended contact") has been shown to be effective, the role of ex-prisoners in symbolic interaction can be particularly valuable. Researchers have suggested ways in which direct and extended contact can be practically combined.[43] In NI, we argue, the role of the ex-prisoner in preventative work is an illustrative example of the practical extension of the Contact Hypothesis in action.

There is also evidence in the analysis that participants are managing their entitlement to engage in preventative work (legitimacy concerns). The legitimacy concerns of ex-prisoners have been well documented in the literature, particularly among Loyalist ex-prisoners.[44] However, we argue that "legitimacy" is not a static concept (that is either present or absent) but is something that participants negotiate in the interview and in everyday interaction. For example, participants use their display of positive interaction with the other group to demonstrate that they do not just "talk the talk" and are therefore genuine and credible in their role as "peace practitioners." Additionally, participants draw on the notion of sacrifice and victimhood as a tool to account for their entitlement to have a role as a community activist. They appear to distance themselves from their account of their involvement, particularly when discussing restorative practices, thereby illustrating the way in which they *do* restorative work. We reiterate the legitimacy concerned noted in the literature but also note the ways in which participants proactively manage these concerns.

Finally, this article has demonstrated that perhaps in an effort to manage accountability, participants attribute responsibility for their violent past externally through reference to the provocateurs who inspired their violence. By positioning themselves as having sacrificed their youth, health, freedom, and so on, they construct their involvement in terrorism as an artefact of the times in which they found themselves. They were *victims of circumstance* and the context to the Troubles is a key aspect of their narrative. As part of the preventative narrative, the ex-prisoners draw on this issue of context to delegitimize the role of violence contemporaneously.

In trying to understanding the issues of desistance for ex-prisoners and the prevention work carried out by these same individuals it is possible that in the case of NI, that process of desistence and prevention is one and the same. In considering the work of ex-prisoners with at risk youth in NI, it is clear that in the process of *doing* peace work, or *doing* counter-terrorism is at the same time the very process that allows ex-prisoners to continually reinforce their identity as *peace makers* while protecting their violent past as a legitimate part of this process.

In attempting to understand the grass-roots ex-prisoner-led initiatives underway in NI in light of the broader debates on de-radicalization from terrorism, there are important lessons that can be learned. While cognizant of the idiosyncrasies of the Troubles and the peace time environment in NI, there are many opportunities for the application of ex-prisoner-led violence prevention in NI to terrorism prevention elsewhere. A key lesson lies in the issue of so-called cognitive de-radicalization and its absence in the NI process. The absence of such an initiative in NI, and the arguably successful efforts of the ex-prisoners (given the status of the peace process) brings such a notion into question as a universal phenomenon. Related to this and emerging from the criminological literature is the notion of temporary desistance. The ex-prisoners do not attempt a frame breaking shift in youth cognitions, beliefs, and ideology. A recognition that all desistence is in effect temporary[45] may be a more appropriate frame for dealing with perpetrators of political violence in that a tailored lifespan approach can then be taken rather than seeking cognitive and behavioral change in one concentrated intervention.

Finally, we suggest some potential avenues for future research. As ex-prisoners themselves outlined in their interviews, it is often difficult to evaluate their work or, in their own words "how do you measure the absence of something" (Loyalist ex-prisoner)? Further research could systematically measure the effects of "symbolic contact" at both a local and a regional level to determine the effect, if any, that both victim and ex-prisoner education sessions have on attitudes toward outgroup members versus sessions led by neutral speakers. Future research could also involve interviews with young people who have participated in an education session led by a mixed-group ex-prisoner. It is worth considering the effect of *witnessing* direct contact between victims and ex-prisoners, as well as subgroups of ex-prisoners, on young peoples' perceptions of conflict transformation, the legitimacy of the speaker, their own perceptions of ingroup and outgroup members, as well as the possibility for positive intergroup contact.

Funding

This research was conducted as part of a larger study that examined the role of victims and perpetrators in violence prevention, funded by the European Commission through the Specific Programme "Prevention of and Fight against Crime," HOME/2012/ISEC/AG/RAD

Notes

1. John Horgan and Kurt Braddock, "Rehabilitating the Terrorists?: Challenges in Assessing the Effectiveness of De-Radicalization Programs," *Terrorism and Political Violence* 22 (2010), pp. 267–291.
2. John Horgan, *The Psychology of Terrorism* (London; Routledge, 2006).
3. Sarah Marsden, "Conceptualising 'Success' with Those Convicted of Terrorism Offences: Aims, Methods and Barriers to Reintegration," *Behavioral Studies of Terrorism and Political Aggression* 7(2) (2015), pp. 143–165.

4. Paul Mandeville, "Muslim Transnational Identity and State Responses in Europe and the UK After 9/11: Political Community, Ideology and Authority," *Journal of Ethnic and Migration Studies* 35 (3) (2009), pp. 491–506.
5. Peter Hopkins, "Young Muslim Men in Scotland: Inclusions and Exclusions," *Children's Geographies* 2 (2) (2004), pp. 257–272; Laura McDonald, "Securing Identities, Resisting Terror: Muslim Youth Work in the UK and Its Implications for Security," *Religion, State and Society* 39 (2–3) (2011), pp. 177–189.
6. See for example this British initiative, available at http://www.thesundaytimes.co.uk/sto/news/uk_news/National/article1433673.ece (accessed 13 November 2016); Orla Lynch, "British Muslim Youth: Radicalisation, Terrorism and the Construction of the 'Other.'" *Critical Studies on Terrorism* 6(2) (2013), pp. 241–261.
7. Jonathan Githens-Mazer and Robert Lambert, *Islamophobia and Anti-Muslim Hate Crime: UK Case Studies* (Exeter: EMRC, University of Exeter, 2011); Laura McDonald, "Securing Identities, Resisting Terror: Muslim Youth Work in the UK and its Implications for Security," *Religion, State and Society* 39 (2–3) (2011), pp. 177–189; Paul Mandeville, "Muslim Transnational Identity and State Responses in Europe and the UK After 9/11: Political Community, Ideology and Authority," *Journal of Ethnic and Migration Studies* 35 (3) (2009), pp. 491–506.
8. Basia Spalek. "Community Engagement for Counter-Terrorism in Britain: An Exploration of the Role of 'Connectors' in Countering Takfiri Jihadist Terrorism," *Studies in Conflict & Terrorism*, 2014. doi:10.1080/1057610X.2014.941436; Abdul Hakk Baker. *Extremists in our Midst. Confronting Terror* (London: Palgrave McMillan, 2011).
9. Cornelia Albert, *The Peace Building Elements of the Belfast Agreement and the Transformation of the Northern Ireland conflict* (London: Routledge, 2009); Peter Shirlow, Brian Graham, Kieran McEvoy, Feilim O hAdhmaill, and Dawn Purvis, *Politically Motivated Former Prisoner Groups: Community Activism and Conflict Transformation* (Belfast: Northern Ireland Community Relations Council, 2005).
10. Peter Shirlow, *Politically Motivated Former Prisoners: Evaluation of the Core Funding Project 2006–2008* (Belfast: Community Foundations of Northern Ireland, 2008); Peter Shirlow, Brian Graham, Kieran McEvoy, Feilim O hAdhmaill, and Dawn Purvis, *Politically Motivated Former Prisoner Groups: Community Activism and Conflict Transformation* (Belfast: Northern Ireland Community Relations Council, 2005); Peter Shirlow and Kieran McEvoy, *Beyond the Wire: Former Prisoners and Conflict Transformation in Northern Ireland* (London: Pluto Press, 2008).
11. Spalek, "Community Engagement for Counter-Terrorism in Britain," *Studies in Conflict & Terrorism* (2014). doi:10.1080/1057610X.2014.941436; Basia Spalek, *Governing Terror: Trust, Community and Counter-terrorism* (London: Bloomsbury Academic Press, 2013).
12. Brian Gormally, Shadd Maruna, and Kieran McEvoy, *Thematic Evaluation of Funded Projects: Politically-Motivated Former Prisoners and their Families* (Belfast: Institute of Criminology and Criminal Justice School of Law Queen's University Belfast, 2007). Available at PN_%5b+Thematic+Evaluation+of+Funded+Projects+Politically+motivated+former+prisoners+and+their+families%5d_020210-1.pdf (accessed December 2015).
13. Ruth Jamieson, Peter Shirlow, and Adrian Grounds, *Ageing and Social Exclusion among Former Politically Motivated Prisoners in Northern Ireland* (Belfast: Changing Ageing Partnership, 2010). Available at http://www.law.qub.ac.uk/schools/SchoolofLaw/Research/InstituteofCriminologyandCriminalJustice/Publications/worddocs/Filetoupload,226499,en.pdf (accessed 24 June 2015).
14. John Horgan, "De-Radicalization or Disengagement? A Process in Need of Clarity and a Counterterrorism Initiative in Need of Evaluation," *Revista de Psicologia Social*, 24 (2) (2011), pp. 291–298.
15. Dena C. Carson, Dana Peterson, and Finn Aage Esbensen, "Youth Gang Desistance: An Examination of the Effect of Different Operational Definitions of Desistance on the Motivations, Methods Associated with Leaving the Gang," *Criminal Justice Review* 38 (2012), p. 510.
16. Ibid.
17. Kieran McEvoy, Peter Shirlow, and Karen McElrath, "Resistance, Transition and Exclusion: Politically Motivated Ex-Prisoners and Conflict Transformation in Northern Ireland," *Terrorism and Political Violence* 16 (3) (2004), pp. 646–670.

18. Bertjan Doosje, Naomi Ellemers, and Russell Spears, "Perceived Intragroup Variability as a Function of Group Status and Identification," *Journal of Experimental Social Psychology* 31(5) (1995), pp. 410–436; Naomi Ellemers, Ad Van Knippenberg, and Henk Wilke, "The Influence of Permeability of Group Boundaries and Stability of Group Status on Strategies of Individual Mobility and Social Change," *British Journal of Social Psychology* 29 (3) (1990), pp. 233–246.
19. Henry Tajfel, ed., *Differentiation between Social Groups: Studies in the Social Psychology of Intergroup Relations* (London: Academic Press).
20. Gabi Haager, Amelie Mummenden, Rosemarie Mielke, Mathias Blanz, Uwe Peter Kanine, "Zum Zusammenhang von negativer sozialer Identität und Vergleichen zwischen Personen und Gruppen: Eine Felduntersuchung in Ost-und Westdeutschland," *Zeitschrift fur Sozialpsychologie* 27 (1996): 259–277.
21. Kieran McEvoy, Peter Shirlow, and Karen McElrath, "Resistance, Transition and Exclusion: Politically Motivated Ex-Prisoners and Conflict Transformation in Northern Ireland," *Terrorism and Political Violence* 16(3) (2004), pp. 646–670.
22. Kieran McEvoy and Peter Shirlow, "Re-Imagining DDR: Ex-Combatants, Leadership and Moral Agency in Conflict Transformation," *Theological Criminology* 13 (1) (2009), pp. 31–59; Clare Mitchell, "The Limits of Legitimacy: Former Loyalist Combatants and Peace-Building in Northern Ireland," *Irish Political Studies* 23 (1) (2008), pp. 1–19; Kieran McEvoy, Peter Shirlow, and Karen McElrath, "Resistance, Transition and Exclusion: Politically Motivated Ex-Prisoners and Conflict Transformation in Northern Ireland," *Terrorism and Political Violence* 16 (3) (2004), pp. 646–670.
23. Mitchell, "The Limits of Legitimacy."
24. Community Restorative Justice Ireland, *Standards and Values of Community Restorative Justice Practice*. 2010. Available at http://crji.ie/wp-content/uploads/2010/12/CRJI-Standards-and-Values.pdf (accessed December 2015).
25. Virginia Braun and Victoria Clarke, "Using Thematic Analysis in Psychology," *Qualitative Research in Psychology* 3 (2) (2006), pp. 77–101.
26. Kenneth L. Pike, *Language in Relation to a Unified Theory of the Structure of Human Behavior* (2nd ed.) (The Hague: Mouton, 1954).
27. Braun and Clarke, "Using Thematic Analysis in Psychology."
28. Charles Antaki and Sue Widdicombe, eds., *Identities in Talk* (London: Sage, 1998); Jonathon Potter, *Representing Reality: Discourse Rhetoric and Social Construction* (London: Sage, 1996); Derek Edwards and Jonathon Potter, *Discursive Psychology* (London: Sage, 1992).
29. Dena C. Carson, Dana Peterson, and Finn Aage Esbensen, "Youth Gang Desistance: An Examination of the Effect of Different Operational Definitions of Desistance on the Motivations, Methods Associated with Leaving the Gang," *Criminal Justice Review* 38 (2012), p. 510.
30. Ken Pennington and Orla Lynch, "Counterterrorism, Community Policing and the Flags Protests: An Examination of Police Perceptions of Northern Ireland's Operation Dulcet," *Studies in Conflict & Terrorism* 38(7) (2015), pp. 543–559.
31. Shaun D. Bushway, Terrance P. Thornberry, and Marvin, D. Krohn, "Desistance as a Developmental Process. A Comparison of Static and Dynamic Approaches," *Journal of Quantitative Criminology* 19 (2003), pp. 129–153.
32. Erving Goffman, *Forms of Talk* (Philadelphia: University of Pennsylvania Press, 1981).
33. Steven J. Heine, Travis Proulx, and Katheen D. Vohs, "The Meaning Maintenance Model: On the Coherence of Social Motivations," *Personality and Social Psychology Review* 10 (2) (2006), pp. 88–110.
34. Richard English, *Armed Struggle. The Story of the IRA* (London: Palgrave MacMillan, 2003); Shirlow et al., *Politically Motivated Former Prisoner Groups*.
35. Goffman, *Forms of Talk*.
36. Ibid.
37. Samuel L. Gaertner and John F. Dovidio, *Common Ingroup Identity Model. The Encyclopedia of Peace Psychology* (2011). doi: 10.1002/9780470672532.wbepp041
38. Michael Wenzel, Amélie Mummendey, and Sven Waldzus, "Superordinate Identities and Intergroup Conflict: The Ingroup Projection Model," *European Review of Social Psychology* 18(1) (2007), pp. 331–372.

39. Martin Innes, "Policing Uncertainty: Countering Terror through Community Intelligence and Democratic Policing," *The ANNALS of the American Academy of Political and Social Science* 605 (1) (2006), pp. 222–241.
40. Jonathon Potter, *Representing Reality: Discourse Rhetoric and Social Construction* (London: Sage, 1996).
41. Gordon W. Alport, *The Nature of Prejudice* (Cambridge, MA: Perseus Books, 1954).
42. Shirlow, *Politically Motivated Former Prisoners*; McEvoy and Shirlow, "Re-Imagining DDR: Ex-Combatants, Leadership and Moral Agency in Conflict Transformation," *Theological Criminology* 13(1) (2009), pp. 31–59; Shirlow et al., *Politically Motivated Former Prisoner Groups*.
43. Rhiannon N. Turner, Richard J. Crisp, and Emily Lambert, "Imagining Intergroup Contact can Improve Intergroup Attitudes," *Group Processes and Intergroup Relations* 10 (2007), pp. 427–441.
44. Mitchell, "The Limits of Legitimacy"; Gormally, Maruna, and McEvoy, *Thematic Evaluation of Funding Projects*.
45. Bushway, Thornberry, and Krohn, "Desistance as a Developmental Process."

U.K. Foreign Fighters to Syria and Iraq: The Need for a *Real* Community Engagment Approach

Tanya Silverman

ABSTRACT
A growing number of British youth are traveling to join the Islamic State of Iraq and Syria and participate in the conflict. In this modern iteration of "foreign fighters" community driven countering violent extremism (CVE) efforts remain necessary as the age of travelers to the conflict zone from geographical hotspots in the United Kingdom decreases, and numbers of those going increases. It is their immediate environments—their communities—which can help to prevent violent radicalization and subsequent travel to conflict. Weaknesses in the government's approaches to community engagement can lessen the efficacy of community CVE capacity. This article aims to highlight some of these weaker U.K. government approaches while suggesting ways to improve community engagement that can strengthen CVE efforts.

Increasing numbers of British youth are traveling to the conflict in Syria and Iraq together with their Western counterparts, joining groups such as the Islamic State of Iraq and Syria (ISIS) and Jabhat al-Nusra. The United Kingdom, like many countries across Europe, has begun to implement softer and more holistic measures to combat this phenomenon, alongside punitive measures. This article focuses on the United Kingdom's community-focused measures and engagement with community members and organizations, offering a vision for community engagement that may help to prevent the violent radicalization and subsequent departure of U.K. nationals to Syria and Iraq.

The number of individuals that have traveled to fight or support rebel groups in the conflict zone is unparalleled in U.K. history, at an estimated 700.[1] That such large numbers of British nationals have been radicalized and recruited into violent-extremist groups incites fears for domestic security. The "foreign fighter" phenomenon has made clear that the threat from violent-extremist groups has become multifaceted. While these groups may continue to operate under centralized leadership, they are more unpredictable thanks to their "lone wolf" supporters that carry out attacks on home soil. These fears are not unwarranted and events such as the November 2015 Paris attacks and the March 2016 Brussels bombings serve as a reminder of the capacity of these lone wolves to cause devastation. While "lone actor terrorism" is not a new phenomenon, research suggests the threat is increasing as groups call on their supporters to act alone without direction or support.[2] This makes the group and its U.K.-based "fans" difficult to track or predict.

For this reason softer approaches to countering violent extremism (CVE) and prevention are taking center stage in policy formation in the United Kingdom and across Europe. For example, the United Kingdom's Counter-Extremism Strategy highlights the need to work with those most at risk and places emphasis on the need to counter the ideological narratives of violent-extremist groups.[3] In this current iteration of foreign fighters[4] community-driven CVE remains necessary as a younger demographic of British men and women are traveling to the conflict zone from geographical hotspots. Therefore, it is their immediate environments—their communities—which may have a fighting chance to prevent departure and reduce the capacity of returnees to be a threat.[5] U.K. policy recognizes the importance of the role community plays in countering violent radicalization and safeguarding youth from joining violent-extremist groups. Particular emphasis is placed on the need to build "cohesive communities" and this will be actioned by the government's Cohesive Communities Programme in 2016.[6] This is also evidenced by its Prevent strategy partnerships that outline the need to work at a local and community level with, for example, local authorities and Community Safety Partnerships.[7] However, government's community engagement needs development, especially as the United Kingdom and communities tackle the issue of violent radicalization and foreign fighter departure from different angles. This author uses "community engagement" to mean *positive* engagement, whereby communities are active partners included in decision making that affects them.

From this starting point, this article briefly paints a portrait of the individuals that are going, and where from the United Kingdom they are going from. This will underscore the importance of community work as it is discovered that many foreign fighters are youth that come from geographical hotspots in the United Kingdom. However, demographic factors are not what lead an individual to want to go and fight, but rather mean that a youth may be vulnerable to being targeted by violent-extremist messaging. Instead, it is important to assess their motivations for wanting to travel. There are three main motivating factors. A number of community organizations work to counter these motivations, and three examples will be provided to highlight some of the important work being carried out at a community level. Again, this will consolidate the importance of community and highlight that there are different, valuable ways of tackling the same problem. Despite government's efforts to work with community, there are still weaknesses in this approach. These will be briefly outlined. This article ends, not with a conclusion, but a vision for an inclusive and open approach that may help to strengthen U.K.-wide CVE efforts.

Foreign Fighters: "A/S/L?"[8]

There is no one discernible profile of foreign fighters and demographic characteristics of foreign fighters vary from person to person. Additionally, missed notices or unreported deaths suggest numbers of individual foreign fighters could be far higher than the estimates provided.[9] Still, much has been learned from the heavy social media presence of individuals known to have traveled that can help provide a sound interpretation of who they are and where they are from. Specific push–pull factors vary considerably, and will not be addressed. Demographics by no means dictate whether or not an individual is at risk of violent radicalization; however, violent-extremist groups and recruiters are adept at seeking out who may be vulnerable to their narratives. Instead, understanding the demographics of these often young individuals and where they come from underscore the value of their surrounding community.

Recent studies have found that among those joining Islamist groups men are an average age of 25 and are typically older than women, which average 21.[10] Simultaneously, the age of individuals in the United Kingdom that are the subject of counterterrorism work has decreased, with 1 in 6 under 20.[11] The conflict remains attractive to male and female teenagers, adhering to the general trend that recruits to violent-extremist groups have been getting younger since the mid-2000s.[12] Data further demonstrate that among these individuals are mostly second or third generation immigrants that have few or no prior connections to Syria, while 6 percent converted from an alternative denomination prior to radicalization and departure. The majority have little to no combat experience.[13] The increase in numbers of females traveling is of growing concern, not least because of the risk of rape and abuse in Syria. Up to one-fifth are females and in the last year 40 females left from London alone.[14]

As such, it is also insightful to evaluate the distribution of foreign fighters from within the United Kingdom. This represents a growing trend that despite attention to online networks, offline networks are key and current U.K. strategies toward cities, councils, and boroughs in CVE is failing to prevent violent radicalization and departure. It has been determined "radicalisation and self-recruitment via the internet with little or no relation to the outside world rarely happens."[15] This is axiomatic from the geographical concentrations of departure in the United Kingdom. The European Union's Radicalisation Awareness Network (RAN) states that "the vast majority of foreign fighters consist of inhabitants from a limited selection of cities [and] this selection of cities is not always self-evident, as it does not always concern the cities with the largest Islamic communities."[16] Through an analysis of 160 profiles the BBC highlighted geographical clusters of would-be foreign fighter travel. This revealed that in many cases people have traveled in groups from localized and social networks.[17] The majority foreign fighters have departed from London, Manchester, Birmingham, and Luton. However, these cities are not the only hotspots.

Two female friends fleeing from Portsmouth to Syria[18] and the "Pompey Lads" underscore the insight that many departures are occurring in groups from cities across the United Kingdom. Living in close proximity the six males were known to attend Portsmouth's Jami Mosque and Islamic Centre. They were in close contact with another Portsmouth fighter, Iftekar Jaman, whom had already made the journey to Syria in May 2013.[19] Similarly, Tower Hamlets council raided a school, suspecting links to al-Muhajiroun.[20] Local news stated five schoolgirls—subjected to travel bans due to suspected intent to travel—attended the same Bethnal Green Academy as the three girls who had traveled to Syria in February 2015.[21] Police had sent letters to their parents warning that Sharmeena Begum, a friend of the girls, had left two months before. Research postulates that there "is much evidence to suggest that the nature of this friendship group allowed for rapid and collective radicalisation, with the girls mutually informing and policing each other's views in a closed-community vacuum."[22]

Stuart observes that 46 percent of terrorist offenses have been committed by someone based in the capital: "London will always be at the centre of things because students are coming through and radical preachers are often based there, but the problem has now spread to commuter belt towns like High Wycombe."[23] Located in Buckinghamshire, the area has had a disproportionate number of travelers. Stuart profiled foreign fighters from the area that have departed. Among them was Omar Hussain, a 27-year-old security guard whom threatened to bomb the United Kingdom following his departure to Syria, and grammar-school student Shabazz Suleman. Three homes were also raided, connected to a bombing plot by those suspected of wanting to travel to Syria.[24]

There are a range of narratives that may have catalyzed the violent radicalization of individuals such as Suleman. However, the final decision to travel is largely owing to motivational drivers.

Motivation Gets You Started, Habit Keeps You Going

That many of these foreign fighters are young and leave in groups underscores the need to work locally and at a community level to prevent departure. Interviews with Western foreign fighters from across conflicts and localities suggest three primary motivations for this.[25] These are not the only motivating factors among individuals but were found to be most prevalent: (1) an adherence to the ideology of the group an individual wishes to join, (2) a search for identity and belonging, and (3) outrage toward what is alleged to be happening in the country of conflict and empathy with people being affected. Additional common drivers are: foreign policy grievances, national policy, and intergenerational conflict.

Outlining these, while highlighting community-driven programs that aim to lessen the catalyzing effect of these motivations, will serve to highlight some of the sound work of community organizations aiming to reduce the motivating factors leading to travel. It will also accentuate the United Kingdom's need to strengthen these (and similar) community initiatives' ability to overcome motivations for travel. This will help to underscore the need for a number of community organizations to be funded that have the same overall aim of countering polarization, integration, and countering violent extremism.

Adherence to the Ideology

Adherence to, or at least a lack of antagonism toward, the ideology of a group is a common motivational factor. Ideology is taken to mean a belief—whether inherent or at face value. This encompasses socioreligious and nationalist beliefs.[26] Many that radicalized to groups like ISIS became committed ideologues in part through offline socialization. Groups such as Faith Associations that "aim to meet the needs of ethnic-minority faith-based communities" and "recognise the key roles of Mosques, Madrassahs and Islamic Centres play in providing guidance"[27] can play a key early role by supporting relevant institutions that are best-positioned to counter violent-extremist ideologues by unpacking their self-serving worldview.

Search for Identity and Belonging

As youths look to define themselves, travel to Syria becomes a "coming of age" story. There is the need to achieve a sense of personal fulfilment and to perpetuate self-perceived identity by way of comparing to others. Foreign fighting can be thought of as "inherently related to self-identification"[28] and the concept acknowledges that attachments to both origin and host countries are not necessarily mutually exclusive.[29] Throughout history, insurgencies "recruited by framing local wars as threatening a shared transnational identity group thereby necessitating defensive mobilisation."[30] Given these violent-extremist recruitment narratives appeal to foreign fighters by giving a sense of purpose-cum-identity within transnational groups, the role of communities to do the same becomes apparent. They can provide foreign fighters more reason to stay than to travel.

As such, local communities can outweigh tempting extremist narratives by acting as a counterbalance that can help to realize the gaps of personal fulfilment. MyExtremism aims to help realize these gaps through extreme sports. Clayson is the managing director of the group, who also hails from a professional counterterrorism background. He explains that "an addiction-like craving for [adrenaline] bonds extreme sports athletes of all ages, genders and nationalities and these moments form the core of our identity."[31] Clayson continues that the geographical distance physically separating extreme athletes is reduced by shared identities that transcend these distances. In addition, he explains that it can appeal to the need for adventure in youth that is often manipulated by extremist groups. The United Kingdom's current approach, which aims to tackle the ideology of extremist groups, does not give enough due credit to similar initiatives that do not necessarily focus on ideology.

Outrage at What is Happening

The initial hook that fosters the interest many fighters feel toward a particular conflict does not have to resonate from a detailed ideological theme. It can be a simple emotional reaction to what is professedly taking place in the conflict, that is, violence toward women or children, whether real or manipulated by extremist groups to fit into their self-serving narratives. They aspire to "do something" to stop this violence. The media age hastens this process, allowing images of warfare and discord from a conflict to be readily available.[32] In a world where atrocities, real or imagined, are being carried out and conflicts are readily viewable through media sources it is unsurprising that some feel driven to act.

Given that much of this anger can be a result of foreign or domestic policy that governments have implemented, community approaches may provide better routes to catharsis than government. The JAN Trust, for example, aims to help parents of vulnerable youth to realize how to approach the grievances that these policies might incite. They have "had mothers come to [them] and say 'I've stopped my child travelling to Syria.'" This is largely due to mothers being empowered to speak to their children, taught how to use the Internet, and what signs to look for that may indicate a desire to travel to Syria.[33]

Bomb Blast to Bombast: Stop Talking, Start Acting

The previous section has briefly underscored the value of community organizations in this space by showing that there are different approaches to the same problem. However, different bodies have different standards for engagement, which are more likely to fail as governments and community groups have different ways of tackling CVE,[34] and by extension foreign fighters. While the United Kingdom has made efforts to engage with community organizations and members, there is still room for improvement. This section highlights some weaknesses of the current U.K. approach in three primary areas: open dialogue and transparency, working with the right institutions, and working locally. These factors have been grouped together by the author following a mapping of the problems that many community-based or community-level organizations and institutions have endured, and is by no means extensive.

Open Dialogue and Transparency

Moisi has asserted that communities share emotions such as fear, as well as identities and meaning.[35] This is often overlooked considering the inarguably natural human response that policy language such as "counter-violent extremism" or "counterterrorism" might evoke within people. It is only understandable that communities may be less willing to open dialogue about these issues. This fear is further pronounced in communities that have been witness to violent radicalization and foreign fighter departures, and in some communities even more so following a domestic or even international event that creates subsequent tremors within said community. For example, disgust at the beheading of U.K. humanitarian aid worker David Haines in 2014 sent shockwaves the world over. Those that felt the aftermath of this were Muslim communities for the fear that the finger will be pointed at them by default of their faith.[36] Long-term and transparent engagement will make people more willing to open dialogue, rather than engagement that is clearly reactive and relational to an event.

This dialogue has often discounted many critical voices. Spalek and Lambert note that voices of young Muslims and women that are "particularly likely to be marginalised through usual consultation processes."[37] Further, when one looks at community as a microcosm of society this becomes evident. Their role in CVE has been undermined by a lack of engagement through quality dialogue. The importance of women and youth is however steadily being recognised.

Women can be "agents of change [...] they are the ones who can nurture and safeguard their children."[38] However, a 2011 study conducted by the Association of Chief Police Officers states that Muslim women have had little contact or interaction with the police.[39] While authorities recognize this, a lack of interaction via trust-building was the likely downfall of Bedfordshire's Project Shahnaz that aimed to include local women in CVE work.[40] The Project relaunched as the Women's Network in 2013 and was established to encourage women to "play an active part in the Government's Prevent agenda," while providing a platform for the Network "to participate as equals in decision-making around the development of policy and strategy, in an area of policing which impacts directly upon them."[41] The re-branding of the project into a network has likely helped, reducing the connotations that Muslim women are a CVE "project" and it is more representative of a cross-section of women, not just Muslim, in communities.

While this is a step in the right direction, the process of trust building will still take time. This trust is slowly being built through women's participation in former Deputy Assistant Commissioner (DAC) Helen Ball's "#PreventTragedies" advisory committee that began last year in response to the issue of foreign fighters. Further, it encourages open and honest dialogue between police and community members that attend so that both parties can better understand each other's roles and concerns while highlighting women's roles in "prevention-as-safeguarding" rather than "prevention-for-security" regarding foreign fighters.[42] Briggs and Silverman elaborate on this in their review of community CVE efforts, stressing that a safeguarding role needs to involve and strengthen women and women's organizations' roles to fill the void that government cannot, given their close proximity to the community. However, they explain many parents and community members "lack the knowledge and skills to be able to perform [this] role and need support and guidance from government agencies."[43]

Open dialogue and transparency encompasses informing communities as part of an information exchange, otherwise it becomes a monologue—talking *at* rather than *with*. Trust between communities and police is still lacking and makes engagement harder. Spalek has explained that in a low-trust context it is important for police to focus on trust building before expecting necessary partnerships.[44] This mistrust is catalyzed by the suspicion that the United Kingdom's Prevent strategy arouses in the communities it seeks to work with or, as Spalek and McDonald explain,[45] communities are not being given as much information as they are asked to give. This lack of exchange has resulted in specific communities feeling they are under surveillance, compromising CVE efforts.[46] This was worsened by the failed Project Champion that prioritized surveillance.[47] Information should include not only signs to look out for but also their rights and responsibilities as communities that may feel targeted by CVE policy frameworks.[48] Prevent continues to come under fire from community groups[49] for its branding as part of "Pursue, Prevent, Protect, Prepare," which makes up the United Kingdom's counterterrorism CONTEST strategy.[50] Research found "many interviewees felt that defining the 'Prevent space' internally within the police organisations had negative implications for external public-facing relations" that were exacerbated by a lack of "understanding [of] how it is positioned somewhere between traditional models of 'Pursue' counter-terrorist policing and [...] Neighbourhood Policing."[51]

This underscores that a lack of the standardization of implementation of CVE policy across the United Kingdom's institutional bodies reflects on community groups' inability to work coherently *with* said bodies. From its inception in 2005 to present day attitudes toward Prevent have generally remained negative in the media and among many communities and community organizations. Increasing transparency of Prevent and its Channel intervention project will help in reducing the fear that closed doors can incite.[52] Further, secrecy perpetuates the notion that communities are something to be secretive about. A lack of transparency over "systems, processes and clarity"[53] of Prevent has left the unsavory taste of a "toxic legacy" that has been difficult to turn sweet. These community attitudes have remained unchanged from Pantazis and Pemberton's studies until today, as highlighted by O'Toole et al.[54] whereby many communities still feel "suspect." Positive aspects of Prevent need to be highlighted so that, over time, perceptions change and increasing transparency around policies can reduce the barriers to engagement, opening dialogue.

Working with the Right Institutions

Working with trusted local institutions is recognized as being critical to efficient community partnerships. The Department for Communities and Local Government (DCLG), a ministerial institution aiming to empower local people to shape local issues, discovered that local institutions are better placed to engage with and understand key issues in communities, especially when trust in government institutions is lower.[55] Government needs to allow and encourage local institutions to work with their communities.

Maximizing the role community organizations can play in ensuring certain communities do not feel marginalized or targeted is important. U.K. CVE policy acknowledges that engaging with specific institutions is important to reach some communities but argues that this should not become an obstacle to issues of social integration, which is often seen as a cause of radicalization and later travel.[56] However, there is an ever present question over what community groups or institutions constitute an obstacle to social integration, and extremism in the United Kingdom is often defined by those juxtaposing "fundamental British values": democracy, the rule of law, individual liberty, and mutual respect and tolerance for different faiths and beliefs. The term is inherently linked to the U.K. extremism debate and is criticized as harmful rhetoric that can serve to exacerbate polarization in communities.

Government engagement continues to concern itself with working with select community groups and institutions. Gilchrist observes that this has led to the government discounting the voices of many communities, which is creating an oppressive shared identity.[57] An earlier, un-actioned draft 2015 Counter Extremism Strategy outlined plans to introduce penalties for not learning English and tightening rules on granting citizenship in a bid to improve integration and deal with the perceived growing threat from ISIS.[58] This exacerbates an oppressive shared identity. This is certainly not fitting with the definition of British values, but rather seems as though the finger is being pointed at closed communities. Not only is this counterproductive to addressing the actual needs of certain communities, but this ever present rhetoric only further stigmatizes communities and respective organizations by putting public pressure on ethnic communities to show allegiance to these values.

Gilchrist et al. also suggest that closed communities can feel "secure and can 'be themselves' without fear of ridicule, misunderstanding, or hostility."[59] Instead, rhetoric that builds "a sense of commonality around real life issues—such as life ambitions and local problems—is regarded as having most value" and can break down feelings such as mistrust and embarrassment.[60] Another socializing agent that has "primed Muslim populations to feel further isolated or culturally secluded […] is the media."[61] While government bodies do not have control over the media they need to realize that whatever policy is being introduced or discussed can send the right or wrong message to communities and community-groups. Further, research has shown there is a gross mistrust by Muslims for some Western media outlets, leading them to turn to sources on the Internet, thus breeding discontent.[62] This discontent can exacerbate the issues that lead to violent radicalization and subsequent foreign fighter departure. Reducing negative rhetoric in speechmaking will ensure that the "media monster" is left hungry and does not add to these feelings of discontent.

Further, the rhetoric of British values underpins a strict policy of not working with nonviolent extremist groups. Hesitancy to working with these groups is exacerbated by the "conveyor belt" metaphor to preventing violent radicalization wherein radical views can be a precursor to violent radicalization or terrorism. This view has been promoted by government ministers over the last decade, but it is hotly contested.[63] However, these same institutions now deemed unsavory to work with can facilitate interaction with other communities so that their existence is embedded in a wider, positive, sociopolitical environment. This fosters a "divide and rule" approach as described by Spalek and Lambert and is problematic when considering Lambert's notion, which advocates that nonviolent extremists are best to deal with violent-extremists.[64] Further, by choosing not to work with certain community groups that likely all have an interest in the safeguarding of their children, the United Kingdom's current CVE strategy does not look like one aimed at protecting vulnerable youth but one that is still security-driven. As Moodood explains, working across a range of community groups embedding youth at risk of becoming extremist within those communities is crucial,[65] especially as it is the communities that are marginalized that may hold greater legitimacy to prevent their drift toward extremism, rather than the communities that the government deems "safe" to work with. While steps have been made in the right direction to include some voices, those of other religious strands are still unrepresented and there is still space for communities to be active participants in the delivery of policy outcomes.[66]

The importance of working with the right institutions is highlighted when considering community attitudes toward the implementation of Prevent in local areas. Ivanescu, in 2013, used the example of Leicester to assert that "Prevent came attached with the stigma of the special needs of the populations it was designed for" and that its "effect has been a competition between Muslim groups within the city for the limited resources provided under Prevent."[67] This perception remains present, and recently Prevent is seen to have been forced CVE on educational institutions, fueling debate over civil freedoms. It is not widely understood that this is a misperception among the public and communities, wherein the duty of educational institutions is a set of advice to safeguard children that schools "do not have to follow."[68]

Additionally, working with the right institutions should remain inclusive of working *right with them* and prioritizing not only statutory needs, but community needs, as accurately iterated by Spalek and Baker.[69] Following the codification of the roles of institutions as part of Prevent in the Counter-Terrorism and Security Act 2015[70] the University and College Union (UCU) released a set of guidelines for its branches and members. Education establishments are social meeting hubs within communities. Although UCU guidelines state "there are many aspects of the Prevent duty which remain unclear [...] many colleges and universities are already developing guidance and this briefing is designed to allow branches to engage with that process."[71]

There is a lack of clarity surrounding the role of educational institutions. This again underscores the internal confusion within UK bodies that, by default, causes confusion within the very institutions they aim to work with—i.e. schools and universities. This is problematic, because it can create inconsistencies in institutions' approaches to working with Prevent and a confused attitude toward just how they should work to protect the localities they are in. Although Workshop Raising Awareness for Prevent training is frequently updated, and delivery of training has been supercharged,[72] there needs to be a precursor to the training to ensure that frontline professionals are on board before the training, but also joint training so that frontline professionals across sectors understand what constitutes a "green" or "red" flag in their eyes—what might be concerning to a nurse may not be to a teacher. This can complicate referrals across sectors bottom-up.

Schools are also crucial to community engagement when one considers the important role families can play in preventing foreign fighter departure. An open letter to Members of Parliament from Slough's Chair of Governors of Iqra Islamic Primary School voices such concerns, stating "government appears to be listening to only a few selective groups and this is creating an impression that no one else is participating in making our community safe" and this is causing frustration.[73] Parents are often board members of schools and are more likely to be involved in school activities than when their children are at college or university. As such, positive engagement with schools could create a positive, or less contested, view of CVE work to prevent departures, or at least work toward filtering awareness into parent-communities. Families need to be supported to both interpret problematic language and behavior but they must also be equipped with the knowledge and tools that will enable them to create an atmosphere where discussion and conversation can take place with relatives at risk.[74]

Working with education institutions is especially important when considering the nature of foreign fighter departures as geographic clusters and the peer networks of youth that have departed together, as outlined previously. As Bjorgo rightly asserts, "parents, schools and religious communities play leading roles in instilling moral attitudes"[75] that lead to the development of empathy and can prevent violent radicalization.

Working Locally

The idea of "community" is heavily featured in social policy as a significant resource for tackling crime and social problems by working with a number of government statutory bodies or voluntary sector organizations."[76] However, "this reflects broader developments in governance, whereby responsibility and accountability for crime is increasingly focused towards local levels, whilst at the same time centralised control in terms of resources and target setting is maintained."[77] Adequate decisions about the local level cannot be made without local-level stakeholders.

When remembering that departures from the United Kingdom appear to occur from specific localities the need for working at a local level becomes pronounced. A 2015 report by the London-based community organization Faith Matters argues that the current iteration of the Prevent strategy has moved away from community engagement. They state that while the move toward a more centralized and top-down approach has succeeded in making Prevent more focused, it is "not likely to assemble the necessary resources, partners and stakeholders" to achieve its goals.[78] Further, it reduces funding for important groups working in this field by providing it to "friends."[79] Ganesh asserts that where Prevent engagement was conducted in some partnership with local Muslim communities, it now sees them as recipients of training rather than equal stakeholders, which Ganesh owes to "fixation on ideology" and contributes to a centralized and top-down approach.[80] In the author's discussions with police and security authorities at the Challenge Panel, a quarterly expert and community leader exchange concerning U.K. approaches to the violent-extremist threat, it was evident that security and police were also troubled by this. Unfortunately, policy is created and they have to work with it.[81] Including police and local police in policymaking dialogue will also be fruitful.

A top-down approach becomes problematic when one considers that priorities vary according to local areas and the availability of services. The need for geographical focus and empowering local governments is underscored by the way local communities have begun working more closely with local councils.[82] Following a spate of departures to Syria and Iraq from Tower Hamlets, schools encouraged a Community Plan to be motioned that foremost takes the views of community members into account. The plan builds on previous ones, by setting out key strategic themes and achievements for people in the borough to tackle the threat from violent extremism. It also takes action where previous plans have not by re-initiating old projects that ran 2007–2008, and starts new ones engaging local community groups in preventing violent extremism.[83] However, these positive developments will not continue to have successes unless responses are continually designed in a manner that addresses local problems.

Powers describes a training program in West Yorkshire's Halifax that aims to do this.[84] Developed in 2009, "Things Do Change" sets out to prevent violent extremism in young people and was inspired by 7/7. Three individuals involved in the attack hailed from West Yorkshire, which spurred interest in local government to create a program to deter the ideologies that would lead to such an event. Furthermore, the training program supplements formal education surrounding CVE, which teachers at formal education institutions are still hesitant to discuss. Powers asserts that the program addresses key voids, such as "the lack of bridge building between communities and the need to address enclavisation in immigrant populations."[85] Further, Suleman, the program lead, states this as a result of developing organic, not reactive, rapport in multi-ethnic communities.

Suleman explains that most Muslim communities prefer to solve problems locally by local means, rather than with interference from those outside.[86] This has also been the experience of the South-U.K. Prevent co-ordinator. His thoughts are that it is not necessarily "a matter of not trusting the police or government" but, rather, it is for fear of embarrassing their community and being met with disrespect from the outside."[87]

Working locally encompasses working in all localities. Currently, the U.K. government has outlined a number of "priority cities" that are thought to be hot-beds of radicalization. While at a national level this might be useful to target limited resources, it can also overblow the "threat," thus polarizing communities. Further, priorities may change and it is better to work across localities and with longevity than wait to for matters to deteriorate and become "reactive" to target resources, adding to a cycle of polarization.

Despite Tower Hamlets, London, as a priority area, has been witness to a distinct lack of resources being filtered into community groups there. One community representative explained that 0.01 percent of funding for the third sector went into the Somali community, a demographic that is notably hard to reach, and that there are no Somali youth organizations in the area.[88] She went on to explain that due to the lack of support, whole families have traveled to Syria and Iraq.

This further emphasizes the need for local issues to be dealt with locally, and a top-down approach will not help to achieve this. Evaluating geographically targeted projects or initiatives will be difficult, further adding to the difficulty of rolling out projects nationwide. Those that work in one area may not work in another. Returning to a community engagement style of Prevent could do this by continuing to work on local engagement and empowering local governments to strengthen community efforts. However, yearly government cuts to local services simultaneous to the focused attention on national CVE strategies are not helping to improve engagement.

Moving Toward a Better Approach

This article has argued for the value of community in CVE. However, many community-based organizations and institutions are being incapacitated by the current U.K. approach to CVE and foreign fighters. Community-level work can be strengthened by *real* community engagement that works toward building a process. This process should be ongoing and build permanent relationships, and include decision making at a local level, rather than as a reactive and top-down response. The latter lacks an understanding of critical local contexts. This is a myopic view of what is being implemented at a community level. Through community engagement a collective vision toward the phenomenon of foreign fighters and their prevention will assist in reducing the number of vulnerable youth being violently radicalized and traveling to Syria, as well as future iterations of the same problem. This article draws no conclusions. Instead, it suggests a vision for U.K. community engagement that will not only help to tackle the recruitment of vulnerable youth to groups like ISIS, but inevitable future iterations of this threat.

Although there a number of ways in which this can be done, this article has outlined three primary areas in which the United Kingdom can strengthen its approach and work toward improving community engagement:

- *Opening dialogue and transparency*: It is crucial to have an understanding of how national and international issues can affect a community and make them more closed off. Communities share emotions as much they do identities and the fear that current U.K. policies can incite can only be expected to increase barriers to engagement and be detrimental to CVE. Trust building over time can open dialogue and will encourage community members to be more communicative, rather than feeling the subject of security. Transparency about government policies, which currently add to fears of securitization and arouse suspicion of another mode of governance and control, can reduce these barriers. This is especially so when considering at a local level that many communities want to deal with local issues locally. Further, it is necessary to include all voices in this dialogue and while there have been steps to doing this, as shown by the Prevent Tragedies campaign, there needs to be more of this to avoid ongoing marginalization of some communities. Being transparent about issues at both a national and local level will begin the critical process of trust building that is necessary for this while serving to reduce the "toxic brand" of U.K. CVE initiatives.

- *Working with the right institutions*: working with institutions that are trusted among their communities—as opposed to ones that are just trusted by the U.K. government—will empower people to shape local issues and ensure certain communities do not feel marginalized or targeted. This has been exampled not least with the exclusion of nonviolent extremists that can be legitimate and effective in countering violent extremism. This fosters a shared oppression that can lead to grievances exacerbating isolation and breeding discontent. As it stands, there is also still a lack of clarity over what some policies actually *mean*, which causes incoherence between government agencies and communities, making engagement all the more difficult as issues are tackled from different angles across communities, local institutions, and government. Clearer guidelines that are influenced from a local and community level will ensure everyone is on the same page working toward tackling the issue coherently.

- *Working locally*: There is a need to move away from a centralized and top-down approach to one that includes local voices in the community to shape local issues. The lack of funding for Somali community groups in Tower Hamlets exemplifies this, despite Tower Hamlets being a designated "priority area" for Prevent funding. Over time, this can encourage changing the perceptions of U.K. government strategies from that of a harder security-focused one, to having a softer safeguarding role. Understanding that priorities and resources vary according to local areas should empower local governments to take ownership over local issues within their communities: what might work in one place may not work in another. Additionally, working locally means working with peripheral communities as well as central communities that already have visibility. A genuine community engagement approach to Prevent that is inclusive of a range of, if not all, local actors within communities can strengthen community efforts to fulfill their potential as key players in preventing foreign fighter departure.

Notes

1. Peter Neumann, "Foreign Fighters Total in Syria/Iraq Now Exceeds 20,000; Surpasses Afghanistan Conflict in 1980s," *ICSR* (2015). Available at http://icsr.info/2015/01/foreign-fighter-total-syriairaq-now-exceeds-20000-surpasses-afghanistan-conflict-1980s/ (accessed 20 July 2015).
2. Raffaello Pantucci, Clare Ellis, and Lorien Chaplais, "Lone-Actor Terrorism: Literature Review" (2015). RUSI, Chatham House, Universiteit Leiden, Institute for Strategic Dialogue.
3. HM Government, "Counter-Extremism Strategy" (October 2015). Available at https://www.gov.uk/government/uploads/system/uploads/attachment_data/file/470088/51859_Cm9148_Accessible.pdf (accessed 1 February 2015).
4. For a historical study into foreign fighters see Marcello Flores, "History of Foreign Fighters' Involvement in National and International Wars," in Andrea de Guttry, Francesca Capone, and Christophe Paulussen, eds., *Foreign Fighters Under International Law and Beyond* (London, UK: ASSER/Springer Verlag, 2016).
5. Rachel Briggs and Tanya Silverman "Western Foreign Fighters: Innovations in Responding to the Threat," Institute for Strategic Dialogue, London (December 2014) http://www.strategicdialogue.org/wp-content/uploads/2016/02/ISDJ2784_Western_foreign_fighters_V7_WEB.pdf (accessed 01 February 2015).
6. HM Government, "Counter-Extremism Strategy."
7. See: UK Prevent Strategy (2011)
8. "A/S/L?" is an abbreviation for "Age/Sex/Location?" used in online communications.
9. Kristin Archick "European Fighters in Syria and Iraq," *Congressional Research Service* (April 2015). Available at http://www.fas.org/sgp/crs/row/R44003.pdf (accessed 20 July 2015).
10. Peter Bergen, Courtney Schuster, and David Sterman, "ISIS in the West: The New Faces of Extremism," *New America* (November 2015), p. 8. Available at https://static.newamerica.org/attachments/11813-isis-in-the-west-2/ISP-Isis-In-The-West-v2.b4f2e9e3a7c94b9e9bd2a293bae2e759.pdf (accessed 22 February 2016).
11. Author's correspondence at Prevent Tragedies (September 2015).
12. Raffaello Pantucci, "Foreign Fighters—Battle-Hardened Europeans Return Home from Syria" (2014). Available at http://raffaellopantucci.com/2014/01/14/foreign-fighters-battle-hardened-europeans-return-from-syria/ (accessed 20 July 2015).
13. Briggs and Silverman "Western Foreign Fighters"
14. At time of writing: author's correspondence at Prevent tragedies (September 2015). Forty to 60 are thought to have traveled. See Katherine Brown, "Why Are Western Women Joining the Islamic State," *BBC* (2014). Available at http://www.bbc.co.uk/news/uk-29507410 (accessed 19 June 2015).
15. Tim Stevens and Peter Neumann, "Countering Online Radicalisation: A Strategy for Action," *ISCR* (2009), p. 12. http://icsr.info/wp-content/uploads/2012/10/1236768491ICSROnlineRadicalisationReport.pdf (accessed 1 February 2015).
16. See RAN, "Conference Paper RAN Cities Conference Foreign Fighters," *Radicalisation Awareness Network* (2014). Available at http://ec.europa.eu/dgs/home-affairs/what-we-do/networks/radicalisation_awareness_network/cities-conference/docs/conference_paper_cities_conference_en.pdf (accessed 1 February 2015).
17. Gordon Coerera, "MPs Warn on Growing Number of British Jihadists," *BBC* (2015) http://www.bbc.co.uk/news/uk-32059813 (accessed 8 August 2015).
18. The News Portsmouth, "Teenage Women From Portsmouth 'Have Joined ISIS,'" *The News Portsmouth* (2015). Available at http://www.portsmouth.co.uk/news/defence/teenage-women-from-portsmouth-have-joined-jihadist-fighters-in-syria-1-6020724 (accessed 20 July 2015).
19. Mary Anne Weaver, "Her Majesty's Jihadists," *New York Times* (2015). Available at http://www.nytimes.com/2015/04/19/magazine/her-majestys-jihadists.html?_r=0 (accessed 1 February 2015).
20. Richard Adams, Aisha Gani, and Shiv Malik, "Police Raid Unlicensed Islamic School in London," *Guardian* (2014). Available at http://www.theguardian.com/uk-news/2014/oct/03/siddeeq-academy-radical-islam-group (accessed 20 August 2015).

21. Hannah Twiggs, "ISIS Runaways Attended Same Bethnal Green School," *East London Lines* (2015). Available at http://www.eastlondonlines.co.uk/2015/03/bethnal-green-academy-revealed-as-school-of-teenage-girls-banned-from-travelling-to-syria-after-radicalisation-concerns/; See Priya Joshi, "ISIS: Five Teenagers Banned from Travel after Links to IS Runaways School is Revealed," *International Business Times* (2015). Available at http://www.ibtimes.co.uk/isis-five-teenagers-banned-travel-after-link-runaways-school-revealed-1493925 (accessed 20 August 2015).
22. Melanie Smith and Erin Saltman, "Till Martyrdom Do Us Part," *Institute for Strategic Dialogue* (2015), p. 44. Available at http://www.strategicdialogue.org/Till_Martyrdom_Do_Us_Part_Gender_and_the_ISIS_Phenomenon.pdf (accessed 20 August 2015).
23. Hannah Stuart, "Why Do So Many Jihadists Come from a Single Town in England," *Henry Jackson Society* (2014). Available at http://henryjacksonsociety.org/2014/11/11/why-do-so-many-terrorists-come-from-a-single-dead-end-town-in-england/ (accessed 20 August 2015).
24. Vikram Dodd, "Arrests in London and High Wycombe over Alleged Islamist Terror Plot," *Guardian* (2014). Available at http://www.theguardian.com/uk-news/2014/nov/07/alleged-islamist-terror-plot-arrests-london-high-wycombe (accessed 20 August 2015).
25. Based on interviews with FFs across ideologies. See Ross Frenett and Tanya Silverman, "Foreign Fighters: Motivations for Travel to Foreign Conflicts," in Andrea de Guttry, Francesca Capone, and Christophe Paulussen, eds., *Foreign Fighters Under International Law and Beyond* (The Hague: ASSER/Springer Verlag, 2016 March).
26. Author uses definition: Tetsunori Koizumi, "Nationalism as Ideology, Nationalism as Emotion, and the Pitfalls of National Development," *Cybernetics and Systems: An International Journal* 25 (1994), pp. 747–761.
27. See: http://www.faithassociates.co.uk/about-us/
28. Melanie Smith, "'Syria is not for the Syrians, and Iraq is not for the Iraqis': The Islamic State 'Foreign Fighter', Transnationalism and Baghdadi's 'Khilifah.'" MA Dissertation, Kings College London (2014).
29. Klaus F. Zimmerman, Laura Zimmerman, and Amelie F. Constant, "Ethnic Self-Identification of First-Generation Immigrants," *International Migration* Review 41(3) (2007), pp. 761–781.
30. David Malet, "Why Foreign Fighters? Historical Perspectives and Solutions," *Foreign Policy Research Institute* 97 (2010).
31. Personal correspondence with Benjamin Clayson, managing director of Victvs Ltd., registered name for MyExtremism (20 September 2015); see http://www.myextremism.org
32. Gabriel Weimann, "The Emerging Role of Social Media in the Recruitment of Foreign Fighters," in Andrea de Guttry, Francesca Capone, and Christophe Paulussen, eds., *Foreign Fighters Under International Law and Beyond* (The Hague: ASSER/Springer Verlag, 2016 March).
33. See "Our missing girls," posted 21 May 2015. Available at https://jantrust.wordpress.com/
34. Basia Spalek and Robert Lambert, "Muslim Communities, Counter-Terrorism and De-Radicalisation: A Reflective Approach to Engagement," *International Journal of Law, Crime and Justice* 36 (4) (2008), pp. 257–270.
35. Dominique Moisi, *The Geopolitics of Emotion: How Cultures of Fear, Humiliation, and Hope are Reshaping the World* (London: Doubleday, 2009).
36. Interview with Prevent Coordinator (10 March 2015).
37. Spalek and Lambert, "Muslim Communities, Counter-Terrorism and De-Radicalisation," p. 264.
38. Vikram Dodd, Sandra Laville, and Helen Pidd, "Syria Crisis: Stop Your Sons Joining War, Urges Met Police," *Guardian* (2014). Available at http://theguardian.com/uk-news/2014/apr/23/sons-war-syriametropolitan-police (accessed 8 August 2015).
39. Martin Innes, Colin Roberts, and Helen Innes, "Assessing the Effects of Prevent Policing," *Universities' Police Science Institute* (2011). Available at http://www.npcc.police.uk/documents/TAM/2011/PREVENT%20Innes%200311%20Final%20send%202.pdf (accessed 1 February 2015).
40. "Engaging Women in Prevent," *Bedfordshire Police* (2015). Available at http://www.bedfordshire.police.uk/tackling_crime/counter_terrorism/prevent/engaging_women_in_prevent.aspx (accessed 8 September 2015).
41. Ibid.

42. Author's correspondence at Prevent Tragedies (December 2014).
43. Briggs and Silverman "Western Foreign Fighters", p. 42.
44. Basia Spalek, "Community Policing, Trust, and Muslim Communities in Relation to 'New Terrorism,'" *Politics and Policy* 38(4) (2010), pp. 789–815.
45. Basia Spalek and Laura Zahra McDonald, "Preventing Religio-Political Extremism amongst Muslim Youth: A Study Exploring Police-Community Partnership," *Institute of Applied Social Studies* (2011), p. 5. Available at http://www.youthpolicy.org/library/wp-content/uploads/library/2011_Preventing_Religio-Political_Extremism_Muslim_Youth_Eng.pdf (accessed 1 February 2015).
46. Centre for Human Rights and Global Justice, "Women and Preventing Violence Extremism: The U.S and U.K. Experiences," *CHR&GJ* (2012), p. 10. Available at http://chrgj.org/wp-content/uploads/2012/10/Women-and-Violent-Extremism-The-US-and-UK-Experiences.pdf (accessed 20 August 2015).
47. Sara Thornton, "Project Champion Review," *Thames Valley Police* (2010). Available at http://www.statewatch.org/news/2010/oct/uk-project-champion-police-report.pdf08/08/2015 (accessed 20 August 2015).
48. Institute for Strategic Dialogue, "The Role of Civil Society in Counter-Radicalisation and De-Radicalisation" (2010), p. 4. Available at http://www.strategicdialogue.org/PPN%20Paper%20-%20Community%20Engagement_FORWEBSITE.pdf (accessed 20 August 2015).
49. Author's own discussions at Challenge Panel committee; see also Tufyal Choudhury, "Impact of Counter-Terrorism on Communities: UK Background Report," *Institute for Strategic Dialogue* (2011). Available at http://www.strategicdialogue.org/UK_paper_SF_FINAL.pdf (accessed 20 August 2015).
50. HM Governent, "Pursue Prevent Protect Prepare," *HM Government* (2010). Available at http://www.youthpolicy.org/library/wp-content/uploads/library/2011_Preventing_Religio-Political_Extremism_Muslim_Youth_Eng.pdf (accessed 31 January 2016).
51. Innes et al., "Assessing the Effects of Prevent Policing," p. 18.
52. Centre for Human Rights and Global Justice, "Women and Preventing Violence Extremism: The U.S and U.K. Experiences," p. 12.
53. Innes et al., "Assessing the Effects of Prevent Policing," p. 18.
54. Christina Pantazis and Simon Pemberton, "From the 'Old' to the 'New' Suspect Community Examining the Impacts of Recent UK Counter-Terrorist Legislation," *The British Journal of Criminology* 9(5) (2009), pp. 646–666; Therese O'Toole, Nasar Meer, and Daniel Nilsson DeHanas, "Governing through Prevent? Regulation and Contested Practice in State-Muslim Engagement," *Sociology* 1(18) (2015), pp. 160–177.
55. Department for Communities and Local Government, "What Works in Community Cohesion," *DCLG* (2007), p. 10. Available at http://www.tedcantle.co.uk/publications/025%20What%20works%20in%20community%20cohesion%20Commission%20on%20Integrati.pdf (accessed 20 August 2015).
56. Alison Gilchrist, Magaret Wetherall, and Melanie Bowles, "Identities and Social Action: Connecting Communities for a Change," (Swindon, UK: Economic and Social Research Council) (2010), p. 30. Available at http://www.cdf.org.uk/wp-content/uploads/2012/07/Identities-and-social-action-Connecting-communities-for-a-change-A-Gilchrist-M-Wetherell-and-M-Bowles-08.09.10-for-web.pdf (accessed 31 January 2017).
57. Ibid., p. 21.
58. Andrew Sparrow, "Anti-Extremism Plan to Push 'British Values' and Link Benefits to Learning English," *The Guardian* (March 2015). Available at http://www.theguardian.com/politics/2015/mar/08/anti-extremist-plan-to-push-british-values-and-link-benefits-to-learning-english
59. Gilchrist et al., "Identities and Social Action," p. 13.
60. Department for Communities and Local Government, "What Works in Community Cohesion," p. 6.
61. Smith and Saltman, "Till Martyrdom Do Us Part," p. 10.
62. Zafar Ali, Chair of Governors of Iqra Slough Islamic Primary School Letter to Members of Parliament "Addressing Radicalisation" (July 2015).
63. See Jamie Bartlett, Jonathan Birdwell, and Michael King, "The Edge of Violence," *Demos* (2010); Donatella della Porta, *Social Movement Studies and Political Violence* (Aarhus: Centre for Studies

in Islamism and Radicalisation, 2009), p. 9. Available at https://www.demos.co.uk/files/Edge_of_Violence_-_web.pdf (accessed 31 January 2016); Marc Lynch, "Islam Divided between Jihadi and the Muslim Brotherhood," in Assaf Moghadam and Brian Fishman, eds., *Fault Lines in Global Jihad: Organizational, Strategic, and Ideological Fissures* (London: Routledge, 2011), p. 176.
64. Spalek and Lambert, "Muslim Communities, Counter-Terrorism and De-Radicalisation," p. 267; Robert Lambert, *Countering Al-Qaeda in London: Police and Muslims in Partnership* (London: Hurst, 2011).
65. Tariq Moodood, *Multiculturalism* (Cambridge: Polity, 2007).
66. Basia Spalek and Lynn Davies, "Mentoring in Relation to Violent Extremism: A Study of Role, Response, Purpose and Outcome," *Studies in Conflict & Terrorism* 35(5) (2012), p. 365.
67. Carolina Ivanescu, "Leicester Muslims: Citizenship, Race and Civil Religion," in Jorgen S. Nielsen, ed., *Muslim Political Participation in Europe* (Edinburgh: Edinburgh University Press, 2013), p. 287.
68. Department for Education, "Protecting Children from Radicalisation: The Prevent Duty" (2015). Also, author's own discussions at Challenge Panel (June 2015). Available at https://www.gov.uk/government/uploads/system/uploads/attachment_data/file/439598/prevent-duty-departmental-advice-v6.pdf (accessed 31 January 2016).; attendees expressed their communities' concerns over this.
69. Basia Spalek, *Terror Crime Prevention with Communities* (London: Bloomsbury, 2011); Abdul Haqq Baker, *Extremists in Our Midst* (Basingstoke: Palgrave Macmillan, 2011).
70. See Counter-Terrorism and Security Act (2015). Available at http://www.legislation.gov.uk/ukpga/2015/6/pdfs/ukpga_20150006_en.pdf (accessed 31 January 2016).
71. See University College Union, "The Prevent Duty: A Guide for Branches and Members" (2015). Available at http://www.ucu.org.uk/media/pdf/8/i/Prevent_duty_guidance_Jul15.pdf (accessed 20 September 2015).
72. Challenge Panel (June 2015).
73. Ali, Chair of Governors of Iqra Slough Islamic Primary School Letter to Members of Parliament "Addressing Radicalisation."
74. Personal correspondence with Channel Intervention Provider (February 2015).
75. Tore Bjorgo, *Strategies for Preventing Terrorism* (Basingstoke: Palgrave Macmillan, 2013), p. 14.
76. Spalek and Lambert, "Muslim Communities, Counter-Terrorism and De-Radicalisation," pp. 257–258.
77. Ibid.
78. Bharath Ganesh, "Implementing Prevent: From a Community-Led to a Government-Centered Approach," *Faith Matters* (2015), p. 3. Available at http://faith-matters.org/wp-content/uploads/2015/07/As-Prevent-Centralises-Community-Engagement-and-Local-Capacity-To-Implement-Local-Tailored-Solutions-Falls.pdf (accessed 20 February 2016).
79. Centre for Human Rights and Global Justice, "Women and Preventing Violence Extremism: The U.S and U.K. Experiences," p. 7.
80. Ganesh, "Implementing Prevent," p. 3.
81. Challenge Panel (June 2015).
82. See "Strengthening Government Partnerships to Build Resilience: The Challenge of Foreign Fighters," *Institute for Strategic Dialogue* (2015). Available at http://www.strategicdialogue.org/ISD_BXL_Report_PPN.pdf (accessed 20 February 2016).
83. See Tower Hamlets Strategic Plan 2015–16 (2015). Available at http://www.towerhamlets.gov.uk/lgsl/800001-800100/800022_community_plan/strategic_plan_2014-15.aspx (accessed 20 August 2015).
84. Samuel T. Powers, "Expanding the Paradigm: Countering Violent Extremism in Britain and the Need for a Youth Centric Community Based Approach," *Journal of Terrorism Research* 6(1) (2015). Available at http://ojs.st-andrews.ac.uk/index.php/jtr/article/view/1074/862#fn:2 (accessed 10 August 2015).
85. Ibid.
86. Innes et al., "Assessing the Effects of Prevent Policing"; Also see Simon Clarke, Steve Garner, and Rosie Gilmour, "Imagining the 'Other'/Figuring Encounter: White English Middle-Class and

Working-Class Identifications," in Magaret Wetherall, ed., *Identity in the 21st Century: New Trends in Changing Times* (London: Palgrave, 2009).
87. Interview with Prevent Coordinator (10 March 2015).
88. Prevent Tragedies (22 September 2015).

Index

Note: Boldface page numbers refer to tables and page numbers followed by "n" denote endnotes.

Abbott, Tony 49n23
Abdulmutallab, Umar Farouk 27
Abu Nidal 83n40
Active Change Foundation (ACF) 59
affect regulatory system 13
AFP *see* Australian Federal Police (AFP)
airports, stop and search process 19, 21, 28–31
Alkhatib, Ihsan 48n6
al-Muhajiroun 107
al Mujahiroun 61
Al Qaeda 5, 9, 54, 58, 59, 62, 76, 78
Aly, Anne 48n18
Anderson, David 22, 23, 29
anti-Muslim groups 62–3
Australian Electronic White Pages 39
Australian Federal Police (AFP) 38, 46, 47, 49n33, 49n34
Australian Muslims, police and community relationship 3; Community Liaison Team 46–7; cooperation 42–3; engagement practices 45–7; ethnic naming system 39; face-to-face survey 39; fear and anxiety 40; "feeling targeted" 39–41, **42**; hyper-legislation 39–40; participants and data collection 38–9; police practices, types of 42; procedural justice policing (*see* procedural justice); regression analysis 43–5, **44**; trust building 42–3, 45–7; willingness to work with police 45

Bail, Christopher 62, 63, 65n6
Baker, Abdul Haqq 78, 113
Bjorgo, Tore 114
Blair, Ian 70, 77, 79, 80
Blair, Tony 79
Blears, Hazel 75
bomb blast, bombast: open dialogue and transparency 110–11, 116; right institutions, working with 111–14, 116; U.K. approach, weakness of 109; working locally 114–16
Bovenkerk, Frank 47n1, 50n37
Briggs, Rachel 210

British antiterrorism legislation 21
British Muslims 55; civil society organizations 20; in counter-terrorism policing 19; in higher education 20
British National Party 24
"British values": definition of 112; interpretation of 8; rhetoric of 112
Brodeur, Jean-Paul 74
Brown, Gordon 79

Caldicott inquiry 27
Cameron, David 72, 75, 79
Central Intelligence Agency (CIA) 53
Centre for Social Cohesion, London 27
Channel Programme 9–10
Cherney, Adrian 48n8, 48n9, 49n31
Chisti, Mak 76, 78
CIA *see* Central Intelligence Agency (CIA)
circumstantial evidence 23
civil society organizations 21
Clayson, Benjamin 109
closed communities 112
CLT *see* Community Liaison Team (CLT)
cognitive-behavioral approach 14
cohesive communities 106
Cohesive Communities Programme 6
Common Ingroup Identity Model 96
communities defeat terrorism 8, 72, 74
community-based approach 38, 47
community-based counterterrorism policing: application of 70–1; implications and limitations 71–5; legitimate religious beliefs 75–9; London 75–6; partnership policing 79; threads 69; United Kingdom, citizens from 80
community-based intervention providers 10
community-based resources 2
community capacity building 93
community engagement programs 115, 116
community/government engagement 2, 6–7
community-led counterterrorism 3, 53–4; clear-eyed recognition of 60; and community

INDEX

policing for counterterrorism 53, 55, 56; conception of 54–7; "Contest" strategy 57; elements of 62–4; ethical anchoring 59–60; evaluation of 60; ideological competition 57–9; implications 55; potential efficacy of 60–1; state endorsement of 63; utility of 60–2
Community Liaison Team (CLT) 46–7
community policing, for counterterrorism 53, 55, 56
compassion-focused therapy 12, 13
complexity theory 14
conflict-related community identity 97
connectors, role of 14–15
Contact Hypothesis 98, 100
"Contest" strategy 57
Cottage, Robert 23–4
Counter Extremism Strategy 6, 8–9, 10, 106, 112
countering violent extremism (CVE) 7, 53, 55, 56, 106, 107, 109–13
counterradicalization 74
counterterrorism 110
Counter Terrorism and Security Act (CTSA) 2, 18, 19, 26, 113
Counter-Terrorism and Security Powers 28
counterterrorism investigations 76–7
counterterrorism investigation team 10
Crelinsten, Ronald D. 11
Crenshaw, Martha 11
Criminal Law Act, Section 3 (1967) 72
CTSA see Counter Terrorism and Security Act (CTSA)
CVE see countering violent extremism (CVE)
cyclical violence 95

Department for Communities and Local Government (DCLG) 111
Department of Homeland Security (DHS) 53
de-radicalization programs 9, 86–8, 95, 99
DHS see Department of Homeland Security (DHS)
discrimination 27, 28, 62–4, 93, 94

EDL see English Defence League (EDL)
Empowering Local Partners strategy 8, 9
"Empowering Local Partners to Prevent Violent Extremism in the United States" 56
English Defence League (EDL) 69
Epictetus 14
Equality and Human Rights Commission report 28, 29
ethical anchoring 53, 59–60
ethnic naming system, Australian Muslims 39
European Court of Human Rights 30
Explosive Substances Act (1883) 24

ex-prisoners, in Northern Ireland see Northern Ireland, ex-prisoners in
extremism 25–8; spectrum of 6

fairness, procedural justice 42
Federal Bureau of Investigation (FBI) 52, 53
Federation of Student Islamic Societies (FOSIS) 2, 19–21, 24–5, 27, 31; campaign 30; civil liberties officer 29; and student Islamic societies 21, 25, 28
"feeling targeted," Australian Muslims 39–41, **42**
Finsbury Park Mosque 77
foreign fighters 105–8, 112; community engagement 115
foreign fighters phenomenon 5–6
FOSIS see Federation of Student Islamic Societies (FOSIS)
Freedom of Information Act 29

Galam, Salim 11
Ganesh, Bharath 114
GFA see Good Friday Agreement (GFA)
Gilbert, Paul 13
Gilchrist, Alison 112
Good Friday Agreement (GFA) 89
government/community engagement see community/government engagement
government-led de-radicalization programs 87
government-sponsored de-radicalization programs 9
grassroots community groups 21, 28
Green, Alan 78
Grieve, John 80
Griffith University, Australia 3

Haines, David 110
Hamlets, Tower 115, 116
Hegghammer, Thomas 54
Hizb-ut-Tahrir 20
Hogan-Howe, Bernard 73
Home Affairs Select Committee Report (2012) 27
Home Office contract 74
Hopkins, Nick 49n25, 49n28
Horgan, John 59
House of Lords 30
Huq, Aziz Z. 55, 65n5
Hussain, Dilwar 78
hyper-legislation 39–40

identity continuity 92
identity transformation 89
identity transitions, managing 91–5
ideological competition 53, 57–9
Imtoual, Alia 63, 67n58
Independent Reviewer of Terrorism Legislation 22

INDEX

Innes, Martin 70
integrative psychotherapeutic approach 13
international terrorism 18
Iraq 5; automatic legal presumption 73; conflict in 105; Muslims, mistreatment of 59
ISIS *see* Islamic State of Iraq and Syria (ISIS)
Islamic State (IS) 5, 52, 54
Islamic State of Iraq and Syria (ISIS) 40, 76, 105, 108, 112, 116
Islamist extremism 6
Islamist legacy 19
Islamist terrorists 27
Islamophobia 28, 31
Ivanescu, Carolina 113

JAN trust 109
jihadis 54, 61, 62, 73

Kelly, Ruth 75
Kundnani, Arun 11
Kurzman, Charles 54, 55, 58

Lambert, Robert 48n7, 55, 110, 112
Lammy, David 30
London: community-based counterterrorism policing 75; Metropolitan Police 52, 58; principle of policing 71; Provisional Irish Republican Army 70; terrorist attacks 73
London bombings (2005) 20, 25; violent radicalization 27
London policing 73, 77, 79–81; adage 72
lone actor terrorism 105–6
lone wolf 105
Lord Carlile 23, 27–8
Loyalist ex-prisoners 3, 89, 93–7, 100
Lynch, Andrew 48n19
Lynch, Marc 58

McDonald, Laura Zahra 63, 65n18
Macdonald, Stuart 23
McGarrity, Nicola 48n19
Mann, Simon 24
Mayne, Richard 71
MCU *see* Muslim Contact Unit (MCU)
Meaning Maintenance Model 94
Metropolitan Police Authority (MPA) 29
Moisi, Dominique 110, 118n35
Moodood, Tariq 112
Motivations factors: conflict, fighters feel 109; identity and belonging, search for 108–9; ideology, adherence to 108
MPA *see* Metropolitan Police Authority (MPA)
MSF *see* Muslim Safety Forum (MSF)
Murphy, Kristina 48n8, 48n9, 49n31
Muslim-Americans 53, 54

Muslim communities 1–2; in Europe 63; in North America 63; in United States 62
Muslim Contact Unit (MCU) 55, 58
Muslim minority communities 53
Muslim Safety Forum (MSF) 75, 76, 79, 80
Muslims' willingness, work with police 45
mutatis mutandi 55
MyExtremism 109

Naqshbandi, Mehmood 76, 77
National Offender Management Service (NOMS) 10
national security 21, 24, 29, 40, 56, 61, 63
National Security Agency (NSA) 61
neutrality, procedural justice 42
NOMS *see* National Offender Management Service (NOMS)
nongovernmental organizations (NGOs) 86
non-violent extremism 75
Northern Ireland, ex-prisoners in 3, 87–8; accountability management 91; Contact Hypothesis 98, 100; legitimacy, notion of 100; Loyalist ex-prisoners 89, 93–7, 100; managing identity transitions 91–5; peace-promoting activities 97–9; perspective of 90; preventing the transgenerational transmission of political violence 95–7; Republican ex-prisoner 91–7; research methodology 90–1; restorative justice 89; superordinate identity 96–7; symbolic contact 99–101; three-tiered approach 91; violence prevention and community development initiatives 88
NSA *see* National Security Agency (NSA)
Nur, Abdi 52

Obama, Barack 53, 54
Office for Security and Counter-Terrorism (OSCT) 26, 82n24, 83n26
Osman, Mohammed 59

Palestinian refugee camp 57
partnership: policing 79; potential benefits of 18
peace practitioners 90, 99, 100
Peelian policing model 6
Peel, Robert 6
PIRA *see* Provisional Irish Republican Army (PIRA)
police and community relationship *see* Australian Muslims, police and community relationship
police practices, types of 42
Police Services of Northern Ireland (PSNI) 89
policing, evolution of 3
political ex-prisoners 90, 98
post-crime society 23
precursor crimes 23
"preventing terrorism" 25

INDEX

Preventing Violent Extremism (PVE) 25
Prevent policy 19, 20
Prevent Strategy (UK) 8, 9, 25, 27
"#PreventTragedies" 110
principles of policing 71
procedural justice policing 38, 41; elements of 42; incorporating 45, 46; measuring 43–5; police and Muslim communities 43; principles of 46
Provisional Irish Republican Army (PIRA) 70, 83n40, 89
PSNI *see* Police Services of Northern Ireland (PSNI)
psycho-behavioral change 13
psychoeducation technique 2
psychological anchoring effect 59
psychotherapeutic approach 2, 12, 14, 15
PVE *see* Preventing Violent Extremism (PVE)

Quilliam foundation 78

radicalization 9–10, 12–15, 25–8 *see also* de-radicalization programs
"Radical Thinking" conference on extremism (2011) 20
Rafiq, Haras 72, 77
Rammell, Bill 28
Reicher, Steve 49n25, 49n28
Reid, John 76
Republican ex-prisoner 3, 91–7
Republican violence 23
Research, Information and Communications Unit (RICU) 82n24, 83n24
respect, procedural justice 42
retributive justice model 7
RICU *see* Research, Information and Communications Unit (RICU)
Roy, Olivier 58
Rumsfeld, Donald 8
Russel Group of Universities 26

Salafism 77, 78
Schedule 7, of TA 2000 28–31
Schengen Agreement 5
Schulhofer, Stephen J. 55, 65n5
section 44 (s44), of TA 2000 29–31
security seeking 15
Security Service (MI5) 53
sense of duty 8
sense of security 6
Silverman, Tanya 210
social creativity 89
social identity theory 88–90
soft power mechanism 7, 11
Somali community 115, 116
Spalek, Basia 63, 67n58, 70, 110–13
Spinzak, Ehud 58
stop and search powers, at ports 19, 21, 28–31

Strasbourg Court judgement 30
Stuart, Hannah 107
student/government relationship 2
suicide terrorist attacks, Brussels (2016) 69
Suleaman, Nasreen 48n2
Sydney, counterterrorism operations 40
Syria 5; coming of age 108; conflict in 54, 105; and Iraq 114

TA 2000 *see* Terrorism Act 2000 (TA 2000)
Tablighi Jamaat 58
takfiri 75
"targeted" community, Australian Muslims 39–41, **42**
Terrorism Act 2000 (TA 2000) 21, 22, 25; definition of terrorism 21–2; offense 29; Schedule 7 of 28–31; section 44 (s44) 29–31
Terrorism Act 2006 (TA 2006) 24
terrorism offenses 21–5
Terrorism Prevention and Investigation Measures (TPIMs) 21
terrorism studies 87
terrorist recruitment 52–4
Thatcher, Mark 24
Therapeutic approaches, for communities 12–15
Tower Hamlets council 107
TPIMs *see* Terrorism Prevention and Investigation Measures (TPIMs)
Transtheoretical Model (TTM) 13
trust building 45–7
TTM *see* Transtheoretical Model (TTM)
Tyler, Tom R. 55, 65n5

UCL *see* University College London (UCL)
UCU *see* University and College Union (UCU)
U.K. Contest counterterrorism 70
UKIP *see* United Kingdom Independence Party (UKIP)
United Kingdom *see also* Federation of Student Islamic Societies (FOSIS): community engagement 105, 106, 116; "Contest" strategy 6, 57; Counter-Extremism Strategy 6, 9, 10, 106; countering violent extremism policy 111, 112, 115; counterterrorism policing in 19; counterterrorism strategy 57; counterterrorism workers age 107; extremism 111–12; federation of student Islamic societies 19; foreign fighters distribution 107; fundamental British values 112; government and community partnership 8–10; ideology of extremist groups 109; Islamist terrorists 27; Muslim Brotherhood 20; Muslim communities in 55; National Offender Management Service 10; preventative programs 87; prevent program 53, 55; prevent strategy 8, 9, 111; Security Service (MI5) 53; sense of duty 8
United Kingdom Independence Party (UKIP) 69

INDEX

United States 54; "Countering Violent Extremism" program 53, 55, 56; counterterrorism strategy 57; Muslim communities in 55, 62
United States Department of Justice 53
University and College Union (UCU) 113
University College London (UCL) 27
University of Queensland, Australia 3

Vermeulen, Floris 47n1, 50n37
violent-extremist groups 105–8, 114
violent radicalization 105–8, 112, 114
voice, procedural justice 42

Walton, Richard 73
"War on Terror" 38, 40
Weeks, Douglas 16n10
White House, National Security Strategy 56
White House summit (2015) 53
Williams, George 48n19

Yusuf, Abdullahi 52
Yusuf, Hamza 30